MW01110024

NO HOME FOR US HERE

NO HOME FOR US HERE

THE MASS ANNIHILATION OF THE FINNISH BORDER-HOPPERS IN THE URALS IN 1938

by
Jukka Rislakki and Eila Lahti-Argutina

Translated from the Finnish by
Richard Impola

NORTH STAR PRESS OF ST. CLOUD, INC.

Copyright © 2002 Jukka Rislakki and Eila Lahti-Argutina

Copyright © 1997 Jukka Rislakki and Eila Lahti-Argutina, published as
Meillä ei kotia täällä
by Otava Publishing Company, Ltd., Helsinki, Finland

Translation Copyright© 2002 Richard Impola

ISBN: 0-87839-176-2

First English Translation and First American Edition: July 2002

All rights reserved.

Printed in the United States of America
by Versa Press, Inc., East Peoria, Illinois

Published by
North Star Press of St. Cloud, Inc.
P.O. Box 451
St. Cloud, Minnesota 56302

Contents

Preface vii
Chapter 1   Border-Hoppers 1
Chapter 2   "It Would Be Nice to Get Home" 23
Chapter 3   The Monastery Prisoners 43
Chapter 4   Into the Ural Trap 63
Chapter 5   "They Were Some Bunch" 85
Chapter 6   A Place Named Kamensk 95
Chapter 7   The Rise and Destruction of Nizhni Tagil 121
Chapter 8   Escapees and Embassy Prisoners 135
Chapter 9   Operation Finns 149
Chapter 10   That New Year's Night 165
Chapter 11   "Where Does This Road Lead?" 173
Chapter 12   Amen! 205
Chapter 13   The Children of Kamensk 221
Chapter 14   Camp Inmates 243
Chapter 15   The Wind Blows over Them 255
Notes 287
Sources 309
Index 315

Preface

SOMETIMES IDEAS JUST SEEM TO BE IN THE AIR, and two people come up
with the same idea at the same time. In the early winter of 1995, I called Eila
Lahti-Argutina in Petroskoi and suggested the we begin writing a book about
the Finnish border-hoppers who had wound up in Ural. She told me she had
just sent a letter to me asking if this wasn't the time to investigate the fate
of the Ural Finns of the 1930s.

There has been a good deal of research on the fates of the American Finns
and those who left Finland in 1918, but much less is known about those who
went to the Soviet Union in the 1930s. Up to now, sources regarding them
have been hard to find. We do know something about the Soviet Karelian
Finns. But to my knowledge no one has tried to investigate the events in Ural,
which reached a climax in 1938, although they involved a large number of
Finnish citizens who became the victims of mass annihilation.

In the early 1930s, thousands of Finns skipped across the border into the
Soviet Union on their own, without permits or passports. This group had the
fewest legal rights and were the most unprotected of all the Soviet Finns.
Large groups of them were ordered to work and live in segregated areas,
where they could easily be kept under surveillance. Unprotected by the law,
they were the first victims of the security police's activities.

We are interested in the easily-distinguished and little-known group of
border-hoppers, whose fate was particularly dramatic—the thousands of

Finns who were taken to Ural to work and who were there annihilated quickly and thoroughly in the winter of 1937-1938. Their relatives, even their own children, often did not know their fate.

In 1995, I wrote "The Children of Kamensk," a two-part article for the *Helsingin Sanomat*. After that, many newspapers took up the subject, and so did television. As we were writing the book, we heard that TV 1 was preparing a new documentary on the Finns of Kamensk.

Our work was divided in the following manner: Eila researched the archives and interviewed people in Russia, and I did the same in Finland. Then I combined the material we had obtained and wrote it up in literary form. We collected the list of names of Ural Finns on both sides of the border. We had thought there might be a thousand names, but we found many more than that, and it became clear that many more names and human destinies remain obscure. In addition, we decided to concentrate especially on two of the most important Finnish centers, in both of which there were mass arrests: Kamensk and Nizhni Tagil.

The time was propitious for us. We were able to use a number of archives previously inaccessible to researchers.

In Sverdlovsk, old KGB interrogation records were just then being moved to the Government Agency Archives (GAAOSO). Eila went with her husband to study them, and we continued to acquire further copies of records whenever possible. From the archives of the Karelian Security Service, we found information on those who had been in Ural, tried to escape from there via Karelia and had been captured.

The papers of the Finnish embassy in Moscow were burned in 1939. However, long-forgotten cards and files on the border-hoppers were recently discovered in the archives of the Finnish Foreign Ministry. The state police archives were also fruitful. In addition, we obtained permission to use the archives of the Finnish security police. We also unearthed a lot of letters sent from Ural to Finland. In addition we interviewed people who had been saved from the blood bath and collected photographs from the victims' families. Eila also photographed the scene of our story in Ural as it looks at present.

We had begun to explore nearly virgin ground. Auvo Kostiainen had, of course, published his trail-breaking research entitled *Border-Hoppers* in 1988. The work defined the causes, nature, and scope of the crossings. On the other hand, it did not mention Kamensk, for example, or the mass arrests and executions of the Finns. Kostiainen did not have a clear idea of the total number of Ural Finns.

This is natural: a historical researcher writes what the sources show to be true, and in those days, the available sources were the Finnish archives. Finnish officials had lost sight of the border-hoppers quite early in the 1930s. The extent of the murderous rampage could only be guessed by those in Finland. For decades Soviet officials gave false information about the fate of those who were arrested, that is, if they gave any at all. The interest of Finnish officials in the border-hoppers and their children declined, then ended as the years passed.

In 1995, Hannu Rautkallio published a book called *The Great Wrath*. It does not live up to the subtitle "Stalin's Finnish Victims in the 1930s." The writer forgot about thousands of ordinary Finns in the prisons and discussed only the Finnish communist leaders, particularly Otto Ville Kuusinen and Arvo Poika Tuominen, who were hardly victims. He bypassed the Ural Finns altogether, concentrating only on Karelia and Leningrad.

Ural researchers have done only general studies into the persecutions and "expulsions aimed at specific groups." The Finns belong to the latter group. They are not mentioned separately but are included in the group labeled "others." Researcher Viktor Kirilov mentions the Finns in only one of his many books—and then only because Eila Lahti-Argutina showed him the records on the arrests of Finns.

In the course of our research, we ran across much surprising information, but the most dramatic for Eila was finding records dealing with her own father. Only then did it become clear to her that he, Eino Lahti of Kemi, had died in the forced labor camp at Chelyabinsk during the war, along with 660 other Finns, American Finns, and Ingrian Finns.

We are grateful to the publisher who decided to publish the book exactly sixty years after the death of the Ural Finns. We began the actual work of writing in the fall of 1996 by chance at the same time as the last cargo of atomic waste was leaving Finland for Chelyabinsk, which became one of the end points and mass graves for the border-hoppers. Funding for our work was provided by the Finnish Scientific Writers Guild, the Ministry of Education, and Otava.

We wish to thank the archival personnel for their help, and also Kristofer Gylling, Timo Laakso, Erja and Pentti Peltomäki, Irina Takala, and Kristina Wallendorf. We thank our spouses, Anna Zigure and Ilja Argutin, for many kinds of help and support. Thanks also to Markku Koskela, Reuben Rajala, and Osmo and Pekka Turtiainen for technical help (computer and electronic mail). And finally our thanks to Eila Wahlstén. If she had not contacted me, I would never have heard of the fate of the Ural Finns.

In the spring of 1997, I was sitting in the coffee shop of the Helsinki Swedish Theater thinking about this preface. I heard a woman sitting behind me saying to her companion: "Ural stones make fascinating jewelry. It's just as if there were little red blood vessels in them."

The reader who wishes to see the lists of names and the personal information we have collected regarding the Finnish and Finnish-American victims of Stalin's persecution, both in Karelia and Ural will find it worthwhile to become acquainted with this book by Ella Lahti-Argutina: *Olimme vieras Joukko vain. Venäjänsuomalaiset vainouhrit Neuvostoliitossa 1930-luvun alusta 1950 luvun alkuun.* (Siirtolaisinstituutti, Turky. Vammala 2001.) [*We Were Only Outsiders. Russian-Finnish Victims of Persecution in the Soviet Union from 1930 to 1950* (Institute of Migration, Turku. Vammala 2001)] This Finnish-language book has an alphabetical listing of some 8,000 names. The lists may be found on the website of the Turku Institute of Migration. The URL is: http://www.migrationinstitute.fi.

The Ollikainens in Kotka. The mother did not go with the family to Russia.

Chapter One

Border-Hoppers

But only one pathway of hope or struggle lay open to him: to cross the border. That too was a leap into emptiness. New forms of misery and suffering were likely to await him there.

Pentti Haanpää: Sorcerers' Circle (Manuscript 1931)

EEVA MARKKANEN AWOKE AS SHE and the other children were being lifted from the motorboat into a rowboat. She was frightened; they were rocking out on the open sea with no shore in sight. Before heading back for Kotka, the pilot of the motorboat pointed out the direction their rowboat was to take, and the men in it bent to the heavy Savo oars. The rowboat was heavily loaded; it contained four families along with their children and at least a half dozen unmarried men, twenty-two to twenty-three people in all. The youngest traveler was Eeva's one-year-old little sister.

It was morning on the last day of August in 1932.

The Ollikainens, a father and three children, had left from Kotka on the same vessel. Soon after they left the island, their fifteen-year old, Sylvi, had fallen asleep. She awakened when shoemaker Robert Markkanen shouted: "Now the cops are on our tail!" But it was only the light from a lighthouse, not from a police boat, that he had seen. Sylvi was disappointed; she did not want to go to Russia. She had heard that children did not even get milk there.

1

Seven-year-old Eeva Markkanen had fussed about it too: "I'm not going to Russia!" Her mother explained to her that they could always come back if things went poorly there. Eeva had run away from home when the family made its first attempt to cross the border; they had been caught and the whole family of five had spent a night in the Kotka jail. The police advised the father, whose brother had crossed over earlier: "Don't take your family into that misery; go alone if you go."

Markkanen was fined 500 markkas, which he did not pay. The VALPO (Finland's secret or political police) file card has the same record for his wife. On the second attempt, the parents deceived their children by telling them, "We're going to the islands," and dressed them warmly. Because of Eeva's fussing, the others in the border-crossing group had to wait for days on Viikari Island, and the desire to go, especially among the women, began to weaken. The money the group had paid did not satisfy their escorts, who tried to take even the rings and watches from the women.

Now it was too late for regrets. A speedboat approached the fully loaded rowboat from the south. It sped past them, caught up with the motorboat that was heading for Kotka, and forced it to turn around. Then a small white boat came steaming toward them, and a man in it began shouting questions at the rowers.

"*Straastui! Finlandia!*" shouted forty-nine-year-old Albin Ollikainen, who had once worked in Russia and knew a little of the language. "*Rabota jest?*" The answer from the boat was, "*Jest!*" There was work. "*Hleb jest?*" "*Jest!*" There was bread, too.

A tow rope was tossed to the Finns, and they continued their journey to the south shore of the Gulf of Finland. The wake of the boat seemed threatening. "They're going to drown us!" one of the women cried.

On the shore, the first thing Eeva saw were people wearing birchbark shoes and quilted coats. She burst into tears; they were in Russia. Her mother Aili too began to weep.

The workers' hall in Karihaara had been almost a second home to a family from Kemi. The father, Juho Lappalainen, had been a logger for the Kemi Company, and the mother, Anna, a worker in their plant. After a strike, the father was blacklisted and was unable to get any work except for brief odd jobs. The family embarked on their attempt to cross into Russia in the fall of 1932. Selling what little they had at auction, they took a bus to Petsamo without telling even their relatives where they were going.

The group they joined in Petsamo ran into a snowstorm while rowing across its fjord-like bay. Discouraged by the difficulties, the group shrank, and soon only the Lappalainens were left to go on. They had no compass and burned their sewing basket in order to heat something to drink.

After the young guide they had hired in Liinahamari left them to find their way to the Soviet side by themselves, the Lappalainen family—mother, father, and three children—became lost in the hills near Petsamo. When evening fell, they realized that they had been traveling in a circle. They spent their first night in the hills wrapped up in their father's ulster.

Before leaving: the Lappalainen girls in a school picture in Kemi. The Lappalainen family skipped across the border by way of Petsamo in 1932.

After spending the night outdoors, they ran across a small fisherman's shack. With no wood to be had, they burned boards from its walls. On the morning of October second, the father set out to look for help. Fifteen-year-old Salli begged in vain to go with him. They never saw him alive again. Later he was found dead in the hills on the Russian side.

Reindeer men helped the mother and children, advising them to return home. But the mother was sure that her husband had made it over the border, and so the family set out toward the east with a paid guide to lead them.

When they were forced to cross icy waters, they went barefoot, carrying their shoes in their hands. "Drink coffee now," the guide advised them. "Soon you won't get any."

On the night of October 12, the mother and daughters crossed the border under the very noses of the Finnish border guards. On the other side, the Lappalainens were detained and taken to Murmansk on a ship full of Finnish border-hoppers.

The Wahlsténs were from Toukola in Helsinki. Their father, William, was a carpenter whose hobby was playing music and singing. He was an active and enterprising man; his papers show that in the early 1930s he had tried unsuccessfully to rent a kiosk from the city. With his wife he joined the Hiilet (Firebrands) organization, founded by people of a leftist orientation, which soon fell under scrutiny by the authorities and was disbanded.

The mother, Kirsti, was a seamstress. Under the name of Armida Valaskivi, she wrote poetry that was published in weekly papers—she continued to send poems to Finland from Russia. The small, blonde and slender Wahlstén girls resembled her. Eila was six years old, her little sister Irma only five.

The Wahlstén family at home in Toukola just before they crossed the border. Father and Mother were executed within three days of each other in 1938. The daughters have now returned to Finland.

Their third effort to cross the border in the summer of 1932 was successful. A relative, who made good money at this sort of work, took the Wahlsténs and a good-sized group of others across the Gulf of Finland on a boat. He left the border-hoppers on an island where they were picked up by the Soviet border guard.

The nature of the very first interrogations at the border station was such that Viljo Wahlstén would have turned back. He was forced to spend three months in a Leningrad jail before the family was together again.

The Wahlsténs departure did not remain a secret from the Central Investigation Police (EK—later known as VALPO). One of their informers, presumably a trade-union official, reported that Viljo's mother had mentioned the Wahlsténs' secret departure for Russia on the second of July. "The Wahlsténs are not likely to be party members," the informant continued.

Wahlstén's mother immediately began a tireless campaign to get the family back to Finland. By January 1933, at the latest, she is known to have gone to the Foreign Office in Helsinki for help, which was promised to her.

The Swedish-speaking Saari family from Porvoo skipped across the border in mid-July of 1932. The father, Aleksis Saari, had worked at the Porvoo steam sawmill, until the depression struck there too. The mother, Gerda, along with her sisters, had scoured the villages in the Porvoo area seeking day work. Among those who went to the Soviet Union on the same boat were working companions of Aleksis.

Besides his wife, Saari had with him his three daughters, eleven-year-old Lea, seven-year old Rakel, and three-year-old Etel. The journey over the stormy Gulf of Finland lasted nineteen hours. Everyone was thoroughly drenched and some of the group became seasick. According to their escorts, the boat had never been in a storm of that sort.

Tahvo Kakkinen, an unemployed mason, left Viipuri with his ten-year-old boy, Viljo, who had already learned the mason's trade. Anna Kakkinen stayed in Finland. In Viipuri, they had listened on their crystal set to Finnish language broadcasts from the Soviet Union, which created the impression that there was plenty of work and bread to be had in their eastern neighbor's country.

In March 1932, the Kakkinens, along with a worker they knew, set off skiing across the Gulf of Finland. Near the Kronstadt Fortress island the guard halted them and ordered them to lie down on their skis. Having searched their bodies, he alerted others to come to his help by firing his rifle in the air.

In the fortress, the Kakkinens were blindfolded as they were led from one room and floor to another. Soon they were taken to Oranienbaum, where a Finnish-speaking officer interrogated them. A pistol lay on the desk in front of him. He wanted to know if they were spies.

The gates of heaven seemed to have opened up for the Partanen children. It was Tyyne's fifteenth birthday when they walked across the border at Suojärvi—a mother, three children, their new father, and a few other men from Suojärvi. A harsh and hungry depression winter lay behind them. Their father had traveled far from home to get relief work, and Tyyne had done her best to feed her younger sisters without any money. She went for flour slips to the township office and baked bread for them.

In a village on the Russian side they were fed a wonderful meal, millet porridge with canned meat mixed into it. The children could not remember when they had tasted anything so good. The only sad thing was that Tyyne's school reports, of which she was justly proud, had been taken away from her.

Even at the camp, the porridge and soup arrived regularly. This was certainly better than conditions at home! Still another pleasant surprise awaited them in a cell in the Leningrad prison: there they met the Lintunen sisters, whom they knew from Suojärvi: Hilja Jelonen, Esteri Lintunen, and Eevi Räty. And at last, in the quarantine camp, their father appeared. The family was together.

Thousands of border-hoppers left Finland for the Soviet Union in search of bread in the depression years of the early 1930s. Most of them went in 1932, the worst year of the slump, when social welfare was practically non-existent. A record unemployment figure—81,350—had been reached the previous year.

It is difficult to determine the exact number of border-hoppers, for the only ones who are recorded are those who, for various reasons, had later made contact with Finnish officials. Researchers have come to the conclusion that there were about 15,000 of them, without taking the American Finns into account. This number jibes with the Central Police (EK) estimates; the Foreign Ministry did not believe the number to be as great.

What we are dealing with is a rather rough estimate, and the border-hoppers who have been "left in obscurity" may well raise the figure. We have come to this conclusion because Auvo Kostiainen, who in 1988 published the results of an extensive investigation, arrived at a total figure of 15,000. But the border-hoppers from Ural, the area that we know best, appear to be missing from his statistics. In addition, the alphabetically arranged records of the VALPO end after the letter "N," so that one can only guess how many names there once were in the card file.

U.A. Käkönen, a legal military attaché who interviewed border-hoppers in Moscow, claims in his memoirs that there was in the embassy in the 1930s a card file of over 20,000 names of people who had gone to the Soviet Union. According to Käkönen, the figure did not include those who left Finland in 1918. On the other hand, they did include the 1,400 who had gone there with passports from 1930 to 1935.

Johan Nykopp, a diplomat who also served in Moscow, writes that ". . . during the depression years of 1931 to 1932, several thousand people skipped across the border." According to him, they were routinely condemned to three years of banishment to labor camps (in fact, only a part of them were condemned), at first in Karelia and then in Siberia. "Gradually letters asking for help began arriving at the Finnish embassy from there."

In 1935 the Finnish Communist Party received information from Soviet security officials that fully 10,000 border-hoppers were then in the country. According to the history of the Soviet border guard establishment, the guards detained a total of 12,950 people at the Finnish border in the early 1930s. The activity was clearly at its peak in 1932; over half were detained then. The Finns also detained more people that year by a broad margin than in any other year of the decade: over two thousand.

According to the Russian work cited, the number of arrests at the border break down in the following fashion; the vast majority of these were undoubtedly border-hoppers:

1930	1,174
1931	2,488
1932	7,207
1933	1,361
1934	720
Total	12,950

Where did the border-hoppers come from then? Many were from Kymenlaakso, especially the Kotka area, and from Kemi, from the Oulu area and from the entire province of Oulu (which also included Lapland). About sixty percent of the illegal crossings occurred, according to Finnish statistics, in the Kainu border-guard area. Border-hoppers left from places along the entire eastern border: from Viipuri, Suojärvi, Kuusamo, and Kuolajärvi (Salla). Many walked across the border over the Petsamo Hills. In Kotka, the best known crossing areas were Hovinsaari, Kymi, Katariina, Metsola, Popinniemi, and Sunila. Economic reasons were the greatest inducement for crossing the border. In the spring of 1932, according to official statistics there were 405 jobless in Kymi and 237 in Kotka.

If people left from the Kotka area when the water was not frozen, they would generally travel a little east along the shore and then head for Narvi Island. They would pass Lavansaari, and then aim at the mouth of Laukaanlahti (Luga). From there the border-hoppers would be taken aboard Russian paddle-wheel craft to Kingisepp for interrogation. Some of the border-hoppers sailed from Finland to the Leningrad harbor. In the winter, they skied over the ice on the Gulf of Finland or Lake Ladoga to the neighboring country. Some hid on ships ordered by the Soviets from the Turku shipyards and reached their destination in that way.

Some boatloads were lost; others were driven up on the shores of Estonia and tried to go on from there. For example, before Christmas of 1931, Tallinn informed Helsinki that "a new group of twenty-one people" had come ashore in Estonia and had immediately been sent back to sea. Four more boatloads were said to be on their way. During the next summer, six men from a boat that strayed to Estonia were left on shore; the rest fled toward the east. The Foreign ministry informed Estonia that it would not pay the cost of returning the six to Finland. The men bought a boat and continued their journey.

Toivo Laine from Tampere related that when he left Helsinki, thirty-two people were packed into a twenty-eight-meter open boat, and "several had too many bundles with them." Weather forced the leaky boat to make an emergency stop in Estonia, from where the group continued their journey to Russia after being interrogated.

In early June of 1932, the Finnish Coast Guard stopped a motorboat and the rowboat it was towing between Pirttisaari and Söderskär. In it were thirty-seven people, three of them children. According to one report, some forty people, all of them men, left Helsinki in a motor boat on the twenty-ninth of September. The Kotka newspaper *Eteenpäin* reported that a yawl had left

Kymi on independence day, taking forty-two border-hoppers to Seiskari. The ship ran aground on the rocks and all were arrested.

Aino Saarela (now Peltola) relates that in the early 1930s, a real "Russian fever" developed in Kemi. Neighbors disappeared at night; they were said to have gone in search of paradise. Her husband caught the fever and persuaded his young wife and baby to go with him. Arthur Saarela's decision was not swayed by the fact that the *Pohjolan Sanomat* had published a warning by a returned border-hopper. According to him, ". . . prisons and hunger awaited them there." Aino stated: "Eino Anttila's wife read to me from one of his letters that her husband was planning suicide. Things were so wretched in Russia that he could not go on living."

The city of Kotka was in crisis because of "Russian widows." The city board, charged with caring for the poor, authorized its chairman to negotiate with the Russian embassy over means of sending money from the border-hoppers to their families in Kotka—or for sending the wives and children to Russia after the men.

Thus, according to the officials of both countries, 1932 was the most active year for border crossing. In the early part of that year, however, a subdivision of the Viipuri EK reported that when the ice froze over, only a small group of reckless young men had dared trying to reach Russia on skis or kicksled. The Kemi division reported that "only a few solitary groups of reckless loggers" had crossed the border at Petsamo.

Nonetheless, it was reported from Petsamo that "a really extraordinary number of men and even women had begun going to Russia." Terijoki EK reported that daily it was detaining workers who came from different parts of the country and were trying to cross the border in groups. In January, their subdivision had arrested 100 people, most of them border-hoppers. Joensuu reported that in January some fifty men had gone across by way of Jonkeri on the Kuhmo peninsula.

At approximately the same time a group of sixty men had tried to cross the border at Ilomantsi; all were captured on the Finnish side. In January the *Helsingin Sanomat* reported that 1,000 people had already set out for Russia, ninety percent of them from Kotka, and that the police had succeeded in detaining a fourth of them.

With the coming of spring and summer, the volume of traffic increased. According to EK reports, at least sixty Suojärvi residents crossed the border in July. At the end of the month it was calculated that 926 border-hoppers had tried to cross in the area for which the Terijoki division was responsible.

"In the last two weeks, a third of the population of Kuolajärvi has emigrated to the Soviet Union," the newspaper *Vapaus* wrote on July 18. In certain areas of Sodankylä the emigration was said to be just as extensive. *Uusi Suomi* claimed that 300 people must have left from Haukipudas during the summer. The fall session of the Suojärvi court sentenced to jail 150 who had attempted to cross the border illegally.

"Illegal emigration from the land on such a scale must be considered a national disaster," a 1932 EK memorandum declared, expressing the hope that the traffic would decline since letters from the other side of the border had told of the border-hoppers' miserable fate. It happened otherwise, however; as the autumn nights grew darker, the crossings continued, perhaps at an even faster rate.

Tracking down the border-hoppers was a futile task, for the same person would head for the border again after being detained, interrogated, and fined. Tenho Ylätupa from Hamina was caught at least three times attempting a crossing but succeeded in slipping through to Russia an equal number of times. After crossing back to Finland in 1938, he was given a jail sentence.

It even happened that a family was not convinced after the first time but skipped across the border again. The Oskar Manninen family from Viipuri, for example, was able to get back to Finland from Leningrad in the early 1930s, but, disillusioned by the depression and the prejudice they encountered, they went back. The family came close to dying of hunger at a work site in the Soviet Union before they were able to return; the father had to wander through snowy woods from the Murmansk railroad to Finland— there the EK arrested him under suspicion of being a spy.

Seaman Rudolf Kukko was another of the same ilk. He had crossed into Russia secretly via Seiskari at the close of the 1920s, had been in Siberia, and returned to Finland legally in the early 1930s. In June of 1932, Kukko and five other men sailed to the Soviet Union in a stolen boat. He too was sent to Ural and suffered the same fate as the others there.

In Ural, Siberia, and Karelia there were several Finnish-American "double border-hoppers," if one may use the term for those who came on legitimate passports. Suoma Lahti (nee Laine), a native of Michigan, about whom there is more later in this book, went to the Soviet Union with her parents in the 1920s. Father Laine was in the Kuzbas mines there, but was not intimidated by the experience, although conditions were terrible and the work was hard. The family returned to America via Finland, but when the Depression struck, they went back to Russia in 1931, this time with fateful consequences.

Edith Jääskeläinen, who left from Kotka in the 1930s, was not happy in Finland for long. Her husband had been tortured and executed in the Soviet Union in 1938, and she herself returned to Kotka in 1963 wearing the same dress she had worn thirty years earlier. She missed her children, who had remained in the Urals. Soon she moved back to Omsk and died there in 1976.

Kaarlo Hartikainen, a worker from Liperi, along with his wife, crossed the border from Finland into the Soviet Union and back on three separate occasions, if we are to believe his memoirs, published by WSOY under the name of Juho Harri. It was never easy. On the third trip in 1931, Hartikainen went on a hunger strike and once attempted suicide.

Perhaps the strangest of the border-hoppers was Jaakko W. Keto, a "gentlemanly dry, researcher type." The son of a city mayor, he had studied in a business college. He crossed by way of Suojärvi in 1934, declared himself a communist, petitioned for Soviet citizenship, and asked for work. Keto was suspected of being a Finnish spy. He was pumped for information about the Finnish Army, and in the autumn he was sent back across the border and reportedly told that he could return if life in Finland proved difficult. In 1957 Keto became the section head of the political department of the Finnish Foreign Ministry and an ambassador in 1975.

The border-hoppers got money for their passage by selling their property. The trip was expensive, and many were penniless after they had paid for it. For example, the Helsinki EK received a report that a group of Helsinki communists were going to cross en masse, and that the cost of the trip was 500 markkas for each person.

The cost of transportation by water was generally from 300 to over a thousand markkas, depending on the number in a boat. The transporters, many of them bootleggers who found themselves unemployed with the repeal of prohibition, apparently earned good money. However the risk of their being caught on either shore was great, and sometimes the Russians fired on the boats which had turned around, killing the transporters. The border-hoppers were left at a distance of forty to fifty kilometers from the Soviet shore. From there they were forced to go on alone in rowboats or motorboats they had purchased.

Esko Riekki, the chief of the EK, reported to the Foreign Ministry in 1932 that one could get from Kotka and Koivisto on Lavansaari for seventy-five markkas with the help of fishermen, who also sold the border-hoppers old wrecks of rowboats, later reporting them as having been stolen.

Lauri Seppälä left Pyhtää in November of 1931 with a group of twelve others on a motorboat owned by a man of the same village. The trip was said to have cost 400 to 500 markkas per person. The crew, which consisted of the boat's owner and motor operator, Kalle Aho (a communist from Kotka), and a third man, had landed the group at the mouth of the Laukkaa River.

> . . . there the Soviet border guards arrested them. They had, however, run ashore by mistake, for the motor operator had intended to turn. around at sea and have the travelers row the rest of the way. When they were captured, Kalle Aho nevertheless told them—the men running the boat, that is—that they were sure to be released soon, for he was acquainted with GPU officers in Leningrad and had given one of their names to the border-guard officer. The next day the group was taken to Jamburg (Kingisepp), but the boat operators remained at the guard station.
>
> At the Russian border guard station, the officers asked the boat owner why he was collecting so much money from the travelers . . .

During the course of this investigation, the EK was told that a man named Koivuranta, who had been to America, lived in Pyhtä. He had financed the men's border-crossing trip, saying, he was "helping a very good cause."

A couple of weeks before Midsummer's Day, the Murtos skipped from Mussalo in Kotka. They were a really large family, probably the largest that wound up traveling to the bitter end the road that led to Ural and the fateful year of 1938.

> The Murtos and two other men who skipped with them had come from Kotka on a motorboat, paying its owner, a certain Ingrian chauffeur, a total of 6,000 markkas for their ride. They had gone from the Merikylpylä shore to Ingria, where they were arrested. The motor boat and its operator were allowed to return at once to Kotka.

This is the account of a journey the EK heard while interrogating a Russian who had met twenty-four-year-old Urho Murto in a Leningrad jail. Crossing the border along with Urho were the father, carpenter Kalle Murto (formerly Flinkman), who at fifty-three was one of the oldest border-hoppers; the mother, Vilhelmina; Urho's wife, Ebba, and their child; his sister, Rauni, and brothers, Erkki, Reino, Veikko, and Väinö; plus Ilmari's wife, Elma (probably married in the Soviet Union). At seven years of age, Rauni was the youngest of the flock of siblings. Seven of the Murto children went to Russia; the two oldest stayed in Finland. As for Ilmari, he had escorted border-hoppers to Russia and had been caught there. Apparently the rest of the family set out to find him. The children's cousin, Tauno Flinkman, who had been captured while attempting to cross the border in 1931, was also in the boat.

The Murto family in Kotka. Twelve members of the family and close relatives crossed the border in the summer of 1932. Most of them perished in the Soviet Union.

In 1931, listening to Soviet radio broadcasts was declared illegal in Finland, but the border-hoppers recall that during church-going time on Sundays, Leningrad Radio's Finnish-language programs were followed eagerly. In Russia there was said to be no unemployment and plenty of food. Medical care and education were free.

Propaganda broadcasts from Leningrad and Petroskoi led people to conclude that the young socialistic state was badly in need of labor from abroad.

The first Five-Year-Plan, with its dizzying growth objectives, had gone into effect in October of 1928, and the country was being industrialized. In the country next door, they were building Soviet Karelia under the leadership of Edvard Gylling and other Finnish communists.

On April 30, 1931, Petroskoi radio said on the subject of "Preparing for the Log Float." "To date, the preparations have been quite old-fashioned, so that there is not enough of a work force in Karelia. More must be gotten from elsewhere."

> This spring [ninety-five] million cubic meters of wood products have to be floated. Getting enough labor will cause difficulties. There has been negligence in this respect. Barely [forty percent] of the necessary work force has been hired for the float, some 50,000 people, a completely inadequate number. . . . It is time to stop dawdling and start hiring more labor for the Soviet Karelian log float.

On Mayday evening of 1933, Leningrad radio discussed unemployment in Finland, stating that "even the university-educated are looking for house-cleaning jobs."

> The whole world knows that we are progressing with giant strides, while in the bourgeois countries, capital and the fascists have doomed millions of workers to hunger. Workers! Don't be scared off, even if they try to blacken us in every way. You know that the workers' conditions in the Soviet Union are so good that we can never praise them too much. Comrades! We have made Russia a free country for workers and farmers. We have tractors, motor vehicles, airplanes, trains, locomotives. We have large factories.

Finnish newspapers reported the decision of the labor union conference in Moscow "this winter at least 300,000 workers must be hired and given a binding assignment to forest work." (The Soviet motor vehicle industry was also reported to need thousands of workers.) Here is a quotation from a report by radio monitors in Finnish military intelligence:

> Leningrad radio February 1933 on Soviet Karelia's forest riches and forest work: Because of this steady growth, the shortage of loggers has increased. Karelia needs a cadre of 15,000 woods workers.

The truth was different from the propaganda, and at least some people in Finland knew it. EK scrutinized the mail coming from the Soviet Union and copied, among other information, the following from a letter sent to Terijoki from near Moscow in October of 1932:

> . . . *potatoes and cabbage are the only foods on which people in the USSR can now live. In spite of the fact that these foods have been the cheapest so far, and that now it is the potato season, the price has risen to [fifty] rubles a sack (three puuta), and we need at least [five] sacks for the winter, for we have to manage on potatoes alone. . . . Up to now, we have earned three sacks. But I couldn't do any more, and now my wife is digging by herself. . . . We've long since forgotten about animal fats. . . . Isn't this a nightmare. . . .*

Finland's official representatives in Russia kept track of the situation. When border-hopping was at its height in 1932, chargé d'affaires Rafael Hakkarainen reported to the Foreign Ministry from Moscow: "This country will never be able to work in an organized manner." Grain production "is a mess." Chaos prevailed in the land, and the Finnish diplomat warned against trusting official production statistics. "Enthusiastic communistic experiments" had brought the country to "a poorer and poorer economic condition."

> . . . *artfully and skillfully the communist leaders of Moscow promise better days to the unfortunate millions in this land. . . . The numbers the party rulers present in their speeches are truly miraculous. . . . They do not shrink from comparisons: they have already surpassed America in the rate of technical and industrial development. Above all, they have decided that in 1932 they will complete the home stretch of the previous "five-year plan," which began early in 1929, and of which three years have thus been completed.*

Speeding up the five-year plan increased the pressure on the people. The groundwork for industrialization had to be completed. Iron and steel fabrication had to be increased many fold, as did coal mining, and the railroads had to be gotten into shape. Millions of people were drained from the countryside and forced into cities and factories. Caring for them became difficult when agricultural production crashed.

In June of 1932, Envoy Aarno Yrjö-Koskinen's report was captioned: "Hunger crisis in the Soviet Union." In large parts of the country, there was absolute famine. The situation was catastrophic. Soon Yrjö-Koskinen related that "anyone who lagged in working had his bread ration cut." According to him, people were driven to work by hunger more than by fear of the GPU.

Just as 1932 was ending, the Russian communist party (RKP) decided to draw the line which brought famine to many grain areas. Millions of farm families, or *kulaks*, were moved from their farms, which were confiscated. The country people who remained were then concentrated into collective farms under party control. The growers were assigned unrealistically high grain quotas, other sources of food were eliminated, and outside aid to the starving areas was interdicted. Robert Conquest, who studied the catastrophe, calculates that the famine killed five million people in the Ukraine in 1932-1933 and a total of three million elsewhere. 3.5 million perished in the concentration camps in 1930-1937, so that altogether the pandemonium in the countryside and the campaign against the *kulaks* claimed, according to his "conservative estimate," 14.5 million human victims.

Aino Saarela, who listened with her husband in Kemi to Soviet broadcasts in 1932 claims that Otto Ville Kuusinen spoke on the radio asking skilled Finnish workers to come to Soviet Karelia. According to the broadcasts, women would be freed from home slavery and could go to work; children would be sent to children's homes.

Even as late as the end of 1933, the English-language *Moscow Daily News* wrote that "Soviet Karelia hopes to develop its natural resources mainly with the help of immigrants from Finland, Canada, and the United States."

At the same time, a very dark picture was painted of conditions in Finland. The *Red Karelia* newspaper had a regular vignette, "News From Fascist Finland." This was the style of their headlines: "Workers die of hunger," "Conditions of political prisoners aggravated," "Priests prepare people for war," "Girl dies on her begging rounds," "Finnish woods work worse than slavery," "Hordes of police hounds at work sites."

Occasional surreptitious recruiters were said to be circulating in Finland. Sirkka Laurila (now Karjalainen) reports that a recruiter from Kemi sent her and her parents, both sawmill workers, to Russia. The recruiter went with them to the border to show them where to cross.

Finnish-Americans were publicly and officially recruited to Soviet Karelia and to Ural and Siberia at first. As early as 1921 Lenin and Yrjö Sirola negotiated about American Finns who were working in the Kuzbas area. Gylling and Kustaa Rovio's project of recruiting them to work in Karelia had both Lenin and Stalin's blessing, and soon they began to arrive.

Tens of thousands would have been accepted! From 1930 on, the recruiting of experts from abroad was official Soviet policy.

In 1932, Rovio, the Finnish-born party leader in Soviet Karelia, wrote to Stalin: "Karelian organizations do everything in their power to benefit and serve the labor force coming from abroad, and to create such a model socialist republic that it will create revolutionary sentiment among workers in Finland and the other Scandinavian countries."

The "Karelia fever" of the United States and Canadian Finns was at its height and the traffic the liveliest in 1932, just as it was in Finland. By the end of October, there were already 4,399 American Finns in Karelia. However, in that same year many already became disillusioned or had returned. The Leningrad GPU and military circles opposed the arrival of immigrants and ordered that they not be stationed near the border.

The American Finns were a desirable work force. Professionally skilled and well-off, they brought their own tools and other possessions with them, automobiles, even tractors, and money. They paid their own passage, and bound themselves to contribute money to the machinery fund. Those who came from America were also treated well at first, but their better living conditions aroused the envy of both the local inhabitants and the border-hoppers from Finland. The latter's monthly ration in Karelia—five kilograms of flour, 900 grams of grain, 900 grams of fish, twenty-five grams of tea, 200 grams of soap, and 240 grams of sugar for the children (all largely theoretical)—could not compare to the food norms for American Finns. Eino Rahja, a well-known St. Petersburg Red Finnish officer once asked angrily: "Why are those who come from America greeted with brass bands while those from Finland are put in jail?"

The emigration from North America slowed down in 1933 and ended in 1934, when the recruiting also ended and when the return movement was perhaps the liveliest. There are no exact figures, but researchers Reino Kero and Irina Takala and writer Mayme Sevander estimate that 6,000 to 6,500 American Finns arrived in the Soviet Union. According to various sources, perhaps some twenty to forty percent of them managed to get back to America. What finally happened to the others is mainly conjecture, so that the question involves an unknown group. Kero wrote in 1983 that it is impossible to say "whether hundreds, perhaps thousands of United States and Canadian Finns wound up in forced labor camps." Mayme Sevander has already found 853 who were executed.

According to Takala, information about the American Finns is quite contradictory. By the fall of 1935 the number who had left Karelia was 1,500.

By the end of spring, the NKVD reported having jailed 342 American Finns. From then on practically nothing is known of this group.

Those who were leaving had to buy their own passports and visas with gold rubles. Most of them were pressured to take a Soviet passport or to renew their contract when their term of work expired—and then when their contracts were invalidated it was too late to try to leave the country. Although Finland helped its own citizens to return, it hampered the return of Americans.

In December of 1933 the *Moscow Daily News* wrote that there were 5,000 Finnish-Americans working in the woods of Karelia and that they had donated a half million dollars to the industrialization fund. Although they had encountered "some difficulties," they were said to be doing well. At the same time, EK reported that disgruntled and disillusioned American Finns were bewailing their destiny in Soviet Karelia. The Finnish embassy reported that many American Finns whom the Russians had persuaded to change their citizenship had turned to them for help. They wanted to get rid of their Soviet passports and return to America or Finland.

The situation of Finns from Finland was much worse. It was soon made clear to them that border-hoppers, even skilled workmen, were not particularly welcome. Even the underground Finnish communist party (SKP) had forbidden workers to go on their own, so that it was easy for the naturally suspicious Soviet officials to distrust the newcomers.

Työ (Labor), a paper circulated in Viipuri, wrote in 1931 that it was wrong to flee the battle in Finland and go to Russia. "Let us also fight against those who abandon the front lines." That same autumn, the SKP's (Finnish Communist Party) Karelia area committee headlined one of its publications: "Halt, Front-Line Deserters!" According to the leaflet, the border-hoppers were "self-seekers," since they went to the Soviet Union in order to enjoy the advantages the Russian workers had achieved through great sacrifice. The workers were urged to fight in Finland instead of "growing fat and complacent in Russia."

In June of 1932 *Vapaa Työ* (Free Labor) warned that only those whom the Komintern and the Finnish Communist Party needed were welcome, and then only by special invitation. Those who went on their own would be adrift and subject to harsh interrogation.

That same month the Central Committee of the SKP published its decision that a "self-generating stream of refugees to the Soviet Union" was not consonant with the revolutionary struggle. According to EK reports, the Kymenlaakso party organization held a grave discussion on the immigration to Russia and concluded that it was a "crime against the party." Among Kemi workers a proclamation was circulated with this caption: "TO THE WORKERS, AGAINST GOING TO RUSSIA—FINLAND TO BE A SOVIET REPUBLIC."

Suspicions were expressed publicly that the Soviet Union was recruiting Finns to work, but in its memoranda EK emphasized the fact that there was very little of this: the true cause of the emigration was need and the depression. Although it was not recruitment per se, radio propaganda also had an effect. So did letters from across the border, which at first praised conditions and urged others to follow. As the Oulu EK reported: "There is no active recruitment, but unemployment and letters from friends are recruitment enough."

In the spring of 1932, Riekki reported that the Soviet embassy in Helsinki was bluntly rejecting the granting of visas for the passports of Finns seeking employment. Riekki had heard of an unfortunate applicant—a leftist worker—who had gone to the embassy in the winter of 1932. There the ambassador himself, Ivan Maiski, had said:

> One should not try to get into Russia nowadays. Altogether too many Finns have already gone there illegally, and among them there are many suspicious characters, about whom we need information.

Another man, whose boat had been taken by the border-hoppers—it was then confiscated in Russia—also went to the Russian embassy for help. He was reportedly told that the embassy would in no way get involved with these trips and that "the individuals who went to Russia without permission would themselves have to suffer the consequences."

EK tested the Soviet consulate at Kotka by sending one of their men who pretended to be a worker to ask for a visa there. He was not even let in, but advised at the door that there was no possibility of his going without a recommendation from Russia and other documentation. In the autumn of 1932, when perhaps 10,000 had already skipped across the border, Finnish officials noted that "passports are no longer denied, but the Soviet embassy will not grant visas." The passports and visas were indeed expensive, if one could get them, and that is surely why so many went secretly, without any papers.

Some Finns were greeted at the border by the shout: "Why are you coming here to a place in this condition?" A border-hopper by the name of Jaakko Seppänen related that a Finnish-speaking Red Army officer who interrogated him in Petroskoi wondered why the Finns were coming there.

"Russia is the most miserable place on earth, and the discipline here more devilish than anywhere else." The officer urged him to apply for return to Finland—later it would be impossible.

Karin and Niilo Puonti of Kotka. Karin has a wedding gift, a piece of golden bracelet on her wrist. A piece at a time was cut from it for sale to keep the family from starving to death.

Niilo Puonti, a mason from Kotka, skipped with his family across the Gulf of Finland in May 1932. As soon as they reached the Ingrian shore, a local resident said to him in Finnish: "You poor people, why did you come here?" Puonti would have turned around then and gone back, but it was too late.

The paper of the Finnish Organization of Red Trade Unions wrote in 1932 that it was absolutely against going to Russia on one's own hook. "Furthermore, one must take into account that the "butchers" try in every way to send their agents across the border for anti-Soviet activities."

The SKP's *Työmies* (Vol. 2, No. 33), wrote that the party had already prohibited workers from going to the Soviet Union on their own. There was no possibility of "organizing and sheltering hundreds of thousands of refugees there." Therefore, some had returned disappointed, and others had been transported to interior Russia and Siberia to huge refugee camps where they suffered from shortages. *TASS* and *Pravda* gave prominence to a news story according to which criminals had conned money in Helsinki from at least a hundred people who wanted to cross the border. Sometimes smugglers tricked the border-hoppers by leaving them on a barren island in the Gulf of Finland and returning home.

The EK had heard of a wire arriving in Petroskoi from Moscow in 1932 which strictly prohibited any further recruitment of labor. The report may refer to the fact that in January, Rovio was informed of "the GPU and the military's view of Canadian immigrants." The minutes of those groups questioned the rationale for recruiting labor and strictly forbade locating foreigners near the border. Rovio then sought support from Stalin and probably received it; at least American Finns arrived after that date and border-hoppers were permitted to remain in Karelia. According to a later memorandum of the Finnish Foreign Ministry, "Soviet civil officials consider illicit immigration into the Soviet Union a phenomenon which is to be resisted in every way."

On May 11, 1932, Petroskoi radio forbade workers from the capitalist countries to come to the Soviet Union: "You are not to believe all the agitators who urge you to leave your country. The Soviet Union is not the garbage dump for all the bourgeois countries' trash." Those who came secretly would not be accepted. *Red Karelia* wrote at the same time: ". . . in their private letters some people urge their Finnish friends to come here. This kind of 'recruitment' is not permissible and cannot continue." Two weeks later *Red Karelia* wrote that it "again had reason to announce that workers were not to try entering the Soviet Union on their own initiative."

Such were the prevailing conditions when thousands of unsolicited border-hoppers from Finland arrived in an unknown land, eager for work and feeling that they had already suffered enough.

Chapter Two

"It Would Be Nice to Get Home"

IMMEDIATELY UPON ARRIVAL, all the border-hoppers were imprisoned for weeks or even months of investigation and interrogation. It was a bitter pill to swallow, for they had believed they were welcome in the Soviet Union. But the truth soon became abundantly clear. The men's reasons for coming were especially suspect, and their wives and children had to wait for long-drawn-out investigations to take place.

The interrogations were exhaustive. The prisoners were questioned over and over about their reasons for coming. They were also forced to reveal whether they had previously been arrested, what their political affiliations were, who their close relatives were, where those relatives lived, and what Civil Guard officers they had known.

Toivo Lehikoinen, who had come from Varkaus to look for work, said later in Ural that he "had often been severely beaten" during interrogations in Petroskoi in the winter of 1933. Another man who wound up in Ural, Viljo Saaristo, a fifty-year-old automobile worker from Tampere, said that:

> when he came to Soviet Russia he was suspected of being sent there by the Finnish secret police, was beaten during interrogations in Petroskoi, was held for [six] days in a cellar among men condemned to death, and for three days in a cell without food, where there was only room enough to stand up.

SKP member Hilja Ojala crossed the border with her husband. The *lapualaiset* (a right wing group) had abused him in Tampere, threatening to send him east by force. She related that in June 1931 an interrogator at Kingisepp had shaken his fist before her face and shouted: "Why the hell do you come here where everything has been done! You should have continued the class struggle in your own country." In Kingisepp, the prisoners were marched to the jail and threatened that if anyone took a step to one side he would be shot without warning.

The previously mentioned Mrs. Vilhelmiina Murto confessed through an interpreter that she was guilty of crossing the border illegally and swore that "We have come only in search of work and will stay and live in the Soviet Union. We don't want to go back to Finland."

> In 1932 life in Finland became difficult; there was no steady employ-
> ment for husbands and sons. For that reason, the whole family decid-
> ed to go to the Soviet Union, where we heard on the radio that there
> was no unemployment and workers were needed. Selling our property,
> a house, cow, furniture, and different things, we went from Kotka to
> the Soviet Union on June 6 of this year.

According to Aino Saarela, one had to learn these Russian phrases in a hurry: "The women want to go to the toilet," and "The children need milk." After going to the delousing sauna, the women were shaved clean of all bod-ily hair. "Our first meal was a stinking broth, worse than dishwater. We poured the food onto the ground, and the Russians said, 'You'll learn to eat it yet.'"

The border-hoppers were immediately given the opportunity to request Soviet citizenship. Tauno Flinkman from Kotka, who ran ashore in Ingria, relates that even before the interrogation "small slips cut from wrapping paper were distributed to us, on which we were urged to write: 'I ask to be made a citizen of the USSR.'" According to one account, in addition to the Finnish language request, one had to sign three papers written in Russian. It was not a question of being actually forced to do so, but many understood the request as a requirement for admission into the country and a ticket to a better economic future. According to one report, those who applied for cit-izenship bound themselves never to seek the protection of Finnish law.

The small minority of Finns who traveled on passports, mainly border-hoppers' wives, were given a temporary residence permit. They were admit-ted into the country after the men had been "checked out" for a few months.

Border-hoppers coming by different routes wound up in Kresty investigation prison in Leningrad. In the summer of 1932, three floors at Kresty were reportedly reserved for Finns, with room for perhaps a thousand prisoners. According to EK, there were always about 550 border-hoppers there. The interrogations were held at night.

The women and children had to wait in the Shpalernaja prison. According to Siiri Hämäläinen, the food was an "awful swill," and the cells were packed. The children, however, were able to go wherever they pleased, because the bars on the doors were so sparse that they fit through.

August Lehmus tells of going to Shpalernaja as an interpreter when a boatload of border-hoppers was brought in. He was informed that according to the SKP the border-hoppers were "butchers." Lehmus is said to have pointed to a three-year-old girl and asked if she too were a butcher. The warden merely shrugged his shoulders.

Soon the women were moved into the Indoctrination Center for Finns in Leningrad, a former palace assigned to the Leningrad wing of the SKP to take care of Finns. Inmates had to sleep on cold, bare floors in crowded, cold, and noisy rooms. They were, however, free to move about the city. At this phase of the processing, the women already began selling their clothing to get better food for the children.

Bootlegger Matti Nykänen from Kemi sold his gold ring in Leningrad in 1932 in order to get enough to eat. He bought butter, bread, sugar, and pork, and died, one can assume, soon after eating it all.

The Vuorio family from Kemi crossed at Petsamo in July 1932 first by boat and then by walking over the hills. When the barking of dogs at a border-guard hut failed to arouse anyone, they awakened the Russian soldiers sleeping inside. The parents were interrogated at the border post, and diver Juho Vuorio admitted to his fourteen-year-old son Allan that he already regretted having come. Allan, who was taken to Murmansk, related:

> . . . we were confined in a big old stable that had been converted to a prison, each in a different cell holding about [thirty] Russian criminals. It was a horrifying place. I have never seen as many lice, bedbugs, and cockroaches as in those cells. They were so small you practically had to lie down on someone else if you wanted to sleep. Some of the men slept in nets hanging from the ceiling. I couldn't imagine sleeping when I looked at the rag-bags covered with lice and bedbugs lying on the bare earth floor. I stayed on my feet the entire first night in a space of about one square meter at the door of the cell. In the morning the food ration

was brought in—200 grams of wet bread, an aluminum cup of codfish broth, and hot water.

At the interrogations the men were asked about all their acquaintances in Finland. Then came a train trip to Leningrad followed by imprisonment for almost two months. "Father weighed over 100 kilos when we arrived in Russia," Allan relates. "Now he weighed [fifty-five] kilos. For the first time he confessed to me his intention to escape as soon as possible." But that possibility never came. Soon only the young and strong were in any condition to escape.

However, according to Ines Vuorio's letter written in 1933, only she and her daughter Margit would return; her husband wanted to stay in Russia with Allan. To judge by another letter in September, he must have changed his mind. "Jukka is frequently ill, he doesn't want to stay."

The border-hoppers could not look forward to freedom after the interrogations and investigations. Crossing the border illegally usually meant up to three years of compulsory labor under secret police* surveillance.

The border-hoppers were first transported to a GPU quarantine camp, from which, after checking, they were sent in groups either to job sites or to special residence zones, often far from the border—to Ural, Siberia, or Kazahkstan. They had no identification papers, nor could they leave the job sites on their own. Whatever their trades, they wound up in heavy construction, woods, or mine work. In 1932 Soviet Karelia requested and received permission from Moscow to locate immigrants away from border areas.

Hundreds of Finns were involved in the construction of the sports stadium and the GPU "Big House" on Liteinaja Street in downtown Leningrad. In this headquarters building, with which many of them became better acquainted later, there were said to be a thousand rooms. During its construction, there was growing dissatisfaction caused by hunger and working conditions. Even strikes developed in 1933, at which point the Finns were taken away.

During this brief phase in Leningrad, the first deaths occurred among the Finnish children. For example, one of them, according to a border-hopper, "was the only son of a Helsinki cabinet maker, who had been a plump, good-looking boy." In the hospital, he looked like "a ghost raised from the grave."

---

*The secret police were the security force known as the Cheka, which was the precursor of the KGB. It was known by different names at different times. For the sake of simplicity this book generally uses only GPU and NKVD (beginning with 1934).

The hospitals were not necessarily any help, and people soon learned actually to fear them. Some disappeared in the hospitals, and a rumor began to circulate that the children were taken away and given new names. One-year-old Eila Markkanen had to go the hospital, and when her mother, Aili, went to ask about her, she was told that the girl had been buried two weeks before. Selma Helistö went on a hunger strike in the jail because she did not know where her boy had been taken. He was brought back.

Pirkko Puonti (later Kyyhkynen) related that her cousins Erkki Halvorsen and Arvo Jordan died and were buried together in 1932. No small wooden box could be found, and the larger coffin they used did not fit into the grave, for the grave diggers had been told that the deceased were children. "The grave was dug deeper at the bottom, and the coffin was worked into it upright. In the end, a grave digger jumped up and down on the coffin to get it to fit."

Early in 1933 a group of at least eighty-six Finnish women and children managed to get a letter of complaint through to the SKP bureau in Leningrad—we will meet a number of these pilgrims to the promised land later in Ural. According to the letter, "they are systematically trying to make scoundrels of us, to kill our activism with regard to class and the Soviet." Furthermore:

> We are not complaining of our fate to you. If the external peace of the Soviet nation is contingent on this huge working country treating the refugees who have come here so harshly and disadvantageously, then we will happily suffer and bear our burden, so that those who are free can repair the damage and build a foundation for the new.

After May Day, the border-hoppers went on strike along the Mariinski Canal at Vytegra. Some one hundred Finnish loggers had been sent there. After a month, it became evident that the pay promised them was not forth-coming. The Finns stopped working and announced that they would not continue unless they were paid.

Viljo Kartineva relates that a high-ranking Finnish Red Army officer was driven hastily to the place. He berated the border-hoppers soundly. They were told that if they were Soviet citizens, they would be "jailed without fur-ther ado, but that this time mercy would serve as justice." The men were loaded onto a ship and taken to Leningrad for construction work.

In 1932, Aimo Salminen from Kotka was on the Kama River in Ural unloading wood from a barge with other Finns. He reported that they went on strike because of unpaid wages. The men had had to sell their clothes to buy their food ration from the dining hall. The names of ten Finnish strikers were put on a blackboard, Salminen says. They were threatened and berated as mutinous, as men who were acting "the way they do in capitalist countries." The strike was said to be the first in the Soviet Union in fourteen years. The situation was resolved by having the office workers punished and giving the workers an advance payment.

At a logging site in Karelia, a group of border-hoppers went on a hunger strike in order to get back to Finland. All were sent to Siberia, according to the EK. On Christmas morning 1932, three Finns refused to work in Syväri and demanded return to Finland. They were given a tongue lashing and ordered to work. In a few days they left on an escape attempt.

In mid-April of 1932, almost 200 Finnish men went on a hunger strike in Kresty prison after waiting months for an answer to their letter of complaint. They demanded investigation of their cases and either sentencing or return home. On the third day they were promised that they could return home if they started eating. There was great rejoicing. Then one hundred fifty Finns were put on a train, which was surprisingly well supplied for a short journey. In about a month, it stopped at the Omsk station in Siberia.

Finnish girls at a sewing shop in Syväri. Center, Kirsti Wahlstén; to her left, Karin Puonti.

Oskari Frisk from Enso refused to work at Syväri unless he got permission to move to Finland. When he was arrested he went on a hunger strike. After the strike had lasted twenty-three days, Frisk was taken to the hospital where they tried to force-feed him by way of a tube through his nostrils. He refused to submit. Finally he was promised that he could go to Finland if he began to eat. Immediately thereafter, he and his wife were sent to Siberia. Fanni Pyykkö maintains that in Sarov, in 1933, she saw this happen: that a man who had petitioned to return to Finland was force-fed through a tube, and that later he and his wife were banished to Siberia.

Many Finns were sent on from Leningrad to the "Svirstroi free labor site," which was northeast of Lotinapelto in Syväri, and also to Nevdubstroi on the Neva, and far away to Nivastroi, a little north of Kantalahti. In all three places, they lived in barracks villages and built power plants and dams. The first turbine at Svirstroi began turning in November of 1933; the dam was so poorly constructed that the Finns were afraid it would collapse.

Finns flowed into Svirstroi at the rate of up to several hundred a week although the camp was not ready to admit such numbers. At the peak in 1933, they were said to number thousands. In the one-story barracks which were equipped with sleeping platforms made of planks, families and unmarried men lived separately. The workers were given quilted clothing and birch-bark shoes.

Everyone got a food ration card, and attempts were made to assign them to work according to their skills. All had to eat in the dining hall. The Finns generally arrived without any money, so they were given an advance in pay. From then on, so much was deducted from their wages that they hardly saw any money. There were also prisoners at work in Syväri; the Finns did not belong to that group, although their freedom of movement was restricted.

In 1938 Finland's *Social Democrat* published a drawing of the barracks in which Finnish border-hoppers lived at the site of the Svirstroi power plant.

There were many unmarried men at Svirstroi who soon tired of the barracks life. The border was enticingly close. The men got themselves skis, and it was a rare morning when someone was not found to have left in the night on a "search for butter"—that is, fled to Finland. In Nevdubstroi, too, the

In 1933 *Hakkapeliitta* published a photograph of ragged border-hoppers who had returned to Finland from Syväri.

unmarried men's barracks were "half empty every morning" because of the flights. Those who did not make it to Finland froze or were captured and sentenced to banishment.

The *Helsingin Sanomat* reported in 1933 that during that spring, 150 border-hoppers had returned to Finland from Syväri. That year a total of 711 returned from Russia. There were even escapes from Nivastroi, although there the situation with regard to flight was more difficult. The Karelia NKVD reported having arrested some 900 border-hoppers by May of 1937 for attempting to return to Finland.

The Sortavala subdivision of the EK reported that those returning to Finland were "in general the worst kind of citizenship material—adventurers, almost all communists, or lazy, useless, and criminal types." The writer of the report expressed a fear that they would become agitators in Finland. General opinion was said to favor "letting those who wanted to go to the Soviet Union go."

In the spring of 1934, the Svirstroi paper published a statement on how the 183 Finnish border-hoppers there were regarded. According to the statement, the people who had crossed the border secretly were "degenerate individuals who could not endure the conditions involved in building up a true socialistic society."

According to Pyykkö, a certain "man of ideals" said in a speech given in the "red corner" that those who tried to flee would wind up "keeping the long-tailed wolves in Siberia company." Tauno Flinkman related that he was threatened with a pistol while being interrogated after an escape attempt. When he called the interrogator "comrade," the man shouted: "The Siberian wolf is your comrade!" Flinkman did wind up in Siberia. (The Russian saying is "Tambovski volk tebe tovarishtsh"—"The Tambov wolf is your comrade.")

One of the many who fled was Helsinki border-hopper Uljas Vasenius. His wife had left their children in Finland, come on a passport, and gotten work in a dining hall at Svirstroi. It was agreed that she would follow her husband when she received a letter from him from Finland.

Vasenius traveled through the woods for three weeks, living on the berries he found. His shoes fell apart, and he went on walking barefoot. In a swamp close to the border, he fainted from hunger and exhaustion. He was awakened by a border guard's dog. After sentencing, he and forty others who had been caught trying to escape were sent by train to Siberia. There too Vasenius escaped and headed for Ural. Again he was captured and sent to Tara, where he was seen walking around in birch-bark shoes and torn quilted clothing.

Deportation to Siberia for three years was the normal punishment for attempting to escape—"small potatoes," as the more experienced said scornfully. One border-hopper reported that many from his group had already died on the month-long train journey to Irkutsk. When it ended, they still had a 650-kilometer trek on foot to the gold mines, wearing birch-bark shoes in bitter cold. Of the sixty-six Finns in this group, only twenty reportedly reached their destination.

In Svirstroi, the Finns were divided into work brigades. Work was done five days at a stretch, with every sixth day free. The "strike force" workers had their names written on a red tablet, the malingerers on a black tablet.

In addition to work, free-time activities were organized for the border-hoppers. They were expected to join political and para-military organizations. The atheists league proselytized among the Finns, and every barracks had its "red corner" or meeting room with its flags, red stars, loudspeaker, bulletin board, as well as its cultural committee, posting committee, and its political education circle. Everyone had to participate in a nightly political meeting. The camp's propaganda group prepared programs and presented them during evening gatherings. At Svirstroi there was even a Finnish newspaper of which 800 copies were printed.

Russian workers and Finnish border-hoppers at Svirstroi.

Osoaviahim* was a civil defense organization with an operative in every barracks. According to Finnish officials Oso trained and armed the border-hoppers so that they could fight in case of a revolution in Finland.

By means of evening entertainments, solicitations, lotteries, sale of insignias, and volunteer work, OSO collected money for the airplane fund and the Otto Ville Kuusinen tank fund. MOPR or International Red Aid collected funds to support revolutionaries in different countries, and, according to EK, the communist party in Finland as well.

At first everyone was urged to join Osoaviahim and attend lectures, which were held in the "red corner." Marching drills were held outdoors. According to Allan Vuorio, mason Niilo Puonti and others directed the drills. He had been a buck sergeant in the Finnish Army. Later, Finnish officials blocked his return to Finland when they heard about his OSO activity. The returnees who were ascertained to have taken part in OSO and MOPR activities were charged with preparing for treason. Vuorio recalled that the lectures taught the manual of arms and the use of gas masks. He himself stopped attending them when "the whole thing became a mess."

Puonti had crossed the Gulf of Finland with his wife, Karin, and his five-year-old daughter Pirkko. According to the girl, Puonti was a social democrat, so that he did not go to the eastern neighbor's country for ideological reasons. The family had been awaiting a letter from an acquaintance in Russia to tell them whether it paid to go; even at Viikinsaari Island his wife begged him to go back to Kotka to see if the letter had come. Puonti's brother found the letter, which absolutely forbade them to go. When he asked his cousins, who belonged to the Civil Guard, whether he should inform on his brother, they said: "Let the lad find out what it's like." Karin's sister and her Norwegian-born husband, Oskar Halvorsen, and a Jordan family from Mikkeli were in the same boatload.

In March 1933, Karin Puonti wrote that they were all sick of the conditions in Svirstroi and were trying to get home. "This is a marshy climate, we've all come down with a severe cough."

Joining the organizations at Svirstroi was not actually compulsory, but those who did not join might be pressured, labeled, and moved into poorer barracks. Their names might also wind up on the black list. In any event, so much was deducted from everyone's pay for the "voluntary" aid funds and for other obligations that sometimes only the food slips were left in

---

*Osoaviahim (*Obstsestvo sodeistvija oborone, aviatsionnomu i himitsheskomu stroitelstvu*) is, according to the Soviet dictionary, a volunteer organization of Soviet citizens which functioned from 1927 to 1948. It promoted Soviet patriotism and military skills.

their hands. Payments for lodging, clothing, light, and heat were subtracted from their wages. The Finns secretly sold their clothing in order to get money.

People soon learned that they had to beware of informers everywhere. The Wahlstén girl's father was already arrested at Svirstroi; someone had reported his saying that he did not want to work for the good of the Soviet Union. That time he was freed when the information was proved to be false.

Karin Puonti once said, when only Finns were present: "I will not send my child to a Russian school." Someone informed on her because the next day there was a caricature of Mrs. Puonti along with those words on the bulletin board.

The Finns at Svirstroi were under the GPU surveillance of Rudolf Holopainen. (His first name was Ludwig, as Kalle Lehto recalls it—EK-Valpo file 677—but it was Rudolf, according to Karelian KGB archives). Holopainen was a Red Army officer, perhaps born in St. Petersburg. An NKVD operative, condemned on January 1, 1938, he was a "small, erect, and sharp-tongued man who was very much attracted to women." According to Lehto, Holopainen rose to the rank of major in the NKVD. He was reportedly in the habit of boasting, "We Cheka are the terror of the world." Sometimes he would declaim: "Comrades, build! We Cheka members will stand guard so that you can work in peace!"

According to Pyykkö, there was a stool pigeon in every barracks who reported to Holopainen, and men were arrested on the grounds of those reports. Holopainen was soon transferred to Karelia, where in 1938 he met the same fate as his charges. The nighttime arrests were brought up at a meeting in Svirstroi, whereupon the Finns were told that there were spies sent from Finland among them, and that the "red broom" would sweep them away.

In December of 1932, representatives of the Finnish Communist Party made an investigatory tour of border-hopper sites in different parts of the country. According to their report, the camps were in a totally wretched condition: "alcoholism, black marketeering of clothing, brawling, gambling, and other evils were widespread among both Finns and Russians." The work supervisors, however, blamed only the Finns, which "smacked of 'Great Russia' chauvinism." The next year they looked into the border-hoppers' conditions in the brick plant associated with the Soloma gulag. Housing conditions were miserable, and the Finns were suffering hunger. For his part, the man in charge of the red corner at Nivastroi reported that the Finns were unable to go to work in the cold of winter with summer clothes, lost their food rations, and finally tried to escape to Finland.

The Karelian GPU leadership also noted the border-hoppers' circumstances in December of 1932. According to their report, "recent symptoms" among the Finns might lead to "anti-Soviet eruptions." Conditions at Svirstroi were considered particularly bad. Aarne Kuusela, a man from Viipuri who had crossed the border as a young boy in 1918, was commanded to go there to organize group political activities under Holopainen. Kuusela had been expelled from the Leningrad minority university for drinking. (Kangaspuro 250-52; Rautkallio 65, EK/Kemi interrogation records 47/1937)

The border-hoppers were a motley crew. Kuusela demanded that the SKP send someone to Svirstroi to settle quarrels among the Finns. The workers, he said, were not receptive to ideological work. Among them were some decent workers and a small minority of party and communist youth group members. The rest Kuusela depicted as bootleggers, criminals, "pawns of capitalist" opportunists, and adventurers.

Kuusela admitted that escape attempts continued and that many of the border-hoppers wanted to return to Finland. A "noticeable pessimism" was surfacing among them, which he intended to decrease by political enlightenment. He and his helper began with the young, from whom he hoped a more favorable attitude would spread to their elders.

Kuusela was eager to interpret for and help the border-hoppers, too eager, in the opinion of some. He communicated the workers' hopes and needs to his superiors and emphasized their extraordinary ability to work. On the basis of his reports, the Moscow SKP took a position which advocated workers' being told their rights, and how long their internment would be: "Would they be held for six months, a year, or two years?"

Midway in 1932, representatives of the GPU announced that the stays in the camps, insofar as border-hoppers were concerned, "were limitless." "It was as if the group had been punched in the face," Kuusela observed.

In vain Kuusela asked higher-ups in Leningrad when the Finns could become Soviet citizens and members of trade unions. In January of 1933 he complained of uncertainty and said that things had come to a kind of dead end. After an inspection at Svirstroi, it was decided to send Kuusela to cool off where so many other border-hoppers had been sent: to Ural.

An attempt was made to keep watch over the border-hoppers' correspondence to prevent their sending negative news. Kuusela demanded that the letters were to reflect an "optimistic and encouraging spirit" and chose the people who were permitted to write. Nevertheless, letters did reach Finland, sometimes along with escapees.

Pastimes were forbidden and the GPU announced that the punishment for card-playing was three years. Kuusela reported that "in spite of this, some mule-heads are still slapping down the cards." For New Year, a carload of liquor was sent to Svirstroi. After the celebration, many Finns stayed away from work, lost their jobs and ration cards and began to live as if the end of the world were at hand. "Are they to starve to death, since they are no longer given work or food, and are not taken away?" Kuusela inquired of the party leadership.

As the efficiency of labor declined, the party committee organized meetings as often as three times a week, selling pasties at the club as an incentive to attend. The subject of the meetings was always: Work performance must be improved. The Finns declared that it would not happen until the food was better. The answer was always curt: "We don't discuss such matters at meetings! You can write to the party committee."

"Where will they be discussed then?" insisted one of the workers. "In Finland we always threshed such things out at the meetings."

"We're not in Finland now. What is your name?"

Two hundred Finnish children died at Svirstroi of dysentery and malnutrition. Flinkman went so far as to vow "without exaggeration" that no child under the age of ten survived, but we do know of some who did.

According to Allan Vuorio, some 150 Finns died during the winter of 1932-1933 alone. No proper sick care had been arranged. Even Kuusela reported that child mortality had increased noticeably. "For example, in Barracks 594, [thirteen] children have died within three months. In Barracks 267, three children died in one day." Toivo Laine related that in Nevdubstroi:

> When we had been in the country for only two months, I woke up one night to the hysterical weeping and shrieking of a woman. It was Elli Eskolin. Her little boy had died. "You brought the children and me into this hell," she accused her husband. Her grief was repeated shortly afterwards when her daughter died.

The Finns still took some pride in their craft, and they organized "strike forces" on the job. Their efficiency is said to have aroused envy among the Russians.

Later on, Finnish border-hoppers stated that in the winter conditions at Svirstroi were absolutely wretched and that workers died as a result. Men who worked outside wore burlap rags and birch-bark shoes as footwear. Women had to do the same heavy work as the men, and the workday was long. Diseases spread, the barracks were cold and dirty, there were no blankets, and rats ate their food.

At Nevdubstroi the barracks had no toilets, so that human excrement was everywhere around them. People died in the food line, and Hilja Jelonen, pregnant with her third child, gave birth prematurely when she was trampled on by a group. Children went to sweep the floors of railroad cars which had transported rye flour, and mothers made porridge from the sweepings. Food in the dining hall was said to be wretched. In nearby villages, bread and clothing were exchanged for milk. Some traded their gold rings there or sold them in the Leningrad money exchanges.

Aid packages from relatives in Finland arrived in Svirstroi, even in large quantities to some: household goods, clothing, shoe pacs, bedclothes, and food. It all arrived free: for some reason no customs or freight was charged. The Puonti family even succeeded in getting a radio and skis. Holopainen took the radio away, saying: "You don't need this." Money could also be sent from Finland, but sometimes it did not reach its destination.

One can see from the records that in 1933, a fifty-five kilo shipment was sent to the Hansen-Haugs in Nevdubstroi. The receipt was signed by a representative of the international commerce commission, and the packet was transported by Sojuztrans. Efforts were made later to ascertain the fate of the shipment.

Chief Consul Eino Westerlund reported to Finland from Leningrad that he could not understand how the border-hoppers received shipments because there was no official postal package service between the two countries. "The office of the chief consul does not wish under any circumstances to become the transmitter of such packages."

Kerttu, the daughter of Santeri Norteva, who earlier had founded a utopian Socialist commune in Northern Canada, visited Svirstroi. She wondered at seeing oak furniture, cooking utensils, lovely women's clothing, and babies' cribs "in the wretched barracks of the Finnish border-hoppers." She hoped that visitors might come only when a model city "with beautiful houses, straight streets, and tree plantings" was completed. (Kerttu was detained as a Soviet agent in Finland during the war.)

At first, the border-hoppers gritted their teeth rather than ask for help from Finnish officials. But as early as the end of 1931 the first of their difficult cases were dropped into the laps of the those officials, and a line had to be drawn.

Adam Kaukonen and Väinö Ylén from Kotka had skipped across with their families in 1931. The men were imprisoned in Leningrad, and the others were settled in the enlightenment building, where up to ninety women and children slept on the floor "with newspapers as their bedclothes." The children became ill.

Kaukonen and Ylén asked for help from Finland's chief consulate, when they heard that they would wind up at some faraway job site. They wanted to return home and declared that they would "willingly submit to prison discipline in Finland." At least the children should be saved, the men wrote.

The foreign ministry tried to follow the fate of these families closely, and the case gave rise to a voluminous correspondence. Westerlund reported that the cases of Kaukonen and Ylén were "the most terrible" he had ever encountered in his long career. "After only three months in this paradise, those young men seem to have lost ten years of their life." Westerlund was afraid that his help might be detrimental to the men. He had already lost sight of them and assumed that they had wound up in Siberia. Later he related that Kaukonen's two children had died.

At the same time, the case of seven Finns who had been banished to Siberia was being sifted in Helsinki. A letter from the village of Borisovskoj in western Siberia had arrived there, signed by a group of men who had left from the Kotka area:

> To the Finnish consul: We the Undersigned citizens of Finland turn to you asking to find out how long we have to suffer this cold and filth here. We have been held since last August. We beg you to help us quickly.

Riekki, the head of the EK, who had apparently been asked to comment on the matter, wrote to the foreign ministry on Christmas Eve 1931:

> It is not to the benefit of Finnish officials to embark too willingly on measures to help such people, since such behavior would only serve to incite many more to leave Finland.

Riekki conjectured that there may well have been causes for banishment in the men themselves, adding that they had "left Finland secretly of their own free will" and that many of them had previously been convicted of crimes in Finland.

But the floodgates had already been opened. Soon one border-hopper after another sent to Finland or her diplomatic representatives simple free-form petitions of the following sort:

We petition the Finnish government. We the undersigned ask permission to return to Finland since we have come to the Soviet Russia [November 25, 1931]. Otto Aleksander Paldan and my wife Tyyne nee Kauhanen with my child [June 13, 1932] without official permission.

Otto Paldan Tyyne Paldan
Virstroi 10/14.32
Witnesses to the correctness of the petition
Lehtinen Ester Aaltonen Aleksander

Another later example is even simpler: "I, the below-mentioned person, want to get back to my country, Finland. In Ala Tagil in Soviet Russia. Karjalainen Eino."

Petitioners for return to Finland were "educated, reprimanded, shouted down, and pressured," and some of them withdrew their petitions in fright. They were told that otherwise their pay could be cut or their extra rations card taken away. If the petitioner managed to get the consul to mail him a passport, the local GPU offices would not give him a visa. They delayed the matter by telling the applicant to come back later. Then the GPU began to confiscate the passports at the post offices, saying that the Finns could leave when matters were cleared up. They were given a certificate which permitted them to stay on "without citizenship." It even happened that when a Finn's pass was in an official's possession for the purpose of obtaining a visa, he was shipped to Siberia because he did not have a passport.

In 1932 Tauno Jalanti wrote a secret memorandum on the subject to the Finnish Foreign Ministry. It was based on September information from EK according to which at least ten thousand Finns had already taken off for the Soviet Union. Some 700 of them had been caught on the Finnish side of the border. By January, some 12,000 were reported to have gone. According to the memo, life in the Soviet camps was harsh, worse than in Finnish prisons. Sometimes as many as a hundred people had to live in the same room, and dysentery spread. Only a few escape attempts had succeeded.

In a message to Helsinki, Chief Consul Westerlund stated his opinion that no effort should be made even to help the border-hoppers to return home. He dubbed them the "victims of stupidity" and demanded that the people's "migration psychosis be forestalled." At first he had requested that those who wanted to go be given a passport in Finland. The Russians were unlikely to grant them a visa, but if they had a Finnish passport, then at least an effort could be made to help them in Russia. By the end of 1932, he had already come to the conclusion that no help should be given.

As I see it, for the time being we should take no official action to help the border-hoppers to return, first of all because such actions produce no results and are, therefore, stupid, and secondly their living in the kind of misery one finds here—in hunger and filth—is the very best kind of anti-communist education, and thirdly because things seem to be developing in such a way that the matter may become a scandal for the Soviet government. The border-hoppers now seem to be planning a folk migration in order to return to Finland, which, if it materializes, would be miserable publicity for this country and would surely attract great attention all over the world. I already know that Soviet officials are worried. They are investigating the reasons for the great discontentment among the border-hoppers and cursing the demands the Finns make, who supposedly want "palaces" built for them, and "even" to be fed butter, meat, and milk too.

Let them attend the school they have voluntarily enrolled in, the consul concluded. He was in favor of having the foreign ministry turn a cold shoulder to the border-hoppers' relatives who turned to them for help.

Westerlund repeatedly advocated cutting off the traffic across the border, especially with the help of the social democratic newspapers, which "could save thousands of workers from destruction. All of those who go are at the very least 'pinkos,' although they do 'whiten' when they get here." Finland's *Social Democrat* advised that "it was available" and in the course of time the paper did publish even quite extensive accounts of the border-hoppers' experiences. Officials put "those returning from Utopia" in touch with editors and sometimes provided them with ready-made material.

Ambassador Yrjö-Koskinen also requested in January 1933 that an effort be made to work on the problem from the Finnish side of the border. Contrary to Westerlund, he was of the opinion that the border-hoppers "are to be helped insofar as possible in their efforts to return. There is no other course open to representatives of the country: every Finnish citizen has the right to return to his homeland." Also, in his opinion, "those who might possibly have been recruited" were to be allowed home.

A week later, Westerlund reported having heard that all those who had resorted to the chief consulate for admission to Finland or whose relatives had begun acting on their behalf in Finland, "are being rounded up and taken to a concentration camp south of Moscow where mail service is cut off." When the treatment of the Finns was pointed out to them, the Russians answered: "We can't set up a special regime for them." For the time being,

Westerlund decided against making any further proposals regarding the border-hoppers. Efforts on their behalf were hopeless and would only hurt them, he wrote to Foreign Minister Antti Hackzell.

In May 1933 Westerlund reported that no border-hoppers had sought his help for about a month, which he believed was the result of their having been moved into the countryside far from Leningrad—or perhaps conditions had improved so much that they no longer needed to turn to the chief consulate "which couldn't help much anyway."

Riekki was aware that those Finns for whom an effort had been made to help had been taken to remote OGPU quarantine camps. "Soviet officials have the mistaken impression that a considerable number of the border-hoppers have been sent from here either for spying or counter-revolutionary purposes," he wrote. EK was not, however, completely innocent and unknowing. The Viipuri EK, for example, had at least seventy-four agents who made espionage trips across the border or who lived in the Soviet Union and aided Finnish intelligence. One of them made over 100 espionage tours between 1921 and 1930. In all, Russian researchers estimate that Finnish intelligence sent over some 400 agents, who used the same routes as the border-hoppers.

The Kemi division of the EK welcomed the news that the border-hoppers had been moved further inland. The number returning would decrease, there would be less work when they no longer had to be interrogated, and money would be saved. And so it was.

A recent photo of the Sarov monastery building, where the NKVD stationed the border-hoppers. Sarov disappeared for a time from books and maps; it became war production city Arzamas-16. The old name has now been restored.

Chapter Three

The Monastery Prisoners

THE CAMP OF WHICH WESTERLUND AND RIEKKI had heard was Sarov,* far off in North Mordva and southeast of Moscow. As early as 1931 about eighty border-hoppers had been sent to Sarov, and in the spring of 1933 the majority of Finnish workers at the Svirstroi job site were shipped there by train. At the end of April, hundreds of workers arrived at the camp. They were said to be "from among the most activist group" and had asked troublesome questions. A head count was taken many times; their number was 700. It was at the same time that a couple of hundred Finns were shipped to the same destination from both Nivastroi and Leningrad. It is hard to say whether they are to be included in the 700.

Those who made it back to Finland from Sarov later related that people branded as unreliable for diverse reasons wound up in this camp: grumblers, strikers, those who had tried to escape or maintained contact with Finland or had petitioned for return to Finland by contacting Finnish representatives or the GPU. In addition, Anti-Soviet talk had opened the doors of Sarov to some of them. According to Aino Saarela, "the papers announced in February 1932 that there was no room for foreign spies near the border."

---

*Sarov does not appear on any Soviet maps or in any geographical dictionaries. It became a closed city, the name of which was Arzamas-16. Atomic research was conducted there, among other things. Now it has gotten its old name back. The border-hoppers usually called it "Sarova" as did Kostiainen in his 1988 research.

43

Children of Finnish border-hoppers in a school picture at the Sarov quarantine camp in 1933. The woman in the white coat is Tyyne Pynnönen.

According to one account, the ones who had not participated in the activities of Osoaviahim wound up in Sarov; according to another, it was those who did not want to request Soviet citizenship.

A couple of thousand Finns remained in Svirstroi. One report had it that sixty-seven percent of them had petitioned to return to Finland. Arvo Poika Tuominen, a high Finnish communist official who visited the site on a speaking tour, reported that those who were ordered to attend the meeting merely sat staring dully; no discussion of any kind arose. In 1936, all Svirstroi was emptied of the "untrustworthy," that is to say, not many Finns remained. Another factor was involved: work on the power plant was completed that year.

In the spring of 1933, the names of those going to Sarov were called out. They were paid off and were locked into dark, guarded cattle cars with bars and shutters on the windows. Their rations were herring and bread; the children were given a teaspoon of sugar per day. A few times they received hot water. There was a small barrel stove in the center of the car, but it was so cold on the straw-covered sleeping platforms that a sleeper's hair froze to the wall during the night. A hole in the floor covered with a piece of plywood served as the toilet.

The journey lasted two weeks. For two days, the trains stood in the Moscow railroad yard. Although it was cold, the iron shutters were opened so that the Finns could see the fly-over of army airplanes organized in honor of May Day.

Sarov had been a monastery—Russia's second largest—until the Bolsheviks expelled the monks and replaced them with prisoners. It was situated on a tributary of the Volga River south of Nizhni Novgorod. A temporary narrow-gage railway sixty kilometers long had been built to it from the Shatki station. The official name of the quarantine camp can be seen in letters sent from it by Finnish prisoners: quarantine lager OGPU.

With the arrival of the large new "detachment," the women were at first kept outside the camp but in barracks surrounded by barbed wire. The food was millet and buckwheat porridge. The walls and floors were icy, and many of the children contracted pneumonia. Later the children were lodged in a church. When the women were put through the delousing sauna, all their body hair was shaved off, including the hair on their heads.

The central yard, where the men were held, was surrounded on all sides by buildings, and by a wall many meters high. Entry to this area was by two guarded gates. There were three churches in the camp. The main church served as the dining hall; there was still a bell in its tower and over the door was a picture of the Virgin Mary, with what appeared to be bullet holes in it. Mealtimes Lauri Patrikainen handed wooden spoons to the men at the door, which were taken away when they left.

There were no criminals sentenced by the courts in the monastery area itself. The border-hoppers were mostly Finns, but there were also Poles, Jews, Germans, Czechs, and perhaps a number of Estonians. All told, there were said to be over 3,000 inmates, and according to one person who returned, there were at the height, in the summer and fall of 1933, that many Finns. Others considered the figure to be exaggerated, that so many people could not have fit into the monastery—at least not at the same time.

The border-hoppers had no personal documents, but later they were given a "Sarov Pass," which mentioned (in Russian) their "serving a term at Sarov lager." Some of the Finns who went out to work were described as "free men"; others were the so-called "kremlin men," who had to remain constantly in the central yard (*kreml*). They could not go outside the walls to work, not even if they were accompanied by guards. Underneath the monastery lay a network of bat-infested passages, through which some of the men tried to escape.

The men lived in the churches and in the monks' cells. The children, who were lodged in a children's home, were sometimes allowed to see their fathers and mothers. According to Eila Wahlstén, she got to see her mother only once. Pirkko Puonti remembers that her family met for a short time in a monk's cell "with horrible scads of fleas and a picture of God on the wall."

The nationalities were mingled in the children's home, so that some of the children began to learn Russian. To pass the time, they made up songs and sang them. A song by Irja Pekala was set to the tune of "Vagabond King," and told of life in "Sarov lager, a terrible place, like a human hell." Another of her songs began:

> Now I've come to Russia, where hunger turns the screws,
> I get a sliver of herring and a little piece of bread.
> Hey diddle diddle day, while the Russian plays us dirty tricks.

Some ten Finnish teen-age boys were separated from the others. They were often entrusted with responsible tasks. Apparently they were meant to be raised as obedient Soviet citizens. The boys were given kitchen duty and all the necessary keys so they were able to pilfer extra food from the stores for themselves and their families at night.

Weakened by hunger and disease, some 400 Finns are said to have died at Sarov. During the summer of 1933 alone, according to EK reports, 300 died of dysentery and starvation. According to one man who returned to Finland, "total famine" prevailed. Many of the victims were children; it was hard to get them to eat the strange food.

Ellen and Hiskias Närvänen from Kemi had walked across the border with their two boys. Alpo Närvänen died at Svirstroi; his parents got a wooden coffin for him but could not be present at the burial. Alpo's older brother died in Sarov at the age of six. Kerttu was born in Sarov but died in Magnitogorsk when she was a few months old.

While others kept watch, Salli Lappalainen once bolted down a dish of farina and a large slice of bread and butter that had been brought to her in the children's room. She nearly died. The woman doctor, who saved her, offered this good advice: "Never eat when your innards are starved."

Not all the border-hoppers who returned to Finland were willing to tell of having experienced misery. As to the others, one should take into account the possibility that some of them may have exaggerated the squalor during the EK interrogations. For example, Tyyne Leskinen (presently Kannas) now says: "The children at least did not go hungry in Sarov. Anyone who claims they did is lying!" The Tervonen children remember having eaten rice pud-

The Närvänens and Valkonens observing Christmas in Finland in 1930. Hiskias Närvänen (on left) and three children died in Russia, and Finnish officials were unwilling to admit Mrs. Ellen Närvänen (second on left) back into the country.

Three of the Närvänen children died in the course of a year. This is Alpo's funeral in 1932. The next to die was Alvari, who is standing before the cross.

ding and gotten tomatoes for the first time in their lives. But again it should be noted that what was enough for children did not suffice for men doing heavy outdoor work.

"When you look at those men, you want to scream, they are all like skeletons already," a woman wrote in 1933. "But still there is a bayonet at their back; a guard takes them to work and back and carefully checks to see that all of them are there."

All the adults brought to Sarov were questioned again. The interrogators were GPU officers Nikolai Fomkin, who was called "Vonkkin," and Hattunen.

After the initial check and quarantine assignment, the men were divided into three groups according to age and strength, and work norms were set accordingly. The men in the first class were ordinarily assigned to work in the woods. The day's norm was to cut three cubic meters of firewood or seven compact cubic meters of timber. The guards accompanying them were strict: "A step to the right or left will be considered an attempt to escape and you will be shot." Women were put to work in the fields. At one time, they went on strike for permission to cook potatoes out in the fields.

Wake-up time was 4:30 A.M., when the inmates began to line up at the dining hall. For breakfast there was porridge, which was more like a gruel. The day's work ended at 4:00 P.M., at which time the bread ration was distributed according to how well the work norms were met. Even the bread was watery. For lunch there was sour cabbage soup, which many threw away, contenting themselves with bread alone.

The best "strike force" workers were given as much as a kilo of bread a day and a fried fish to boot. In addition the rule was that tea, sugar, and a small piece of soap were to be distributed to every worker monthly. No wages were paid, but some spoke of getting coupons from which rationed goods could be bought at the camp store, for example, sugar, tobacco, envelopes, and postage stamps.

During the summer the workers supplemented their diet with snakes and frogs, and with clams that they found in the river. Some even managed to steal food from the watchdog's dish. In the autumn, they pilfered root vegetables while working in the fields. Allan Vuorio tells of saving the life of a Finn suffering from dysentery by bringing him beets hidden in his pants. Allan's father, who had once weighed 100 kilos, was now down to forty-five.

Those too weak or too sick to work were given 300 to 400 grams of watery bread and a little bit of broth. A "majority" even of those who worked were soon so weakened that they mainly just stood around on the job sites.

The sleeping facilities were cold and dirty. There were no mattresses or bedclothes on the tiered sleeping platforms. Once in every two weeks the inmates we were able to go to the sauna. The hospital at Sarov was crowded and dirty. The inmates suffered chiefly from dysentery, edema, and stomach ailments. Every night Finnish boys hauled away several corpses with a horse and wagon and buried them in the railway embankment where the sand was soft. The Finns called the deceased "railway guards."

Some border-hoppers maintain that if the board coffin was too small for a corpse, its legs were chopped off with an ax. On the other hand, Allan Vuorio says that nude bodies were taken to the track, toppled off the wagon into a pit, and covered with sand and lime.

> *Two hundred Finns died of hunger and disease within a few months. I remember how mothers would come into our hut weeping and telling us that their son or daughter had died and asking that one of us go and take care of the burial, and see to it that the body was covered with the clothing they brought.*

According to the Finns, the camp commandant was an officer with two straight bars on his collar (the rank of adjutant regimental commander or special battalion commander). According to others, he was a general who spoke Russian but also understood Finnish. Taking care of such a large number of people seemed to exceed his abilities.

When the working day was over, everyone was practically forced to go to the clubhouse for political education. The subjects were the communist party, the development of the Soviet Union, increasing work efficiency, and related topics. Once they even got to see Charlie Chaplin's film, *The Gold Rush.* At first they wondered at it, but then some scoffer concluded that it was meant to teach them that they could even get a meal from a shoe if it was cooked long enough.

> *The state of mind among the Finns is gloomy and sullen, and almost the only subject of conversation is memories of what they used to eat in Finland. Escapes are frequent, although mainly among the Poles. The Finns seem to be waiting for the end of summer when berries are ripe and it will be easier to succeed.*

It was later reported that many Finns had tried to escape, but that almost all of them had been captured. According to one Finn who returned, a new law was announced in the fall of 1934: every attempt to escape brought a sentence of five to ten years of forced labor. Many also sought official permission to go to Finland—without results.

In Sarov there were also units of the party, the MOPR, and the Osoaviahim, although membership was not compulsory. Membership and aid fees were drawn from those who joined. It appears that a purging of some organizations began as early as 1933; border-hoppers were expelled from the military Osoaviahim.

There was no longer as much interest in the political meetings as there had first been, and complaints abounded among the Finns.

> The trade union and "red corner" meetings have gradually degenerated into tongue-lashing sessions during which the leaders heap abuse on the lazy and the malingerers, who, because of their hunger, had not completed work norms which exceed their strength. When better food is demanded of the leaders, the answer is always, "it's coming tomorrow," but the promises have never proved true.

Ilmari Kanerva, a masseur and physical therapist from Helsinki, was the Sarov political club instructor. Russian was taught by Kustaa Adolf Toijonen, the director of the children's home, who had lived in Russia as a child. A former seaman (Kola), Nikolai Gavroi of Viipuri, who spoke eight languages, directed the staff in charge of Finnish affairs at Sarov. He was also recalled to have had charge of the kitchen, and to have been the lover of the camp commandant's wife. The above-mentioned Fomkin and Jalmari Kosonen were in charge of ideological instruction for the Finns.

Their acquaintance with Second Lieutenant Nikolai Prokopyevitch Fomkin, who was authorized by the NKVD, turned out to be fateful for the border-hoppers. They believed him to be a Karelian Finn and a former member of the Red Guard, but according to KGB papers, he was a Russian citizen, born in Livonia in 1901. During the Russian civil war, he had served with the Finnish Reds, and he had learned more Finnish in a border-guard detachment on the Finnish border. He was said to have lost one of his collar bars because of strikes among Finns.

Kosonen was a small and slender worker from Savo. He was a former Red Guard member who was later testified to have disseminated "bolshevism" in the army. In 1922 he was sentenced to prison and spent years in the Tammisaari compulsory labor center. Kosonen had also been an itinerant political speaker in Finland. He had been asked to speak at the funerals of those who had left the church, and was said to be able to bring tears to the eyes of his listeners. He had come to Sarov by way of Nevdubstroi.

Fomkin's wife had already lived in Russia for years, but Kosonen's wife had remained in Finland and lived near the Imatra workers' home; their son still lives in Imatra. Their passport was in order, and they had applied for a visa, but they never did leave—apparently they did not get a visa. With a wife in Finland, Kosonen married again in the Soviet Union. His Finnish wife warned their boy not to tell people that his father had written about having joined the Russian communist party.

In Finland, the police confiscated the following enthusiastic letter which a Finnish woman sent to Lyyli Kosonen in 1932:

> . . . workers have built once backward Russia into an industrial nation. Such giants as the Dnieper power plant, the Magnitogorsk smelter, and the Kusnets copper mines. This year we are putting 518 factories into operation. They are the flowers of socialist construction. . . . In Nivastroi a power plant is being built which will provide power for the city of Kantalahti, where there are now about 22,000 inhabitants. . . .

A Finn who wound up in Kamensk later told how the political workers at Sarov functioned:

> [At Sarov] the clothing situation was actually somewhat better, but the food situation was absolutely impossible, and the griping kept on getting louder. Party men Jalmari Kosonen and Fomkin held meetings of the border-hoppers here, tried to calm them down, and squeeze the last bit of productivity from them. A film was always shown in connection with the meetings to get more people together.

At first Fomkin was satisfied with the pace at which the Finns worked. Once he said: "Here at the Sarov sawmill we have reached and surpassed the norms in the capitalist countries. Correction, I did not mean norms but work output." Permission was given by Moscow to transfer the first Finns from Sarov to "free job sites" in Ural because of their accomplishments on the job. In his lectures, Fomkin's every second word was said to be "goddamn." On May Day 1933 Fomkin gave a speech to a large group of Finns. One of the listeners was the oldest man in the Finnish kitchen crew, a Red officer named Paavo Varkkinen, who had been born in Rautu and fought in the 1918 war. Fomkin shouted crudely to him: "Do you remember, Varkkinen, goddamn it, when we buried preachers alive and stuffed earth into their mouths?"

The information does not tell us whether Varkkinen remembered, but the next year he was arrested in Kobakovski for "practicing provocation" and speaking abusively to Russians, of which he was quite capable since he knew the language.

Jalmari Kosonen had been sent to Sarov to do woods work, but almost immediately he got into party activities. He actually lived among the border-hoppers. Kosonen was well grounded in socialistic ideology and often corrected Fomkin during his lectures, corrections which Fomkin accepted. According to some of the border-hoppers, Kosonen was a zealous communist; others emphasized the fact that he was very practical and calm and belonged on the map of Finnish leftists to the "waverers" or the Välläri group. In the papers of the Sverdlovsk security command, Kosonen was not listed as a communist.

Once when Fomkin was lecturing on poverty in Finland, he said: "Even engineers there go hungry while they polish shoes." One of the listeners dared to ask: "Well, whose shoes are they polishing?"

According to Veli Hyrsky, Fomkin's attitude toward the border-hoppers was contemptuous. Once at a meeting, he jeered at them when they were complaining about conditions: "You seem to think that we Russians haven't seen hard times. We've eaten horses too!" Hyrsky opined that Fomkin was aware that the border-hoppers, who had to work so hard, did not "even get horse meat, but only a few spoonfuls a day of soup made from the guts of horses and goats."

Another time, when the inmates were grumbling, one of the "bigshots," perhaps Fomkin himself, criticized them as being Finnish-minded: "If Kosola [leader of the right-wing Lapua movement in Finland] were to come here, he'd think he were among his own," to which someone shot back: "And he wouldn't be mistaken."

Some Finns carried tales about the others to Fomkin, who then wrote them in a clean copy and stored them away; they are still to be found in the NKVD/KGB personnel files, along with characterizations of the border-hoppers. For example, Aleksis Saari, who was from Porvoo, "says little, but when he does, he only praises conditions in Finland." According to an informer, Saari's daughter had received money from Finland. The informing seemed to have been done in Svirstroi, and the tale-bearers were given false names.

At some point there was stored in the files a nameless woman's disclosure that she had asked Sylvi Laukkarinen, whom she knew from her work with the MOPR in Finland, to come to the women's meeting. "She answered me that it was useless to invite her, first feed and clothe me, and then feed

me politics. When we sat peacefully in our committees in Finland we agitated for a Soviet state, so that workers would not suffer poverty and hunger,
but here it's just the opposite, the workers go naked and hungry."

An informer related that at the meeting on September 12, 1932, some
women began to talk about their poor living conditions, "but when they got
no support, they gave up the attempt." After this comment, there is written
in Russian: "H. Voutilainen and S. Laukkarinen said that one need not point
to the Tampere jail as an example of wretchedness; life here was worse." And
still another informer told tales of Laukkarinen's talk:

> *They've set the wages so low that we can only die of hunger, and we've
> all grown thin and weak and can't work. We have to get out of here
> and back to Finland. Her husband, Fabian, is also against the Soviet
> Union, but he is very careful and says little.*

The dissatisfaction at Sarov increased; once 300 men refused to go to work.
Because of this—according to another report, because of a complaint made
by the workers—three uniformed inspectors arrived at the camp from
Moscow. Nikolai Gavroi acted as their interpreter. Karin Puonti succeeded
in slipping a letter of complaint into the pocket of one of the inspectors, but
did not know whether the letter had any effect. Toivo Kivistö reports that
just before the arrival of the inspectors, the border-hoppers got straw-filled
mattresses for the first time.

The inspectors shook their heads when the Finns told them of their
death rate, the disappearance of food intended for the camp inmates—
apparently for sale—and of their futile requests to return to Finland. On the
basis of the inspectors' statements, the commandant was relieved of his position and sentenced to ten years of forced labor. He is reported to have shot
himself immediately after the sentence was read—according to other reports,
immediately after the visit of the inspectors. After that, conditions improved
somewhat, at least with regard to the food regimen and family life.

Many practical problems limited the border-hoppers' correspondence.
Sometimes it was impossible to get stationery, envelopes and stamps. The
occasional letter that arrived in Finland was a cramped scrawl on a small slip
of paper. During the early phase at Sarov, they generally did not reach their
destination, and packages from Finland and envelopes containing money disappeared.

Many did not want or did not dare to write about the kind of conditions
they had encountered, but others were unrestrained. Viola Saarenoja wrote to

her mother from Sarov in August 1932 and sent the letter along with a "woman who was leaving with one of the detachments" in the hopes that it would find a way to its destination; it was said that one was not supposed to correspond with one's family. "We're still alive," the daughter wrote, and went on:

> [Eighty percent] of the people here are asking to go back to Finland. Everyone is already sick and tired of this misery. One is supposed to work even if he can' t . . . I'm not able to go out in the fields, and there is no other work. Uuno has worked a little, but he is in a weak condition too. Water is our main nourishment here, and you can guess that it doesn't make a person strong . . . the only thing we talk about is going to Finland.

Saarenoja wrote that she and her husband had applied to return. "We'll see if we get out of here before the three years is up, but at least we will then. It's so terrible to be here; every day I wait anxiously to see how the matter will be decided."

It was said that a passport had been arranged for "the Muuri boys from Kotka." They had cost 250 markkas and were sent to Sarov. There a visa was obtained for them, which cost sixty rubles. The boys thought they were going home—but they were taken away at night. For his part, a certain Arpinen wrote from Perm that his dreams had vanished when his interpreter had disappeared, taking with him Arpinen's passport and those of seventeen other border-hoppers.

Kalle Vartiainen, a carpenter from Savonlinna, a communist and former candidate for the Finnish parliament, went to Ural along with other border-hoppers. His family remained in Finland when he crossed the border on Lake Ladoga, carrying with him a newspaper clipping about the court case in which he was sentenced for intending to commit treason. In Vartiainen's letters, the EK observed that at first he urged his wife to follow him and even sent her money. In a letter from Magnitogorsk in 1933 he expressly forbade her to come and explained that he himself was trying to get back to Finland. Especially in his last letters in 1936 and 1937, he complained bitterly of the conditions.

Helsinki musician Pauli Valkama, who had worked as a cook at Sarov, had, according to the EK, "acted as the leader of the young communists' league in Finland." He had skipped to the Soviet Union in 1932, and already that autumn his mother asked the Foreign Ministry to act on behalf of her son's return. Valkama wrote from Sarov in September 1933: "I've been hoping for this year and a half to get out of here."

Valkama wrote: "News from Finland has reached this monastery that we can be delivered from here through the agency of the foreign ministry." He hoped that his letters would be offered as testimony. He had, he reported, been asking to return "the entire time." The next year Valkama fled to Finland.

Aleksis Saari from Porvoo was voted the elder of the border-hoppers in an election in the Svirstroi barracks. He would tell his children what life had been like in Finland: every morning you had to bow politely to the sawmill owner; only those who bowed were given day labor. The Saaris wrote diligently to their relatives in Finland, and at first the letters, especially the men's, were spirited and downright defiant.

In September of 1932 Saari wrote that "Me and my wife are in the sawmill lumber yard"—at work. "We have free theaters and entertainments, we don't have to pay anything, and the Russians dance in the street every night to accordion music." Reportedly they had to be "under observation" for a year at Svirstroi. "If we serve well, then we can freely go wherever we want to look for work."

On the other hand, he asked: "Please send us some old socks from Finland, three yards of elastic for the children's garters, and a kilo of oatmeal. And shoes, clothing, and woolen yarn. We can't get wool and butter here." Saari would have sent "money, but you're not allowed to send money to Finland from here."

Later, from Svirstroi, in November: the family is well and the parents belong to Osoaviahim.

> ...soon we'll get a uniform and then a rifle, and then the tough training will begin, and we'll soon come to greet you, it would be a nice trip, it will be different from 1918, when I get the uniform I'll go and have a picture taken and send it to you.

"The wife is getting awfully fat, she'll soon be another Rantaska." Saari had hopes of getting out of quarantine soon with the help of a guarantor. The family was still waiting for old woolen stockings from their relatives. A fur hat should be sent by express mail. "You help me now, and I'll remember it when the time comes, and it's coming soon." And further: "The woman is sitting here whining about getting some oatmeal; we do get other grains here, buckwheat and millet."

Daughter Lea was doing well in school and learning Russian—"for us old people it's really tough to learn." Lea and Etel kept asking constantly when they were going to Finland. In one letter, Aleksis castigated a man who had returned to Finland. He declared that he did not miss Finland "as Limberg had. He did a shitty thing when he took off, not in going, but in stooping to lie about it; the poor man didn't think of the consequences; tell him when you see him that some day things will be hot for him in Finland because of his talk." According to Saari, things were getting better day by day in Russia, and he too was getting fat. The work was easy, and they held dances in the "red corner." "We're starting tough training; the gun barrels will soon be hot; it depends a lot on you there."

January 1933: "I got a letter from my sister in America; times are bad there; people are starving to death; some kill themselves because they have nothing to eat." His sister had sent a newspaper clipping with an account of the Finnish border-hoppers in which Saari was actually mentioned by name.

> *The capitalists are really trying in every way to stop the Soviet Union but it's no use, look ahead [two to three] years, things will go otherwise, this land will rise and the capitalist lands will fall, that's clear. Listen Siggi, when you write send a fine-tooth comb in your letter so that we can get the bugs out of the children's heads, there aren't any fine-tooth combs here.*

Saari asked why other relatives in Finland did not write. "You're the only one who writes to me. I consider you a comrade, and you will be honored as a comrade the time is near."

Gradually the tone of the letters changed. The next letter which has been preserved is one in Swedish by Gerda Saari, sent to her sister from Magnitogorsk at the close of the Christmas season in 1934; her husband was writing very little now. "I'm writing a few lines in my sorrow." Life was poor, the family was suffering from cold and hunger and eating salt, bread, and water.

> *We had no bread to give the children on Christmas Day. . . . Every day Etel asks when we'll get to be with auntie and eat potato soup and coffee and coffee bread, and I told her we'll get there soon if we don't die first.*

Gerda Saari hoped to get home and be forgiven by her children. She wrote that all their clothing had been sold for food. "Aleksi has gotten so thin and old-looking because he has to work hard without food. He says that if we get to Finland, we'll never move again. We've learned our lesson now. I just want to cook a meat stew once and tell my children now you can eat as much as you want."

I'm sitting in front of the stove, we burn coal, we are dirty and black, we don't have a bit of soap. I wonder how long a person can live this kind of life. My eyes are swollen from crying so much.

The next letter that reached Finland was written by Aleksis Saari after the family had been in Chelyabinsk for a month. He stated that his sister had not received his last three letters. "They've either been confiscated or lost." He congratulated his sister on the birth of a son. "I'm not able to do it, since our food is *kipetku* [boiled water] and bread; it doesn't stand up; my eyes have gotten so bad that I can hardly see at all to write. . . . I don't dare say what I think; the letter won't get there again." There were again rumors about getting to Finland soon, but Saari declared that he would not believe it until they were at the Finnish border. "It would be nice to get there."

In October 1934 Gerda wrote from Chelyabinsk: things were better since she had gotten work as a cleaning woman. Lea and Rakel were going to school. Etel was in a nursery. "Save a little meat for her, auntie, when she comes to visit, she asks about it every day."

I don't know what to write here, this is the kind of life we live in a room with [forty] people, the children yell and the old women talk and sing; it's like being in a movie all the time, when everyone goes to bed in the evening it keeps on ringing in your ears and head for a long time.

Presumably a long time before this, Aleksis Saari had written the following petition which is preserved in the archives of the Foreign Ministry:

Petition. I, a Finnish citizen, ask to get to Finland with my family on the grounds that I am weak and ill and my wife has pneumonia and my three children are weak and ill.

EK, the secret police whose opinion the Foreign Ministry solicited, had nothing against Saari at first. Later it was recorded that he had participated in left-wing activity at the Porvoo steam sawmill.

Later, Riekki of the EK pointed out to the Foreign Ministry the danger to Finland and the difficulty of surveillance that "a group of many hundreds or thousands of agitators and spies, either recruited or forced into such service in the Soviet Union, would cause." Nevertheless his view was that those who themselves asked for help should be aided to return. He recommended further propaganda opposing border-hopping: such propaganda had already begun over Radio Finland.

Ambassador Yrjö-Koskinen affirmed that perhaps some of those returning had been enticed into promising to further communist activities in Finland.

> *In general, however, you can be assured that those who are trying to get back to their homeland are people who have truly learned through bitter experience here that they went astray in leaving. The descriptions of their present circumstances are so shocking . . .*

The Foreign Ministry's policy memorandum on secret emigration of March 1932 declared that all Finnish citizens had the right to return home. Governmental envoys in Moscow or Leningrad were always to start making arrangements for a border-hopper's return unless an EK statement on him contained "information prejudicial to the state or otherwise."

The results were meager—only two women along with their children received permission to leave. With regard to others, Moscow frequently answered that they had requested Soviet citizenship and could not be granted permission to leave until that matter was settled. But most often there was no answer. "It looks as if the measures Finnish officials take to secure their return may have the effect of making their situation worse."

At the end of August 1933, Aaro Pakaslahti wrote another memorandum according to which by then some 880 border-hoppers had returned to Finland, either surreptitiously or sent back by Soviet officials. Many of the border-hoppers had their applications to the Finnish embassy in Moscow approved, but then when they took them to Soviet officials they got no results. Often these officials "took away from them the passports issued by the Finnish embassy."

When in 1932 and 1933 hundreds of relatives turned to it for help, the Foreign Ministry took other steps. It sent to the embassy in Moscow and the chief consulate in Leningrad the border-hoppers' documents from the church or civil registry in Russian translation attested to as legal by the Soviet embassy "so that action could be taken." (Beginning in 1934, the embassy alone handled the matter.) The border-hoppers had no passports, but with these papers they were supposed to prove their identity.

According to Pakaslahti, it was to no avail. "On the contrary, there is reason to suspect that the border-hoppers for whose benefit the action was undertaken are transferred from job sites to concentration camps." Likewise the proposals made to the foreign affairs commissariat have led to no results. At best, inquiries about the Finns often got the response: "whereabouts unknown."

At the start of 1933, negotiations were begun at Finland's initiative. Finland hoped that the Soviet Union would issue a return visa to everyone who requested it with the embassy's mediation and support and who were not accused of any crime; those who were had most often been captured during the attempt to return.

Furthermore: "As to those who had signed a request to become Soviet citizens, that should not constitute a barrier to their returning to Finland." In the view of Finland, such a request did not yet change one's citizenship, and it had to be revocable. The Foreign Ministry considered a minister's certificate sufficient proof that a man was a Finn.

Soviet officials did not "acknowledge individuals in their territory without passports and visas to be Finnish citizens, but considered them to be 'men without a country,'" the embassy was informed. Even people to whom a new Finnish passport had been sent continued to be viewed as such.

After Finland had requested quicker action from Moscow, the first counter-proposal arrived: "there was a possibility of returning" border-hoppers who had arrived with their families, but contrarily, "those who could not satisfactorily explain their reasons for coming or who had, during interrogation, given reason to suspect their true motives, could not be permitted to return to Finland. They would be placed 'at least for the time being' in some concentration camp."

The Finnish government did not approve a procedure that was so open to interpretation. When there was no progress in the negotiations, in the summer of 1933, Finland began to direct its attention to separate groups: for example, they felt that supporters of a family, minors, women, and the ailing should be allowed home.

The Foreign Ministry also decided that as an experiment they might, as Moscow wished, begin to enclose explanations from the border-hoppers' petitions and letters along with the return requests. If that was actually done, it gave the Soviet authorities damaging material to use against the border-hoppers. The embassy in Moscow later observed in a secret wire that the petitions and letters included such shocking descriptions and complaints that they would "certainly be very damaging to those involved."

Foreign Minister Hackzell almost gave up: he considered the possibility of dropping the matter of the petitions altogether since they were futile. In May Yrjö-Koskinen was in direct contact with Litvinov, the commissar for foreign affairs, after which the required paperwork was simplified. An oral agreement was reached on "a questionnaire to be filled by those who had illegally crossed the border," which was supposed to suffice; Moscow no longer demanded copies of the applications for return.

The embassy immediately requested that the ministry print and send them 1,000 copies of this form plus 1,000 accompanying letters. The ministry sent 3,000.

At the very beginning of 1933, the foreign ministry began sending out a letter which raised the hopes of close relatives in Finland. It was signed by a division secretary named Asko Ivalo:

> In negotiations between the Soviet Union and Finland on the return of Finnish citizens who have surreptitiously gone to the Soviet Union, a resolution has been arrived at by which it is possible to return, provided that application be made on behalf of each so-called border-hopper following the form approved by Soviet officials.

Ivalo related that the ministry would send the information to the embassy in Moscow, which would then forward the petitions to Soviet officials for processing. "For border-hoppers who have been arrested and sentenced in the Soviet Union, there seems to be no possibility of returning to Finland until the time of the sentence has expired."

If the initiative came from relatives, they had to prove that the border-hoppers really wanted to return. Many of them did send to the ministry letters that had come from Ural, which spoke of coming home in various turns of phrase. Not everyone had letters to send: they had destroyed them. Others advised the ministry that one could not mention such matters in letters from the Soviet Union because of censorship.

The Finnish news agency STT announced in November 1933 that Finland and the Soviet Union had made an initial agreement regarding the return of the border-hoppers: thirty-five families were to get home first. Rumors spread everywhere among the border-hoppers that some kind of agreement had been reached and that some people had already traveled to Finland. In their letters, they asked for further information from their relatives and about ways to strengthen their own applications. They complained about being "in the dark"; nowhere could they get any information. "Every Finn has only one hope: to get back to his home country."

At the end of the summer, Pakaslahti had to announce that some 200 petitions following the new form had been forwarded to Soviet officials "but not one border-hopper has yet gotten home by that means."

The embassy did not give up but forwarded the forms of every border-hopper whose address they knew and whom they knew wanted to come to Finland. At the end of September 1933 the Russians informed them that the first group had been granted permission to return, and after a month had passed, they handed a list of thirty-seven names to the Finnish embassy. It was a drop in the bucket—many hundreds were waiting for permission to go back to Finland, and new ones were lining up every day.

After that, small groups returned legally from time to time; meanwhile the illegal flights back to Finland continued. By November of 1934, some 100 adults had returned with permits, and 2,000 applications had been submitted. The foreign ministry complained that the Soviet Union returned by official channels only helpless wives with their children, border-hoppers who had remained waiting in the Finnish embassy in Moscow, and those "whose return to Finland could hardly be considered desirable from Finland's point of view." Some of them the Soviet Union expelled as "undesirable foreigners" although they did not otherwise treat them as foreigners while on their soil, but as "having no citizenship."

At the very end of 1934, Finland sent a note to the Soviet Union in which it requested speedy action so that all the Finns who wanted to return could do so. The note seemed to have no particular effect.

Johan Nykopp reports striving in vain and going often to the foreign affairs commissariat to discuss the border-hoppers. "Our point of departure was that a border-hopper, once he had suffered his punishment, had atoned for his crime and thus should be allowed to return to his homeland." According to Nykopp, the matter was a painful one for everybody, but "no great attention" was paid to it; it was not even discussed in the newspapers.

Nevertheless, it was years before the foreign ministry gave up. It kept sending long lists of names to Moscow accompanied by these words: "The ministry requests that the embassy initiate action for the return of the following border-hoppers" and "requests that the embassy inform us in due time of the results of the actions taken."

It is not known whether the delay in returning border-hoppers was related to the position taken by the Finnish Communist Party. In 1931, the party's attitude toward the intentions of those who fled the Soviet Union became clearly suspicious, and at the end of the year they declared to Soviet officials that they should not let them into Finland to agitate against the party and the Soviet Union. The "horror stories" of the returnees had affected party activity in Kotka and Northern Finland.

Young Finns were sent to trade school in Magnitogorsk.

Chapter Four

Into the Ural Trap

DURING THIS TIME, THE FATE OF THE BORDER-HOPPERS changed decisively: they were transported farther east. In late 1933 and early 1934 over a thousand Finns were shipped in several "detachments" to the city of Magnitogorsk on the east slope of the Ural Mountains. There were already some one thousand Finns and American Finns there. A disillusioned and embittered Isak Kaikkonen wrote to Temmes in the summer of 1933 that he and 115 others had just been sent there; they were the first of the Finns to arrive.

According to one source there were about 1,300 Finns in Magnitogorsk in early 1934, 150 of them children, some 200 women, some 100 youths, and the rest men.

The largest train shipment of "Sarov people" left at the end of November. It was made up of 750 Finns, who were transported across the frozen steppes with little to eat. At the start of the trip, on the narrow-gauge Sarov track, the last car of the train carrying one group caught fire. Since those at the head of the train did not notice the fire, a boy had to climb along the roofs of the cars to sound the alarm and get help.

Upon leaving Shatki, the people traveled in locked cattle cars. They were promised that the children would get sausage at a station along the way. The piece they were given was thumb-sized, which so angered the mother of the Lohilahti family that she threw it at the distributor. Later on she would have been happy to get even that.

Life seemed freer, to the extent that the Finns could travel without guards—the only ones watching them were the Magnitogorsk recruiters. Before Kazan, the train got stuck in a snow bank in the cold and stormy weather of late November, and everyone who could walk was ordered out of the cars to free the locomotive with axes and shovels. A cloud of vapor rose from the hot steam engine. It took the whole day to get the train loose from the snow. The young people sang: "Siberia's steppes are wide, / and there Sonja shovels the snow."

At the Kazan station, the travelers were given wooden spoons and served sour cabbage soup from washbowls. The rest of the journey was made in proper passenger coaches. They arrived on the sixth of December. "This is a good independence day," some of them exulted.

Magnitogorsk was the Soviet Union's largest construction site, the offspring of the first five-year plan. Stalin had decided to concentrate heavy industry far from the borders in a Ural manufacturing area of 1,250 square kilometers. A measure: "To carry out a special colonization in the Northern and Siberian spheres and in the Ural area" was approved by the government in 1930. The area was also a great center of military production. In the 1930s, 200 plants were built there, without regard for the sacrifices involved.

The area needed a work force from all over the country and from abroad as well. Forced migration served economic ends, which were cloaked under a loud propaganda campaign aimed at "destroying the kulaks as a class." A third of the "kulaks" (wealthy and moderately well-to-do farmers) along with others who were singled out for banishment, were transported to the Ural, where a system of camps was developed through which hundreds of thousands of prisoners were reported to have passed. In January of 1933, Stalin ordered the industrialization to be speeded up.

The city of Magnitogorsk had been established only a few years earlier but in size and number of inhabitants it already surpassed Helsinki, the border-hoppers wrote home. It was known to be somewhere on the Asian border in the Ural Mountains. Its exact location was not known. One man reported living on the European side but going to work on the Asian side; another reported seeing camels.

There are no woods here, not even the smallest of trees grow in this area, only mountains as far as the eye can see. Nor is there any green grass here, since the earth contains so much ore that there is only black sand on the surface.

Mining had already begun here in the 1700s, and for a long time the Magnitogorsk iron-ore deposits were considered to be the world's richest. Construction work on the largest European, if not the world's, iron-and-steel combine had already begun at the end of the 1920s, with young volunteers and deported people furnishing the labor. The first iron plant began to spit out ingots from its maw on February 1, 1932. The combine was never completed exactly according to plans, but, nevertheless, it produced almost one fourth of the whole country's iron ore and millions of tons of coke, iron, and steel per year.

Among other structures, border-hoppers built this coking and chemical plant at Magnitogorsk. Photograph taken in the 1930s, from John Scott's book.

The director of the combine was for all practical purposes the dictator of Magnitogorsk. Just as the Finns arrived, the American and German experts were leaving, and all responsibility was being left to the Russians. "There is a building crunch going on," wrote Matti Virkki, who related that he had gotten a chauffeur's license without taking a course. Thirty Finns drove trucks that hauled building materials. "Iron pours out day and night" from the plant, there are no holidays.

Nearly a quarter of a million workers came to Magnitogorsk—according to statistics seventy-five percent voluntarily and twenty-five percent compulsorily. Earlier there had been only the small Magnitnaja community on the steppes, inhabited by the Bashkir and Kirghiz people. There were no regular streets in the city, nor any lighting; admission of the wrong type of current into the circuit had ruined all the lamps. Only the initial steps had been taken in the construction of the projected Socialist model city, so that most of the workers had to live in tents or temporary barracks. A thick black cloud belched out by the smokestacks hung over everything. It was so cold during the Finns' first winter there that the factory's blast furnaces stopped from time to time.

Movement was freer than it had previously been, but the people could not go beyond the city limits and had to report to the GPU. Their range of travel in this "free work area," as Kaikkonen wrote ironically, was a few kilometers. He felt that life here was more difficult than in prison. All food was on ration cards, and everyone had to stand in line for it by the hour. Kaikkonen claims to have eaten nothing but bread for a full month.

Jewelry was sold in case of dire need. Karen Puonti had brought a gold bracelet with her from Finland from which pieces were cut in the currency exchange when the need arose. The women of the Lappalainen family sold their winter coats and their best dresses. They went cheap, since the sellers did not know Russian.

The Finns were lodged in barracks which had a common kitchen. Most of them were not admitted to the most important job site, the iron smelter, which was guarded by soldiers; they were assigned to jobs outdoors. Once a group of Finns who knew the trade was chosen to do the plaster work on a building, but the GPU announced that for political reasons they were unfit for this task.

According to the border-hoppers, a worker earned sixty to eighty rubles a month (100 rubles according to official information), so that materially life was even worse here than at Svirstroi. Pay was seldom on time, and the worker's food rations—thirty kilos of bread per month, three kilos of meat, one kilo of sugar, fifteen liters of milk, one-half kilo of butter—remained largely a dream in almost every respect. There was a good deal of job switching so long as one was free to quit a job.

Military training was no longer given. "Polit classes" were held by Kosonen and Kuusela. Their immediate superior was a Finn who used the names "Ek" and "Sanin"; his real name was Onni Sipinen, and he was from Kotka. Sanin-Sipinen was the "top polit leader and was in command of the foreigners' section."

Sipinen had visited Leningrad in 1927 during the tenth-anniversary celebration of the communist revolution as a representative of the young communists and then lectured in Finland on the "ideal conditions" in Finland's neighboring country. He had moved to Russia permanently at the end of the 1920s and his parents had followed him. Like the other Red officers, he used a cover name. Once an acquaintance called him by his right name in the barracks and was roundly berated for revealing it.

"He was a really confirmed communist and hated the Finns," was how one of the border-hoppers characterized Sipinen. According to others, he was a "reading type and a theoretician." "He was a rabble rouser and would rail against Finland, using foul language," Väinö Murto related. Sipinen had a wobbly gait and was nicknamed "Pincer-legs" by the Finns.

Regular attendance at lectures and propaganda speeches in the red corner was expected of all the Finns. As the border-hoppers recall, even anti-Finnish songs of the following type were composed there:

> When Butcher Finland dares us to war, / we will never refrain from the fight / until the red banner with hammer and sickle / waves over Helsinki, hui jai jekunia rilluma rei
>
> When Kosola's thick stomach feels the point of the bayonet / hui jai jekunia rilluma rei / then in terror Kares the priest / will close his eyes forever.

Fomkin was still in charge of the Finns. Allan Vuorio says that he once refused to go and work outdoors in his ragged clothing, whereupon Fomkin threatened to send him to Solovetski, a prison camp on an island in the White Sea with a particularly bad reputation. "Go ahead. It makes no difference where one dies," Vuorio is reported to have said.

He and all other young Finns, both boys and girls, were sent to the factory FZO trade school. There was a crying need for skilled labor. They could begin this school at the age of thirteen. At fifteen, they would work a half-day in conjunction with the schooling—at grinding and welding—after which they were sent to study mathematics, chemistry, physics, and electricity and the Russian language. Marx's and Lenin's books were also studied, along with Soviet history. Sipinen taught Leninist economics. Escape from such factory schools was punishable by law with a six months' sentence to a camp—the lightest punishment the law recognized. The youngest children were put into Finnish-language schools whose teachers were chosen from among the border-hoppers.

The hunger was so great that it was hard for the young people to learn. In order to stay alive, they had to steal food. The Finnish boys killed the chickens and geese of the original residents, once even a billy goat. They had no luck, however, with the *kolkhoz*'s pig; the wounded animal ran squealing in flight. There were guards in the fields, and one night a watchman shot dead a Finnish man he caught stealing potatoes.

In the autumn, the trade school pupils were taken to the *sovhoz* to work, where at least there was food. In the winter, the boys searched for and ate frozen potatoes and beets which the residents had cached unbeknown to Soviet officials.

Sick care was non-existent; there were no doctors nor any medicines. The health of children was threatened. Sirkka Laurila lay ill a whole year with dysentery, which had afflicted her from the very beginning in Leningrad. The seven-year-old girl was skin and bones. When she got up, she could no longer walk but began to crawl. Pirkko Puonti too had to learn to walk over again after she had suffered from diphtheria and scarlet fever at the same time. Sirkka recalls that one morning when she awoke, Laura Jelonen, who slept in the next bed, was discovered to have died of hunger. The grown-ups did not expect Sirkka to recover either.

The EK Sortavala section reported in the autumn of 1934 that most of the Finns who had gone to Soviet Russia secretly during 1930 to 1932 had been expelled from the border areas up to at least the east shore of Lake Ääninen as supposedly politically untrustworthy and in order to lessen the possibility of escape. They had been sent to different places of banishment in eastern Russia and Siberia.

According to their survey, there were still some 800 to 900 Finnish adults and children in Svirstroi. "Most of them had applied for return to Finland without getting an answer to their applications." There, as in other Finnish places, education in communism had totally ceased. Efforts were made to prevent escape to Finland by explaining that the border was closely guarded; those caught in the attempt were generally condemned to three years beyond Ural. According to EK information up to 200 Finns had been banished as one group to Siberia.

According to EK, the usual place of banishment was Tara, where there were hundreds of Finns. At first they were "free deportees," who had to work but who were free to move about the Tara district. The food ration depended upon the work norms, and those norms were "impossible to fulfill." In 1934 it was decreed that they could not go outside the community administrative area. Those who returned to Finland reported:

> that the banished people were living in the greatest misery, suffering from hunger and contagious diseases, and forced to do hard labor, and that all of them were hoping to return to Finland. Those who have been banished stay alive by wandering around the area and begging. Others get odd jobs on the farms. A large number live by thievery, they break into kolkhozes' and private farmers' storehouses, stealing flour and edibles, clothing, and anything fit to eat. . . .

Escape was also discouraged by saying that those who went back would wind up in jail in Finland. According to the Finns, itinerant "polit teachers" in Ural further explained that when the workers' revolution was accomplished in Finland, all those who had fled without permission would be punished, since they would be viewed as pawns of the secret police.

A letter sent to the Leningrad consulate by the father of a border-hopping family in Omsk leaves little room for conjecture:

> . . . we have come to such a pass that if we don't get help quickly from somewhere we will die of cold and hunger. I have a family of five, a wife and three children, the youngest was born the [twelfth] of June 1933 after we arrived here, and all the time we've been here I've been sick with kidney disease and stomach ulcers and now we're in such a state that I can no longer take care of my family, and my wife is sick too, she can't care for the family either. Our clothes are all rags too; we have no shoes except for my one beat-up pair, and we can't get any new ones because I'm not able to work . . .

In October of 1934 Riekki wrote a report of the border-hoppers' situation to the Foreign Ministry that was based on information obtained by interrogation. According to it, EK did not have accurate information on their numbers. (Neither did the ministry. Pakaslahti conjectured that the estimate of 10,000 "was perhaps exaggerated.")

Riekki complained that his personnel was insufficient for a proper interrogation of the border-hoppers returning from Russia. "1932—1,850 interrogated, 1933—474, up to mid-September of the current year—212 individuals." From the addresses on the petitions sent by those who wished to return, Riekki concluded that they had "largely" been moved to Siberia and other places in the interior of Russia.

Beginning with Sarov, in the Ural work area, and up until the last part of the 1930s, a special GPU organization, the "emigrant sector," was always in charge of the border-hoppers. It was made up of a few Red Army officers plus a few Finnish communists and interpreters. The sector organized the border-hoppers' work, housing, and educational matters. At least Gavroi, Kosonen, Kuusela, Impi Qvintus, Sanin-Sipinen, and Pauli Viuhko seem to have worked under Fomkin in that sector's leadership.

Our old acquaintance Aarne Kuusela was ordered to Magnitogorsk in the fall of 1933 to work among the Finns. Together with Sipinen, he tried to make communists of the border-hoppers and apparently did his best to improve the organization of their work and their training. Sipinen also asked the SKP for permission to send good students from the factory school to the Finnish Language School in Petroskoi and Leningrad. A few young people received that permission and even dared to go.

However, the state of mind of the border-hoppers was declared to be poor. Some ninety percent talked of going to Finland, and many were in correspondence with the Finnish embassy. Sipinen said the negative thinking had even spread to the children, who spoke disparagingly of the "Russkis."

Lauri Patrikainen was a one-legged man who walked on crutches and who supported himself by mending the border-hoppers' shoes. When it was revealed that even he had asked to go to Finland, Kuusela brought up the matter at a meeting "in a really nasty way," as others recall. He reminded them that even as far back as Leningrad, many had had dealings with the Finnish consulate about returning home.

"The more you run to the consulate, the farther into Siberia you'll get," he threatened. Then he added, shouting, to Patrikainen: "You complain of getting bone-rot in your foot here, but what you've got is bone-rot in your brain!"

Later one Thure Palmén from Hollola wound up being sentenced for asking at a meeting: "Who is it that enslaves the people when there are no capitalists here?" Kosonen is said to have succeeded in having charges brought against twenty Finns in Chelyabinsk on the grounds of anti-revolutionary activities.

Anni Ahonen from Tampere was forced to sit in the Chelyabinsk jail for six months in 1932 because of sports and picture magazines she received by mail from Finland. When nothing political was found in the magazines, she was released.

Among the border-hoppers, there were "veterans of Tammisaari," communists who had served a sentence in Finland. They declared outright that life in a Finnish prison was many times better than working in Ural. For talk of this sort one could easily be sentenced to banishment or disappear quietly from the group.

As yet there were not many arrests in Magnitogorsk, although the NKVD files were getting fatter all the time. Only in 1937-1938 did the city experience a huge wave of purging, which did not spare even party members or the factory management.

In 1934 the border-hoppers were allowed to send for a special petition form from the embassy in Moscow, and that year a virtual flood of requests arrived, especially from Magnitogorsk. Presumably most of the Finns who wound up in Ural asked to return home. They apparently did it together, since the papers are filled out in the same way, even in the same handwriting. EK reported that they sent in requests from "everywhere in Ural and from all the way to Siberia, with a few exceptions."

Tauno Törölä, who had returned from Ural, told the EK in 1935 that at the end of 1934 and the beginning of 1935, a "very noticeable 'Finland fever' prevailed" among the border-hoppers. Almost all of them had ordered forms from the embassy and sent them in. Törölä received no other response than that his form had been received. He knew of only a few who had gotten home from Ural—Karin Puonti and her daughter and Riikola's and Kakkinen's wives, who had come to Russia on Finnish passports.

The form which those who wanted to return filled out and to which they attached their own and their children's photographs was by name "a notice to the Finnish embassy/consular office to be stamped for citizenship." Almost everyone also stated at the same time, for the sake of certainty, that they wanted to surrender their Soviet citizenship. They generally did not even know if they had requested that citizenship and been granted it (very few had)—that is, they did not know what papers they had signed.

In the place on the form where it asked, "Have you ever sought to become the citizen of any foreign country, when, where?" young Reino Liimatainen, for example, answered, "Never, and I retract my request."

All possible papers that might be used to prove Finnish citizenship were to be enclosed with the form. Those who had been sent to Ural generally had none except for their "Sarov passport," so they sent that on to Moscow.

"We all plan to return home, since life here seems impossible," nineteen-year-old Armas Pukala wrote from Magnitogorsk. Armas had left secretly from Pispala with his father. Both were masons, and neither was saved in the end.

Kalle Pukala had taken this one son with him; the other children he left in his wife's care. Other enthusiastic young men recruited by Pukala had also left Pispala, among them the unemployed Orvo Virtanen and messenger boy Pentti Haapaniemi, both seventeen. Pukala was like a father to them on their journey toward a common fate. Pukala planned to become a master builder, and his son was to be a flyer.

In the early phases, Pukala played the part of a convinced ideologist, encouraging the others and singing "Free Russia": "The czars are no longer our keepers . . ." His wife, however, emphasized in her petition for aid to Finnish officials that her Pukala was not a communist. Even Pukala's tension gradually increased, however. Once when his food purchases had been slapped into his fur hat at the store, he returned to the camp, threw the hat

The Pukala family home inn Pispala in North-Pirkkala.

onto the floor and cursed: "This country is ruled by devils." He contracted dysentery but recovered from it. He had some gold rings with him, so he lived well at first and helped his comrades—let them wear his good clothing and offered them "sugar-tea."

Armas comforted his mother back home in Pispala. "Don't worry, we're still in good shape." According to the boy, there "was not yet any real need." At the same time, he told of hearing rumors of an agreement between Finland and the Soviet Union and asked her to find out about it and send an application to the foreign ministry.

The mother of Adolf Koskinen of Kotka wrote to the Foreign Ministry that her son "owing to unemployment lost his ability to reason to the extent that he went secretly by water to the Soviet Union with his family."

Anna Orell of Viipuri wrote to Helsinki in April 1934:

> I most courteously beg the Honorable Foreign Minister to assist me in getting my son out of Russia. He went there two years ago to look for work, and there is indeed work there, but the conditions are so miserable that he is on the verge of starving to death.

Mason Kalle Pukala (top) left with his son Armas (bottom), and was also a father figure to many other young border-hoppers from Tampere. Both Pukalas were executed in 1938.

Reino Orell later married another border-hopper, Sanni Lappalainen, and had a child with her. From Magnitogorsk, Reino had written forebodingly to his mother that if the "paper war" (bureaucratic red tape) had produced no results by the end of the summer

> then I'll try it by myself, and I'll go as far as I can, and if I'm caught and sent to jail then it won't be long before it's the end of me. I just can't stay here any longer because it's getting to be too much torture working from morning till night without enough money to buy milk and butter, always when you come home from work in the evening there's nothing to eat but bread and water, there's no place to go, just eat and start killing lice.

The boy added in the letter that "half of our group has no underwear at all."

In March a request for help arrived from the Pekala family, which was headed "Sarov, Soviet Russia 1934." Maunu and Aleksandra Pekala's home was in Käkisalmi. They had their three daughters with them.

> I would like to get back to my home country Finland with my family. I have come to the Soviet Union from Finland without the legal permission of the authorities, and I crossed the border on [March 28, 1932] and my wife and family came after me in the same way without permission, and we have been detained here since then without our doing anything wrong, to our knowledge. They've just taken us from one place to another and our present lodging is the former Sarov monastery. Life here is completely impossible and unbearable. I myself have been very ill and we don't get a doctor's care here. Not at all. And I have two young children, and they lack food and clothing. One is a grown-up girl here. She is ailing and in want too . . . Manu Pekala. Witnessed by Lauri Patrikainen.

The ministry immediately requested a statement from EK, and in May it asked the Moscow embassy to begin measures for the return of the Pekala family.

The Murto family mentioned at the start of this book also tried to get back. The Moscow embassy had already sent them the forms in January of 1934. They are still in the KGB files in Jekaterinburg—not filled out. They were apparently never given to the family.

After the celebration of "Revolution Day," Väinö Murto wrote a letter headed "from Rompikki (Hrompik) in Ural," which did not go to Finland.

Reino Orell was executed. Sanni Lappalainen-Orell was not arrested only because she had a year-old child. Mother and child were not able to return to Finland.

That too was found in the Murtos' KGB file. During the festival, 800 grams of sugar and 300 grams of butter were issued to holders of ration cards, which in Väinö's opinion was too much. He said of his siblings:

> *Rauni and Erkki go to school and get to eat there once a day if they have money but many days it's so that they don't always have money.*

According to the letter, the boundary between Europe and Siberia was fifty kilometers away. "There are many thousands of Finns there who just wander around and beg and lots of them die here."

A woman, one of whose children had already died, wrote to Finland from Ural:

> *I won't write that real letter now even and I can't bring myself to lie. We are in Ural, not in Europe. There are mountains here; we burn coal, our lodgings are barracks; a city is being built here. Pekka is working as a fireman on a locomotive, the wages are really nothing . . . we plan to save Kerttu, otherwise she will die too, we need that certificate soon, we should get things in order so that we can leave here.*

Border-hopper Eino Karvonen, a store manager from Oulu, went via Karelia to Ural, where he was executed. His mother sought the Foreign Ministry's help in the summer of 1934. "The life insurance company wants to know if he is alive." As documentation she sent her son's letter dated in Petroskoi February 1, 1933.

> *I'm so starved that my sight is failing, and I can't hope for anything but bread alone to satisfy my hunger. I get 700 grams of bread every evening, I eat it all at once, and I'm forever hungry.*

The boy went on: "You would hardly know me, I'm so thin." He also told his mother that "the care is so bad you wouldn't treat your pigs this way." The reason for his being arrested: "I asked to go back to Finland and said that I didn't have the strength to do the work. They haven't come for me and my comrade yet."

Kirsti, the daughter of the Katainen family, wrote from Satrinski (Shadrinsk) in Ural at the end of November 1934: "If uncle could see father and mother, he wouldn't know them; they've changed so much you wouldn't believe your eyes. . . . There isn't even a sauna here. You have Christmas; we have nothing. Everything is empty, we have no clothes, no food. Father goes to work and he doesn't even have a coat. Mother is sick and she isn't able to do anything. We've sold our clothes so we have none at all."

In the winter of 1936, Niilo Hansen-Haug and his wife, Kristiina, nee Udd, who were, according to the minister's certificate "vaccinated, attended

The Hansen-Haugs (above) left from a rural Kemi township, and not a single one of them returned. Their daughter Anja (right) is assumed to be living somewhere in Russia, but officials report that they have no information about her. The family picture was probably taken in 1932 before Niilo Hansen-Haug's departure. The rest of the family followed him across the border.

confirmation school, partakers of communion, and enjoying the privileges of citizens in good standing," requested "humbly the help of the Foreign Ministry in getting back to Finland with their family."

The Hansen-Haugs were then living in Chelyabinsk. They had taken with them to Russia their children Anja and Eero, the latter only a year old when they left. "We humbly ask the ministry to lend a helping hand on behalf of my son and his family and all the other Finns," Niilo Hansen-Haug's mother wrote to the foreign ministry.

At first the ministry really tried to help the border-hoppers who were in distress. They and their relatives were given advice, papers were mailed to them, and Soviet officials were repeatedly contacted on their behalf. Money was also given or sent to them.

As early as the winter of 1930, Pontus Artti wrote from Moscow a statement explaining that the embassy felt itself compelled to send fifty rubles to Aleksander Tyyskä, who for months had begged for their help in getting out of "this hell." Similarly, the embassy "could not refuse to give" 100 rubles to seventy-four-year-old William Ahlgren "so that he and his family could be saved from dying of hunger and cold." The recipients were not always obligated to repay the money. It was Artti's wish "to take measures of this kind only in the most pitiful cases, which—regrettably enough—there was now no lack of here."

Over the years, however, the officials' interest in the border-hoppers' cases declined. Some of them wanted to teach the border-hoppers "a lesson." Others conjectured that they had become communists or that there were spies among those who were returning.

Norma Laivo, an American Finn, may serve as an example. She got herself admitted to Finland from Petroskoi in 1938. Apparently she was sent to do some kind of party work. Here she appeared at the door of relatives, but aroused enough suspicion so that they told officials about her. Laivo wound up in jail, and in 1942 VALPO handed her over to the Gestapo, who sent her to a concentration camp in Germany. Along with her, they took Hilda Nevalainen, who had come from Leningrad to visit relatives in Finland, and who had made the mistake of saying that she was an MOPR member.

"Apparently the Russians have succeeded in infiltrating a lot of spies into our country among these 'escaping border-hoppers'" a summary report of the Sortavala district EK stated. Suspicion was also directed at the wives who went legally, with passports, to visit their husbands in the Soviet Union.

Not only were the Finns in Ural forgotten, but the Foreign Ministry also led their relatives astray or actually lied to them.

As indicated, mason Niilo Puonti and tailor Karin Puonti had skipped with their daughter Pirkko in 1932. In 1933 already, a Kotka law firm took up the matter of their return, and in July the foreign ministry took action, since the EK had nothing against the Puontis. Puonti had written from a "'conslager' in the Sarov monastery in back of Moscow" and asked his relatives for help.

In April 1934, Puonti wrote from Magnitogorsk and complained that he had received no answer to his letters from Finland or from Moscow. In May EK had gotten further information about Puonti and informed the ministry that "Puonti had served as an Oso company commander in the Soviet Union, hence indesirable."

In July of 1934, the ministry retracted the recommendation it had sent the embassy a year earlier. They declared that "the officials concerned in the matter had recently sent a further statement about the said individual, on the basis of which information the embassy has no reason to continue measures for the return of Niilo Puonti."

Karin and Pirkko Puonti were able to return to Finland legally during the Christmas season in 1934. The father did not get permission. His wife began to bombard the officials with her letters. She wondered why she had been given permission to leave, but was told that "her husband's case was being discussed." A department secretary "assigned to the case" at the Foreign Ministry answered her question curtly: "The case of your husband's return is under continual discussion." In her next letter from Kotka, the wife asked if there was any hope, relating that her husband had again been moved to a new district, Kamensk, along with other Finns "and they have been thrust into the most miserable of conditions."

The ministry answered in the spring of 1936 that "there is no information now about when your husband can travel to his homeland. This being the case, you can do nothing but try quietly to help him."

In October, when his wife wrote that her husband had almost lost hope, she received a letter stating: ". . . your husband's case is still open" but the measures taken have not "at this point produced any results."

The tenacity of the solitary woman from Kotka began to yield results. In 1937 EK informed the ministry that "although Puonti has participated in actions directed against our country and our societal organization, EK at this point has no special objection to taking measures for his return to Finland."

A few days earlier, Mrs. Puonti had written an appeal to Foreign Minister Rudolf Holsti asking for help. "Don't condemn us poor devils; we've already had to suffer the consequences of that error." At the end of April the ministry replied again, making a point of blaming everything on the Russians: There is no information yet as to when the Russian officials will give him permission to leave. We have made inquiry, we will inform you immediately when an answer arrives.

In November of 1937, the militia in Kamensk had told Puonti that he would be allowed to travel home if he secured a foreign passport. The ministry wrote to his wife: "The embassy in Moscow will see to it that your husband gets the necessary passport and papers."

Time passed. The wife wrote again from Kotka January 10, 1939, declaring that "her husband was supposed to have gotten out of Russia a year ago." The man had received a passport and taken it to the militia for a visa. He was arrested soon after that on December 25, 1937. "I haven't heard anything about him for a full year."

The Moscow embassy recorded this information in February 1939:

> *Kantonen, J.E., no information since December 1937, apparently imprisoned, Kantonen, Aino Maria, perhaps in an exile camp. Children in a children's home. Puonti, no information since November 1937.*

Niilo Puonti had been executed almost a year earlier, March 10, 1938.

Although the majority of the border-hoppers had not been politically active, the foreign ministry requested a statement from EK-VALPO about everyone who wanted to return. Early on, especially, the statement was a stumbling block for many. EK might label them communists, smugglers, or criminals; a crime might be border-hopping, for example, and the consequent failure to pay a fine levied for that offense. When later, as the persecution became more stringent in the Soviet Union, and EK-Valpo would have "pardoned" the border-hoppers labeled as suspicious, it was usually too late.

The Viljamaa family, which had left from Kemi, petitioned in vain from 1933 on. EK stated "respectfully that J.H. Viljamaa had participated publicly in communist party organizational activities." These words were often used to signify the socialist labor party. Eino Johannes Kangas, for his part, had "engaged in secret communist organizational activities" and "is known from his opinions to be a communist."

In connection with the Paldan family petition mentioned in the previous chapter, EK announced that Otto Paldan from 1923 on had belonged to the "Kymi Popinniemi Gymnastic and Sports Society 'Toverit' [Comrades]." The district court had disbanded the society the same autumn (1931) that Paldan skipped across the border. In addition, according to EK, Paldan had had no regular employment for years but had supported himself and his family by smuggling spirits, for which he was often punished. EK had found the same kinds of sins in the background of some Murto family members.

When the Hämäläinen family left Finnish Karelia, there were five of them. Of these five, a boy and the youngest girl had died in Nevsdubstroi of hunger and disease. Three young girls remained alive. After all this, Juho Hämäläinen himself had asked that his family be included in the group being sent to Sarov.

EK did not want to have the parents return. Juho Hämäläinen and his wife Anna had been under surveillance for a long time while still in Finland. There had been floods of "tips" and information about them: a neighborhood

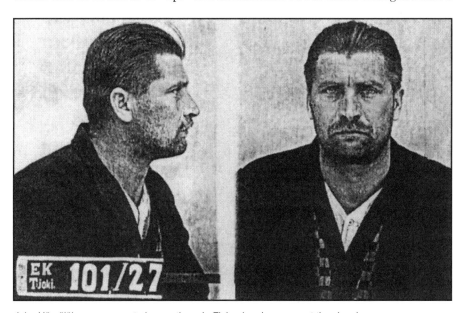

Juho Hämäläinen was arrested many times in Finland and even spent time in prison.

merchant reported someone's saying that Hämäläinen functioned as a paid "agent"; according to another report, he led a "loose life," and "seemed to have plenty of money.'" Juho Hämäläinen had been arrested many times on suspicion of smuggling, spying, and of working for communist border detachments. He had even been jailed for five years. Once when the EK searched his home, his wife, according to the report filed, was given permission to answer nature's call outside along the wall. When the spot she had chosen was later checked, "50,000 Czarist rubles" were found there in the snow.

EK reported briefly on Kaarlo Holopainen in 1934: "The indicated individual has taken part in public communist organizational activity in Finland. In order to earn money, Kaarlo Emil Holopainen has escorted people going to Russia and was finally arrested on one such trip." The paper is in the archives of the Foreign Ministry. Someone has underlined the last sentence and written near it "Notice!"

A woman from Kotka who lived at the "Norska," or the Norwegian sawmill, remembered that Holopainen along with his ten-year-old boy Pertti was constantly ferrying border-hoppers at night one year in the early thirties. Holopainen lived in Puistola, and his large motorboat left from the Norska tar dock. There were continual widespread whispers about his activities in Kotka, as well as about the fact that he and his son did not return from one of his trips. His wife and two daughters were left in Finland. (Interview with a former Kotka resident, GAAOSO f. 1, op. 2, d. 32462.)

Holopainen was not saved either. Five and one-half years later, the Finnish embassy sent the "respectful" notification that nothing was known of his whereabouts or of his fate.

Sortavala EK District Chief Yrjö Kares thwarted the chances for returning from Ural of Arvo Lehtonen, a resident of Suojärvi, in this fashion:

> . . . shown himself to be a communist, led an irregular and alcoholic life, been a constant annoyance to his community. Taking part in a strike at the Suojärvi sawmill brought about by the communists in 1927 and 1929. . . . Finally crossed the border from Suojärvi Parish at Naistenjärvi, his departure probably the result of drunkenness and communist opinions. . . . Winding up at the Nivastroi job site, has indulged in drinking, card playing and has made unsuccessful attempts to escape. Resulting banishment to Siberia, where he has been in Sarov and later, at least on [February 26, 1934] in Magnitogorsk. Regretted going to Russia and went on strike . . . address: Chelyabinsk Stankostroi KBS. kom. 4, where he is known as late as [November 9, 1934] to have been drinking and wearing birch-bark shoes.

Iisakki Malo of Oulu, who was journeying toward his death, was, according to EK "a good-for-nothing guzzler. Supported by his wife." A certain other border-hopper was "left-leaning . . . but belonged for years to the Salvation Army," in addition to which he had "a child out of wedlock with a maid." He was separated from his wife and had "a relationship with a common woman." In May of 1934, EK did not "consider itself able to support the petition of Aleksi Jelonen because he was known as a lazy worker but an ardent communist." During the same month EK commented on another longer list of names, and did not *oppose any but the following: Laukkanen, Anna Maria, who in letters to her relatives in Finland has extolled conditions in the Soviet Union and criticized conditions in Finland in an unsuitable manner. . . .*

And certain other Ural Finns: Jokimies, Kerttu, "known as a common woman in Finland and sentenced several times for immoral living." Tervonen, Isak, "been a member of several communist organizations." Roiha, Jalmari, "has married a Russian woman in Soviet Russia and has written very class-conscious and vengeful letters to Finland."

Chapter Five

"They Were Some Bunch"

THERE WERE 2,000 FINNS IN MAGNITOGORSK when their shipment to Chelyabinsk began in April and May of 1934. The first group to leave was made up of one or two hundred, only four of them women. Other groups followed, so that by the beginning of November there were over 800 Finns in Chelyabinsk. Some fifty to 100 skilled Finnish workmen remained in Magnitogorsk.

Chelyabinsk was no dream place. Back in April of 1932, Yrjö Forström, Emil Härmä, Anni and Veli Hartikainen, and sixteen other Finns had tried to get away from it by signing a letter and sending it to Otto Ville Kuusinen in Moscow. The group complained of their working conditions and of language problems and asked to be transferred to Soviet Karelia. "Many of our comrades could, however, if we worked at our own trades, fulfill our norms and even exceed them." Further on: "At this time some twenty of our comrades' wives are on their way from fascist Finland to this workers' state, so that for the sake of their little children too it would be better to be nearer Karelia."

Before the arrival of the large group in 1934, there had been a few Finnish border-hoppers in Chelyabinsk. On their arrival they had caused a "scandal" by not going to work at the power plant after the first day because not all of them had received the felt boots they had been promised. The representative of the Finns said to the functionary sent to them by the party and the trade union that they would not go to work until the boots arrived. And that is what happened.

The American John Scott, who traversed the town with an acquaintance of his, thus described the bread line they saw in a store:

> At the head of the line, I observed about twenty men, who struck me as being pleasant, and who waited patiently and quietly for their bread. They were Finns. "There are some 300 in Chelyabinsk," said my friend. "They are good workers, but they drink too much. Most of them crossed the border in 1930 and 1931. Many of them were smugglers and oddly enough, they stick together."

Scott related that when a *komsomol* functionary tried to step to the head of the line, only the Finns did anything. They grabbed the man and shoved him out of the line. Furious, he tried again to step to the front of the line, whereupon "one of the Finns shouted out in poor Russian: 'We stand in line; you stand in line.'" The Finns seized the man and moved him calmly but decisively out into the yard.

At the latest, it was during the phase when the new group of border-hoppers was arriving in Chelyabinsk, or, as some recall, it was already in Magnitogorsk, that a Finnish-speaking Red Army officer named Antti Fomin appeared among the Finns as the representative of the GPU. He brought with him his wife and adopted son. Fomin wore civilian clothing without insignias of rank. The border-hoppers got along better with him than with Fomkin. Hannu Rautkallio, who confused Fomin with Fomkin, wrote that Fomin had been assigned to Magnitogorsk as an "SKP instructor" and conversely that Fomin had served before that in "Sarova."

"Jussi" Fomin was, at any rate, an experienced man. He had originally been a Viipuri streetcar conductor who had risen to be a Red Army officer and one of the men in the Finnish Cheka unit in Leningrad. There he served in the investigations branch and also belonged to the party's purging committee.

It was said that Fomin had "pulled a boner" for which he had been condemned to serve in this remote place. According to one report, he had refused to sign the order to arrest one of his subordinates. Conversely Markku Salomaa relates that in 1935 Kustaa Rovio described Fomin—if it was the same Fomin—as "a fearless Chekist, a self-sacrificing fighter for the working-class cause and for the destruction of its enemies."

Finally Kaarlo Hartikainen relates that Fomin was the man before whom the men sent to Shpalernaja had appeared in Leningrad. According to him,

Fomin was "middle-aged, ugly, coarse" and a brutal interrogator. One prisoner had reported that Fomin had made a living as a beggar in St. Petersburg and had risen after the revolution from being a bilingual street informer to an investigative judge. Hartikainen's story changed from one book of memoirs to another.

In the 1700s Chelyabinsk had been founded in a nomadic area as a Czarist military outpost, and had become a stopping-place for caravans. Now a section of a modern city with its several-story factory housing had been built there, which the border-hoppers thought "looked good." Only in April 1934 with the arrival of the first banished group of forced laborers was the transporting of prisoners to the area begun. The Finns got to live in a four-story brick building still under construction. It was located on the "steppe" in a barracks area at the edge of the city. The building was later a women's prison and a center for the care of sexual diseases.

The building housed some 1,000 people, thus 800 would have been Finns. But according to a letter from Kirsti Wahlstén, there were over a thousand Finns all told and in addition "some hundred-odd" Poles, Jews, Rumanians, and "Lord knows what." It was crowded living in "our *komnaa-*

Finnish workers at Chelyabinsk, 1935. Left to right, front: Onni Nissilä, Juho Hämäläinen, and Ahti Pellikka.

ta [a room] too." Unmarried men lived together in one room; a modicum of privacy was achieved for families by room dividers made of plywood or hanging sheets.

The Finns worked as common laborers on a secret building a half-kilometer in length. Officially it was called the Stankostroi tool factory, but it was known that actually a tank and cannon factory was rising there. Viljo Kartineva relates that the Finns were taken away before the building was finished because the Russians did not want them to see it.

A large tractor factory had already been built in Chelyabinsk, in which many Ingrian Finns were working. Now the Finland Finns were also assigned to it. Seventy new American-model Stalinets caterpillar tractors were driven out of its doors daily. They were said to perform well, so there should have been no reason to complain about the factory. Nevertheless, ten of the factory's directors were jailed in August 1936.

Living conditions in Chelyabinsk were, in the border-hoppers' opinion, wretched, and their dissatisfaction was great. Sipinen had promised that school would continue, but soon the Finns were aware that the advantages they had had at Magnitogorsk, such as the Finnish school, the children's nursery, and the trade school, were a thing of the past. For the small children, there was indeed a summer camp. The Finns grumbled at having a part of their pay deducted for the airplane fund, for example. The wages were otherwise so poor and paydays so infrequent that hunger threatened them, particularly the families with children. "Our group was in the grip of panic."

Many requested and were given work building the railroad, or escaped to work in the city. "This place is worse than the other," wrote Adolf Koskinen. "I'm working as a shoemaker in the city, actually it's forbidden, I'm supposed to do construction work, but I can't stand to because it pays really nothing."

"It's not too great here, if I could only get away," wrote carpenter Eemeli Nikula from "Chelapinski" to his brother in Vihanti. The Nikulas had taken a taxi into the Kuusamo wilderness and walked across the border carrying their little girl in a backpack.

According to Nikula the best workers were rewarded and the joiners fared best—they got food and even good clothing, which was impossible in Finland. He himself asked for "some tenners so that he could buy the girl shoes for the summer." One could get everything now without a card, but the prices were too high. Chances for the children's education were said to be good, and Nikula himself thought that he would be getting along better within a year if he could only get a start somehow.

In the margin he wrote: "Tell me isn't it better to stay here once I've come; wouldn't that be acting like a man? Write soon." After four months he had new questions to ask: did it pay for him to get a Soviet passport so that he could work on a locomotive? On the other hand, he couldn't come back to Finland then unless there "happened" to be a revolution. Was there work to be had in Finland?

Eemeli Nikula died in 1936, and Aili Nikula immediately began to make arrangements for the voyage home. She asked for help from Finland, saying "that many widows here have gotten permission to leave." There were many obstacles before her, but within less than a year she was in Finland with her daughter.

"They promised to pay us well here, but now that we've moved it's a totally different story," wrote Viljo Wahlstén, who had left Helsinki with his family. "Now they tell us this is what we'll pay you and not a kopeck more. These Russians are masterful liars if they are not forced to keep their word, and if there is any advantage in breaking it, they will always do so. But anyway, they are a happy people . . ."

Wahlstén affirmed that everything would change for the better. Production figures testified to enormous progress. "It's a sure thing that a panic and its consequences will never happen in this country." Nevertheless, he added: "We keep waiting to see the continually circulating rumors about getting to Finland come true."

"We are not in Siberia, and God protect us from going there," wrote his thirty-year-old seamstress wife, Kirsti. She told her relatives not to cry and wrote them she believed the hardest days were over: "We'll come back from here yet."

"Viljo dreams of fine boots, blue breeches, and furs, and the children and I of silk dresses and other such things," Kirsti Wahlstén wrote in her letter. According to her, spiritual nourishment was "somewhat lacking"—perhaps a hint at the meetings in the "red corner."

The common lodging meant crowding and noise, and diseases spread from one family to another. Eila Wahlstén relates that one night a Finnish woman went crazy, "She screamed, wept, called on God, and wanted to jump out of the window."

Grumbling, lack of discipline, and drunkenness increased among the Finns. "They were some bunch," declared Sanin-Sipinen. "No way in hell would I have turned them loose in Karelia. Laziness and malingering are their basic traits." There were said to be only a couple of SKP members in the large group. Political enlightenment seemed to have no effect on the hooliganism; the Finns were accused of fighting and even of murder. Group doings were not arranged out of fear that the Finns would break them up.

A couple of hundred of the most riotous were isolated, but an attempt was made to keep the "emigrant sector" together at the same factory. Since there were not enough jobs there for everyone, there was a shortage of both wages and food. And everyone was ordered to work: thus no trade school was provided for the young.

A common laborer got sixty to 120 rubles per month. A skilled painter could earn as high as 150 to 200 rubles. Actually the pay was always smaller, since deductions for political funds, taxes, and cultural endeavors were taken from it.

The border-hoppers relate that both at the Magnitogorsk and Chelyabinsk job sites there were a disproportionate number of "bosses" and clerical workers. According to Tuomas Monto, there were only six carpenters at his construction site, while there were twenty bosses. At another site there were twenty-seven carpenters; all of them could not work every day because there were not enough horses to haul the building materials. However, thirty horses stood at the wall of the office building—the directors drove them back and forth to work.

According to Monto, nails were not always to be had, so they were cut from iron wire. "In the fall of 1935, there were no nails at all in Kamensk, and then the lumber ran out too." Decent tools had to be purchased from the American Finns. One of them, Jukka Hämäläinen, was for his part horrified that in Soviet factories "functionaries made up forty percent of the personnel."

John Scott relates that there were ten "office rats" to take care of the work that one decent worker could easily have done. He cites from the Magnitogorsk combine's statistics, according to which in 1933 over forty-two percent of labor time was lost in stoppages, harassment, accidents, shortages of material, and absenteeism.

Everything was on ration cards. Extra food could be had by selling one's clothing and other goods. In Chelyabinsk there was one state store in which the necessities of life were sold "on the open market," but there black bread cost a ruble and a half per kilo, white bread three rubles, and butter twenty-six to twenty-eight rubles. Each worker was provided with quilted pants and a coat, for which he had to pay about thirty-five rubles.

Supervision at Magnitogorsk had not been strict, so that not everyone went to work after getting a bread card, as long as they had money to buy bread. But in Chelyabinsk, on the other hand, close watch was kept over work and food consumption. "Slackers" went without their bread ration, and those who missed work completely had their cards lifted. According to a new law, a worker could be dismissed and have his bread card taken away if he missed even a day's work without a legitimate reason.

> Lately discipline has been made even tighter than before. If someone is too weak for lack of food to go to work some day, this "slacker" is visited by the camp's Soviet taskmasters who, shouting and waving their hands in vintage Russian fashion, berate him as a hooligan and anti-revolutionary. The slightest effort at defense or argument is branded as rebellion. The taskmasters threaten to send such people to a place where they will be taught to work. Many Finns have wound up leaving in "prick detachments," in other words, going off to Siberia in groups closely guarded by soldiers with bayonets and rifles, and nothing is ever heard from them again. The same fate hangs over those on the job or in camp who are dissatisfied and dare to criticize the wretched conditions prevailing in the Soviet Union.

According to the same narrator, one could express his opinion openly only in company of whom he was absolutely sure, for men and women in the pay of the GPU, most of whom were even known to be so, were buzzing around everywhere. Lectures and other functions were held in the red corner only once or twice a month, and the participation was apathetic. Only some twenty Finns were enthusiastic about taking part in political activity.

One of the Finns, whom the GPU tried to recruit as an informer, was Veli Hyrsky, a seaman and policeman's son from Turku. Fomkin called him into his quarters in the late winter of 1935 and asked to be informed if "he heard anyone talking against the Soviet state, or planning to go to Finland, or if he knew that someone was in the service of the Finnish secret police.

According to his story, Hyrsky said that he was the same kind of border-hopper as the rest and did not know of any crimes being committed. Nonetheless, Fomkin often called him in and tried to ferret out information about the Finns, especially about Arthur Friman and Kalle Eloranta. Friman was a seaman who had skipped from a Finnish ship in a harbor. He was sentenced to five years in 1935, and Eloranta was sentenced during the same year. Eloranta, a worker, had followed his wife to the Soviet Union on a legitimate passport, believing that he could just try working there for a half year, but the border closed behind him. He was a marked man—as they said later—because he was married to the "wrong" woman.

Fomkin urged Hyrsky to write a list of Finns who wanted to go to Finland, but the latter replied, "You can put me down first on that list."

Fomkin reportedly threatened him with jail. Hyrsky did wind up being sentenced, but only after attempting to flee.

In the spring of 1935—some remembered it as in the fall—Fomin suddenly died. He fell ill of erysipelas, which turned out to be fatal. Tyyne Leskinen remembers standing in an honor guard beside his coffin, and, according to Fanni Pyykkö, the Finns placed wreaths with memorial statements on the coffin. Fomkin was now the only GPU official left to oversee the border-hoppers. In the opinion of some, Fomin's death was a loss, since he had related to the Finns in an understanding way, and no arrests had been made during his tenure. According to others, "there was no cause to mourn for him. They were both the same."

At least Fomkin had dealt with practical matters which concerned the young Finns in a businesslike way. He had secured Soviet passports and command certificates for all those who wanted to go to Petroskoi for further study beyond the trade school. In the end, only a few went—first Tyyne Leskinen, Esteri Lintunen, and Eero Vahlroos, and later Veikko Ollikainen. The other families did not want to become scattered around the country.

For their part, at least the Puonti family from Kotka remained indebted to Fomin. Karin Puonti had been chosen as his home helper, and she cared for Fomin's ailing wife so well that the officer thanked her, saying he could never repay her for saving her life. At that point Karin Puonti reminded him of their futile petition to return home. Soon the information arrived that Karin and the again ailing eight-year-old Pirkko were to be ready to travel within a week.

Niilo Puonti, who was himself ill, sternly ordered his wife to leave with his daughter: "Forget your feelings! A man can always get along, you're leaving and that's all there's to it!" Mother and daughter crossed the Finnish border on Christmas Day 1934. The woman who locked them into a quarantine cell in Terijoki said: "We observe Christmas, but do you?" Karin Puonti began to weep. Her husband, who had cursed himself for having taken his family to Russia, did not come through alive.

The family's rare good fortune aroused envy and malicious gossip. Later, Fanni Pyykkö wrote bitterly that Karin Puonti's travel arrangements were made secretly, and hinted in addition: "Was the lady able to please Fomkin somehow?"

In October 1935 the entire group headed north to an unknown destiny. They were informed that, under threat of arrest, they were to go elsewhere in Ural to work. Every day a rail carload of workers without passports was taken to a city named Kamensk.

A number of families who had hitherto traveled with the group, some of whom had requested citizenship, remained in Chelyabinsk. Among them were the Närvänens and the Pyykkös.

Allan and Fanni Pyykkö were from Oulu. With their two small children, they had walked across the border to Uhtua. Fanni's brother and sister had skipped across earlier. The Pyykkös' daughter died in Svirstroi, and their son died later. In Chelyabinsk, Allan did not buy the government bonds and urged others to do the same—he appealed to the fact that his family had to live.

One night in January 1936 Allan was arrested in his family's dwelling. Fomkin directed the search of the home. A man named Eskolin was said to be to blame for what happened. He himself did not escape his fate—he was sentenced to twenty-five years.

The night of the arrest, Fanni Pyykkö woke up their acquaintances, the Närvänens, who lived below them. Their three children had died in the Soviet Union; their fourth, a daughter named Raili, was born there. Hiskias Närvänen asked if the people arrested were guilty, "for I haven't been arrested." Fanni said she did not believe they were guilty, and then said jokingly to Ellen Närvänen, "You knock on the ceiling then, when they come to get Hiski." Almost two years after the disappearance of Pyykkö, Ellen woke Fanni up during the night. They had come to get Hiskias Närvänen.

Pyykkö was sentenced to two years and never returned, for having served his sentence he was shipped to a camp in the north for ten years. Ellen Närvänen was permitted to visit her husband twice. He urged his family to try to get to Finland; he himself would follow. He also asked her to "bring a little salt next time." By that time Närvänen himself had disappeared—permanently. Ellen was probably saved by the fact that she had a babe in arms. She moved to Kamensk, and Fanni Pyykkö was left in the big building with the Takalos and the Pynnönens; the men of all these families had disappeared. Soon they were the only Finns in the Chelyabinsk area.

The old part of Kamensk-Uralski at present.

Chapter Six

A Place Named Kamensk

THE CITY OF KAMENSK,* TO WHICH THE BORDER-HOPPERS were moved in the summer and autumn of 1935, lies in what was then the Chelyabinsk District. The city was a hundred kilometers southwest of Sverdlovsk by rail and had a population of nearly 50,000 inhabitants. Kamensk is on the Asian side of Ural, at a spot where the Kamensk River feeds into the Iset River; the latter joins the Irtysh, which flows into the Ob. Kamensk is an old factory town; as far back as 1700, work was begun on an iron foundry there by order of Peter the Great.

A barracks community had been built at the edge of the city on the wooded bank of the river. The first barrack was of sod. There were twenty of the long buildings in all; most of them came to be filled up with Finns. Written records show that they were referred to as *kvens*, which is the name applied to the Finnish minority in Norway. The barracks area got the name of "Finski Posjolok," "Finnish village," although its official name seems to

---

*The name of Kamensk was changed to Kamensk-Uralski in 1940. In the 1930s, the city belonged to the Chelyabinsk District; later tot eh Sverdlovsk District. That fact was to our advantage, for the KGB papers were transferred to the Sverdlovsk GAAOSO archives. The Chelyabinsk archives are under the control of the security forces and not open to research. However, we have received answers to questions from those archives. At present, Kamensk-Uralski has 200,000 inhabitants.

have been "Posjolok TETS" after the nearby power plant. Roll was called there in the evening to see that everyone stayed in the area.

Here, about six miles from the downtown area, UAZ, the huge aluminum plant, which was to process Severouralski bauxite, was under construction. Thousands of prisoners were at work on the site. The Finns, both men and women, were employed as builders, welders, masons, firemen, and drivers at the factory and its power plant, and around the railroad sheds. An engineer named Akulov, said to be of Finnish descent, was sent from Moscow as manager. The road to the job site ran through the woods, and solitary night-shift workers walked it with ax in hand for fear of wolves.

At first the surroundings were pleasant, but when the plant was completed, the air was full of ash and fine dust, which stung the eyes and throat. The snow was like a layer cake—white snow and black pollution in layers. Trees died standing, and the river was colored by pollution. Nevertheless, children swam, women washed their clothing in its waters, and men tried to fish from its banks. They hunted rabbits as well.

People were given coupons at work, with which they could eat in the dining hall; their value was deducted from one's pay. The price of the clothing they received—a quilted coat and pants—was also deducted. The card system and rationing ended in 1935, but at the same time the prices rose.

Kamensk-Uralski aluminum factory today, seen from the area of the former Finnish village.

Bread was available at the barracks village store to those who stood in line. Meat and vegetables were sold at the marketplace.

The necessities of life were expensive, but all in all, the border-hoppers were able to live better during the early phase at Kamensk than at any other time while they were in the Soviet Union. Robberies, fights, and murders happened in Kamensk too, but the life of the Finns seemed to have settled down a little. "We lived sort of like human beings," Salli Lappalainen recalls. "We were beginning to get food and clothing."

Even packages from relatives in Finland found their way here. Letters went quickly: Adolf Koskinen's letter is dated 19 November 1935 and stamped Krasnaja Gorka, Kamensk 21 November, Leningrad 23 November, and Kotka 27 November. But in his letter the shoemaker complained: "This is a poor village; no one is strong enough to do anything. There isn't even enough money to buy bread."

Those who still had jewelry and Finnish money left took the train to Sverdlovsk to shop. There they bought fabric which the tailors among the Finns made into clothing. Kirsti Wahlstén was the head of a sewing workshop where women's dresses were made.

For a while a group of Finnish boys were even allowed to work in Sverdlovsk, where they got into a fight. The militia took them to jail. It was in the house where Czar Nicholas II and his family were shot, and the boys were warned: "Behave or the same thing will happen to you." They were shown the cellar in which the bloody deed is claimed to have occurred.

The border-hoppers were finally able to escape having to live together in common rooms. Families got their own small rooms in Kamensk, where there was a stove and as many beds as could fit on the floor along with the table. "But the rents are so high," Kristiina Hansen-Haug wrote to Haukipudas. "We even have furniture, a pail, and a bucket." Some of the unmarried men got into five-man rooms. The rest of them were housed in two large lodges where there were several rows of beds side by side.

In Kamensk the Finns had a school, library, clubs, an orchestra, and a choir. They participated in gymnastics and sports and even traveled outside of Kamensk to compete. May Day of 1937 was celebrated with a three-day festival. "They must have had their fill of celebrating," Tyyne Paldan wrote to Finland, and then went on: "It's just as bad here, things don't get better when you move."

The children were sent to a Finnish school in the barracks village. Rauni and Erkki Murto, who had learned to speak and write Russian well when their parents were living apart from the others, went to the Russian school in Krasnaja Gorka. The Hansen-Haugs sent Anja there too. "We'll try to educate her so that she won't have to do dirty work."

The smaller Finnish children were taught by Aili Eloranta, a seamstress from Helsinki, and the older ones by Hellä Viuhko, whose daughter died in

The class of teacher Aili Eloranta (right) in Kamensk. Near the teacher is Irma Wahlstén and, behind her, is Maila Laukkarinen. Etel Saari peers from behind, on her right (third from left) Sointu Hölsä. Seated at the extreme left is perhaps Anja Hansen; next to her is Kerttu Jelonen; standing in fur caps are Leo Kurko and Jouko Alhonen. Oiva Ronkainen is wearing a light-colored blouse. Seated in front are (left to right) Ensio Luoto, Keijo Markkanen, Jorma Roiha, and Antti Tervonen. In back of Tervonen is Lauri Vaittinen.

Kamensk. The director of the school was Eloranta's new husband, Jalmari Kosonen, who taught Russian a couple of hours a week.

Aili Eloranta had been left an orphan at the age of three and wound up in the family of a small farmer who already had eleven children. He participated in trade union and workers' activities and acted as a nurse on the Red side in the Finnish Civil War, which landed him in jail. It is said that Kosonen and Eloranta were invited into the Soviet Union as specialists.

One of the buildings in the barracks village had been divided into two, so that one end was a club and the red corner and the other a nursery, where Helmi Laine took care of the little Finnish children. The children were happy to spend their days there, for there were lots of toys.

"Jallu" Kosonen had a room in the same building. He was still talking politics, showing educational films, and luring people into the red corner with a pretext of dances. It was a good drawing card, for there were many boys and girls under twenty among the border-hoppers. Kosonen was the "polit-director and head of the Finnish sector"—according to others, the number two man (under Fomkin). Some called him the commandant. Kosonen was a Russian citizen and an RKP (Russia Communist Party [b]) candidate, that is, he was waiting for admission to Communist party membership.

One finds little trace of the Finns in the Kamensk factory's newspaper. In June 1936, it did publish a news story "Best Stakhanovites [strike-force workers] Rewarded." A meeting had been held of the "strike force" construction workers.

An excerpt from the story:

> The Finnish workers' political director Comrade Kossonen (Kosonen) stated: The Stakhanovite* movement applies to us too. There are dozens of Stakhanovites, whole brigades of them in our ranks. We have studied Comrade Stalin's words and we shall faithfully fulfill them.

In July 1937 the paper criticized a man who set norms for treating the Russians differently from the Finns: "A norm-setter named Belyh who works in the office at the Sojuzvodstroi job site assigns different wages for the same job. Comrade Panova's brigade is paid this: norm 2.2 cubic meters, pay— [two] rubles, [seventy-two] kopecks per cubic meter; and Kaukonen's (Henrik Kaukonen) brigade, norm 1.68 cubic meters, pay—[three] rubles, [fifteen] kopecks."

---

*Stakhanovites were "strike-force" workers who competed in an effort to surpass the work norms. Their model was Aleksei Stakhanov, a miner "discovered" in 1935. As his opposite number, saboteurs were "discovered" on job sites and blamed for accidents, for example.

In September the paper headlined the record of Mason Hapalainen (Erland Haapalainen from Kemi, who had just six months left to live).

> In building the walls of the TETS' boiler section, Mason Hapalainen plastered [twenty-nine] square meters in place of the 16.6 meter norm. Exceeding the norm earned him [forty-five] rubles and [forty] kopecks. It should be mentioned that master builder Vilkin supplied the place well with the necessary materials and thus assisted Comrade Hapalainen to achieve his high productivity.

How many Finns were there then in Kamensk before the imprisonments carried out during the latter half of the 1930s? The estimates of the young people who survived vary from 400 to 700; the last figure was put forth by Annikki Tervonen and Erkki Murto, for example. According to Toivo Laine and Allan Vuorio, the maximum population figure was more than that if children were taken into account. Siiri Hämäläinen spoke of more than 500. Sylvi Ollikainen recalls that at the end 350 Finns were taken and fifty

Finnish workers in Kamensk. Seated at right is Sylvi Ollikainen, who was transferred to another job when she fainted in the factory. Seated at left is Salli Lappalainen, and standing is Helmi Viljamaa. Second from left at the back is Reino Vesterinen, and fourth from left is Kauko Reinikainen.

allowed to remain. In any event, shortly before this many had already been imprisoned, probably dozens. Hilma Vaittinen, who lived in Kamensk from 1936 through 1994, remembered that the lodging of Finns in the barracks was arranged so that families lived in Barracks 4, 8, 9, and 10, and unmarried people in 11 and 12. From the arrest records, one can see that number of barracks went up to 13. Other besides Finns lived in some of the barracks, at least there were Tatars there.

Onni Kauppi, who still lives in Kamensk, wrote in the aluminum plant's paper in March 1989 that "between 1935 and 1937, nearly 500 Finns lived in nine or ten barracks," and most of them were arrested on one night. The Kamensk city newspaper related in 1993 that in "operation foreigner" nearly 500 Finnish residents were arrested; the source of the number may, of course, be the paper cited. Some years after the tragic event, the NKVD operatives questioned said that in the group of prisoners taken by train to the jail in Chelyabinsk there were more than 200 people. They may have had their own reasons for not citing the correct figure.

Armas Jämsä, who returned to Finland in 1936, said that a group of 600 Finns moved from Chelyabinsk to Kamensk in 1935, and that their number

Possibly Impi and Valdemar Riutta, and Paavo, who was born in Kamensk in 1937.

had noticeably decreased before he left. Information from VALPO interrogations in the fall of 1937 relate that some 500 to 600 Finns were brought to Kamensk and that most of them were scattered to other sites to work in factories and above all, in the woods. EK's annual report indicates that discipline slackened in 1936, at which time men went to work elsewhere on their own initiative.

In estimating the number, a problem is posed by the fact that different sources take into account only the adult Finns, although we cannot know this for certain. In any case there were many families with children in Kamensk, some of them large. They remained there while the unmarried men, who were freer to move, had left to work elsewhere or had escaped. Erkki Murto said there were a couple hundred children. We ourselves have calculated the number of children and young people to be over two hundred.

From Russian and Finnish archives and from interviews with those still alive, we have gathered a list of names of 737 Kamensk Finns, and we conjecture that we do not have everything straight. A lot of Finns went to work at logging sites, and some of them returned, so that it is very difficult to ascertain when certain people came to Kamensk or moved away from there. In each of the Kamensk barracks there was a total of thirty-two rooms on either side of a hallway, where the Finns said they lived, "packed in like salt herring." Furthermore, there were two barracks in whose rooms the beds were lined up side by side. If, say, there was a family with one child or a few unrelated individuals per room, and if there were a scant ten barracks, a mechanical calculation leads to the conclusion that a hundred people could have lived in one barracks and that in principle there might well have been room for 800 Finns in the whole village. That ties in well with Eila Wahlsten's recollection that there were over 300 families in Kamensk, in which case there would have been at least 600 adults.

According to EK reports, half of the Kamensk Finns had requested Soviet citizenship, and ten percent had been granted it; in later court records almost all were listed as "without citizenship" or as "Finnish citizen." The test period was a year, and the applicant had to know Russian. The year 1936 was the most active with regard to citizenship applications—and for a time almost the last chance for a Finn to get citizenship. Freedom of movement was also greater in 1936.

It was easier for a citizen to find a job or change it, and to travel, which was crucial in any plan to escape or to visit representatives of Finland. Some even expressed a hope of vacationing in Finland. Applications for citizenship were also motivated by the fear of being sent farther east. According to EK, border-hoppers' passports were exchanged in 1936 for citizens' passports, and if a person did not want one, he was "shipped far away to a miserable logging site."

Although these Finns were held to be particularly dangerous at the time of their arrest, never once was there applied to them the decision approved in 1934, according to which the folk commissariat had the right "to expel beyond the borders of the USSR foreign underlings who are dangerous to society."

Already in 1937 some were said to regret bitterly their request for citizenship. Many definitely wanted to keep their Finnish citizenship in order not to lose hope completely of returning home, and used only the so-called border-hoppers' passport. The Sortavala EK district reported in 1937:

They all want to return to Finland, but no one believes in any other possibility than trying to sneak in.

Diplomats seemed to be of the same opinion. In October 1935, embassy secretary Asko Ivalo wrote in connection with the case of Heikki Niva-aho's return request:

We have made the customary proposal on the matter to the Soviet Union's Folk Commissariat for Foreign Affairs, but usually we get no answer to requests for speedier action on matters that involve border-hoppers. Considering the negative way in which Soviet officials have reacted to such matters for years, it looks as if there is hardly any hope for the case in question to end favorably.

Many were still able to write to Finland and ask for help. Very few border-hoppers returned by legal means. The distances they had to travel did not discourage those trying to escape; particularly during the summer, young men kept quietly disappearing from Kamensk on a flight to Finland.

In the autumn of 1935 a group of Finnish men moved from Kamensk to work in Tashkent. According to driver Toivo Laine, there were some one hundred masons there, most of them from Kamensk. Some went on toward Afghanistan and China, but Laine does not know if any succeeded in escaping to other countries.

Driver's license photo of Toivo Laine taken in the Soviet Union.

Laine and Pentti Haapaniemi, who was a couple of years younger, had come from Tampere with Kalle Pukala's group. From Tashkent the two went on to the Tatar capital of Kazan. Haapaniemi's uncle was a work supervisor at an airplane factory building site, at which a lot of Finns and American Finns congregated.

One night in November 1937, Laine was arrested as a spy, and the frightened Haapaniemi moved back to Kamensk, where he thought he would be safe among the Finns. But of the two, it was Laine who remained alive. Other Finns moved to Komsomolsk-na-Amur, where a "Finnish spy and sabotage group" was also uncovered.

The Tatar NKVD arrested a number of others along with Laine, twenty-five Finns in all, whom "Vilho Kärkkäinen, a Finnish intelligence agent, had recruited into an anti-revolutionary spy organization," or by another agent, Eerik Alatalo from Kuolajärvi. Kärkkäinen was a border-hopper from Viipuri, who in turn had been recruited by "one of the employees of the Finnish Embassy in Moscow in 1925." Furthermore seven other men "recruited as agents" escaped arrest on this occasion since they were working elsewhere, many on the embassy building in Moscow.

The men (and two women) were said to have spied on the manufacture of military matériel—inter alia, the automobile plant at Nizhni Novgorod, the airplane plant at Kazan, and the railway car plant at Nizhni Tagil. In addition, information about the group's political state of mind had been accumulated "their extreme distortion and total slander of the communist party and the Soviet nation." Alatalo's group had communicated military information from White Russia "in the literary code, Kansan Työ"—an apparent reference to the newspaper *People's Work* published in Finland.

Pentti Haapaniemi and Yrjö Nissilä in Ural.

Everyone was made to confess. The greater part (twenty) of these Finns were executed by decree of the *dvoika* or twosome, made up of Nikolai Jezhov and the Soviet Union's chief prosecutor Andrei Vyshinski. Among those shot were Väinö Aaltonen, Taneli Jokiniemi, Väinö Paldan, Hannes Saariniemi, and Matti Tennilä, all of whom had come from Kamensk. Apparently Alatalo had mentioned many of the boys from his area, since many of those executed were from Kuolajärvi and from other places in the North.

One of the few who got a lighter sentence was Toivo Laine. While waiting in his cell, he made the acquaintance of border-hoppers who had come from Karelia to Kazan, mistakenly thinking that Finns would have it easier here. The NKVD troika sentenced Laine to ten years at reformatory labor.

Comrades Bruno Aalto, Toivo Laine, and Viljo Viitanen went to a photographer in Helsinki a couple of days before they crossed the border in 1932. They were all under twenty years of age. Only Laine returned—having served a ten-year sentence at forced labor.

He was sent to the large Uhta camp in Komi, where political prisoners and criminals were held together and where a human life was "not worth a wooden penny." All the work was done by the political prisoners.

For decades, Laine was afraid to tell what he had experienced at Komi. During the first four years, the prisoners lived in army tents, with an oil drum for a stove, where it was so cold that the men's hair froze to their bunks at night. They had no bedclothes at all. While working outdoors, the men wore sandals made from automobile tires. Laine froze his hands and was handi capped for the rest of his life.

According to Laine, the death rate was "appallingly high." On success summers, 1942 and 1943, two Ural Finns died, the Varis brothers Eero Toivo, who were sentenced to ten years on the same day. Before his deat! letter from the home folk in Pölläkkälä had arrived for Eero, which for sc reason is now in Vilhelmiina Murto's KGB file along with a photograph.

In Komi things were stolen at every turn, and the food rations prescribe by the state vanished before they could reach the hands of the eater. The was no soap, and the men stole heating oil to wash with. Then a Polish sur ply chief came up with the idea that soap could be boiled from dead rats. Fc five rats you could get a plug of tobacco. Soon all the rats had disappeare from the camp.

In 1942 American aid arrived at the camp—flour, white bread, and pork. The United States had reportedly demanded certain rights and freedoms for Soviet citizens and foreigners as conditions for getting aid. For that reason it was later easier for the Finnish embassy to distribute passports to the border-hoppers. Tauno Flinkman also reports that the rations continually shrank during the war, until salvation arrived unexpectedly at his camp in Uhta: American canned goods and flour.

Laine served out his sentence to the very last day. Finally he was allowed to choose either Siberia or Kazakhstan as his place of exile. He chose the latter.

People came from other places to check what possibilities life offered in Ural. EK related in its 1936 survey "Finns in the Soviet Union" that because of falling wages many border-hoppers had moved from the Petroskoi area to southern Russia and across the border into Asia "where they imagined that better conditions prevailed than in Karelia. Many of them, however, returned in disappointment to Petroskoi and said that conditions elsewhere in the Soviet Union were no better—on the contrary, they were in some respects worse than in Karelia." For example, in the Ural area there was a shortage of potatoes, sales of which were limited to a maximum of fifteen kilos per person.

According to the report, information received from different parts of the Soviet Union "indicate that efforts to get out of the country have increased extraordinarily of late." EK considered one cause to be that the border-hoppers had heard of improving conditions in Finland.

During the past three years, the number illegally crossing the border from Finland is hardly worth mentioning. Among the Finns there is general dissatisfaction and disillusionment with Soviet rule and with wretched conditions. The political activity and agitation which were evident during the earlier years has—with the exception of a few confirmed communists—practically died out, and indifference and despair have taken their place, causing many Finns to become alcoholics or deteriorate in other ways.

In 1936, for the first time in ages, Gerda Saari received a letter from Porvoo and wrote back to her sister that she had thought everyone was already dead or had forgotten about them. Life was a little brighter now; she had been ill, but she had gotten a job as a dishwasher, and Aleksi had a better job too. The necessities of life were cheaper. They were not able to speak Russian, so fourteen-year-old Lea shopped for them.

In October of the same year Lea wrote to Porvoo from Kamensk—in Finnish, for all three girls had almost forgotten their Swedish—that her mother did not have time to write; she worked twelve hours a day. Her little sisters were in school, Rakel in the third and Etel in the first grade. There was other news to relate: Father had caught no fish, and uncle Allan had frozen to death when he fell asleep drunk in a snow bank. Lea told of missing Finland, thanked her for the glossy picture, and asked for hairpins.

Gerda Saari wrote next that "things are generally good, there is food every day but it's hard to get clothing since this place is just being built." There were again rumors that the Finns would soon be allowed to leave, "so pick some berries for us so we can cook a good berry pudding." She said they had drunk no coffee for five years. Gerda was already planning where the family would live in Finland. She was unable to write more because she could not get paper in Kamensk.

Niilo Puonti wrote a number of letters to his daughter who had gotten to Finland. "Try to be a good girl and work hard in school. . . . Grow up to be a big girl. . . . I hope that some day Pirkko will have her father and that her father will have his Pirkko." He asked her to send some glossy pictures to Eila Wahlstén and regretted that he was not able to send anything to Finland "because he had not been to town."

The family learned later that Kalle Aalto, an acquaintance of his from his army days in Santahamina had urged him to flee to Finland with him. Puonti did not dare. Aalto left Kamensk in 1936 and appeared in Finland in 1937. Veli Hyrsky, who arrived in Finland that same summer, had tried to persuade Viljo Wahlstén, who lived in the same barracks with him, to flee but the latter did not want to set out with two little girls.

Fomkin continued as the NKVD operative authorized to keep watch over the Finns during the years at Kamensk. While there, he is reported to have developed a stomach ulcer. He did not live in the Finnish village, but in the "richer quarter" of Krasnaja Gorka. Hilma Vaittinen kept company with Fomkin's son and stole his food card. Life depended on little things.

Kalle Aalto and Niilo Puonti were army buddies. Aalto urged Puonti in vain to flee with him from Kamensk.

The old, familiar "Finnish sector leaders" were still with them: Kosonen, Kuusela, Quintus, Sipinen, and Viuhko. They were responsible for their "education," their work and lodging, and also acted as interpreters for them. At least temporarily Kuusela was ordered to leave Ural and work in Leningrad. He was shot in 1938. Sipinen moved there too but wrote that he had soon grown tired of trade union work, was going to become an electrician and return to Kamensk. It was his last letter.

For his part, Kosonen returned from Karelia to Kamensk, where he wound up doing painting work. This is what David Sinkko had to say of him to VALPO interrogators in the fall of 1937:

In the winter of 1936 K. committed some thirty Finns to the GPU jail for anti-revolutionary talk. Then K. somehow or other either forced or persuaded the wife of one of them, a worker named Eloranta, to marry him.

Kalle Nestor Eloranta sat in the Chelyabinsk jail for a scant year, but that was enough. According to other information, Eloranta was jailed in 1935 and his wife searched hard for him. Then again, according to her daughter's account, Aili Eloranta had been childless during thirteen years of marriage, so that her husband agreed for her to have a child with someone else. Her pregnancy saved her life; both her men were executed.

Väinö Tiiainen from Lappeenranta was, according to the accounts of others, a GPU agent in Kamensk, and even before that. He testified in court against some Finns who were given jail sentences. In the end Tiiainen was arrested and executed.

The first imprisonments in Kamensk began as early as 1935. In the situation that prevailed after the murder of Sergei Kirov, Fomkin drew up lists, carried out arrests "with Kosonen and some Russian," and interrogated the suspects. The first group arrested included a total of twelve Finns, Toivo Laine recalls. In January there were arrested, as if from an alphabetical list, the following border-hoppers: Laitinen, Lassila, Launonen, Lindstén, Peltoniemi, Tuominen, and one more, perhaps Venho, all of them family men.

The men were taken to Chelyabinsk for interrogation. For her part, Fanni Pyykkö remembers that the fathers of ten Finnish families, one of whom died almost immediately in the prison, were brought there from Kamensk. According to other information, "in the winter of 1936 Kosonen committed some thirty Finns to the GPU prison for anti-revolutionary talk" or "had many sent to Siberia."

Those imprisoned were accused of Trotskyism and contacts with the Finnish secret police, by whom they were supposed to have been assigned tasks and given money. They had spent money very freely, which had attracted attention in an impoverished society.

A whole crew of Finnish workers went to Chelyabinsk to give information to the GPU about the activities of the accused and testified against them when they were sentenced in Kamensk in March of 1937. All received three-to five-year prison sentences, which at least in the case of Lindstén was changed to exile to Siberia.

During that period, the nocturnal fetchers took away some individual men, the father of the Markkanen family among them. Fomkin and two of the militia searched his home, chewing on sunflower seeds and spitting. The children, Eeva and Keijo, watched with sleep-dazed eyes from the bed they shared. Robert Markkanen refused to go until his wife returned from the night shift. They waited. Finally Aili Markkanen arrived, and frightened, began to weep. How long would her husband be gone? "Time will tell," said Fomkin. Markkanen disappeared for ten years to Siberia.

The mother was not able to support Eeva and Keijo and gave them up to a children's home. She and Eeva saw each other once in the fall of 1937. Her mother told Eeva that she was taking her brother home. When they parted, the child began to cry: "What if I never see you again?" The mother consoled her by saying that Eeva would get to come home when winter was over and promised to come again on New Year's.

The bullet meant for Eeva's mother had already been molded. They never saw each other again.

While Robert Markkanen was being held at the Kamensk militia post, his wife was still permitted to bring him a couple of packages. "Dear Aili, I got everything," read a note from him. Later he was kept for ten months in a cell at Chelyabinsk, where his food was tossed in through a trapdoor in the roof so there was no need to open the cell door at mealtimes.

Later Markkanen told his daughters that in Siberia he had to stand in a cell that was so crowded that some of the inmates had to go out into the corridor when the door was opened. Those whose names were called out disappeared forever. In the end, only Markkanen and a few other Finns were left in the cell.

Markkanen had not requested permission to go to Finland, nor did he do so as a prisoner, although he was offered the application blanks. For years he had not written a single letter to Finland, and had warned others against doing so. It is not known whether he ever tried to search for his lost son. He reportedly did not dare return to Kamensk, for he might "even have killed Fomkin" in a fit of rage. When Markkanen died in 1961, he was not yet sixty years old.

At one point, Reino Orell's wife Sanni Lappalainen was offered a "big roll of rubles" for travel money to Finland on condition that she agree to act as an "undercover agent." She would not be allowed to take her little daughter Tamara with her. She refused, whereupon she was threatened with never

Aili and Robert Markkanen. Aili was executed, Robert sentenced to ten years; one child died, two were taken to a children's home, and one of the latter disappeared.

being permitted to go to Finland. Nor was she. According to Finnish security police archives containing information from border-hoppers who returned in the 1950s, the MVD (Interior Ministry) had questioned Sanna Orell about the "life and talk" of those who had left Russia. In another instance, when Emil Aura applied for return to Finland, the MVD reportedly tried to recruit him to help them there.

The Murto family—parents and children—were the only Finns sent from Sarov to Pervouralski. The father, Kalle, was a carpenter at the Hrompik station and the children, Rauni and Erkki, were put into a Russian school. The parents had learned not a word of Russian, and seven-year-old Rauni was already an experienced interpreter who even helped out her mother at the offices.

Rauni was there to help at the Pervouralski NKVD when her mother asked about her husband, who had disappeared without leaving a trace. Kalle Murto had tried to flee, but the messages from Finland said nothing about his having arrived there. He had been stopped at the border, and soon he returned to his family from prison. His son Väinö succeeded in getting to Finland.

The Murtos heard that there were many Finns in Kamensk, among them their sons Ilmari and Urho along with their wives. Kamensk was among the places to which one could move with NKVD permission, and they too traveled there. The youngest children went to the Russian school at Krasnaja Gorka. "There are [forty-two] pupils in the class, and I'm the best pupil," Rauni wrote to her sister in Finland in 1937. She had even won awards. "It's neat to study two languages, Finnish and Russian. . . . After I finish school I go to work in an office."

Their father was forced to work on construction while he was a sick man. Rauni remembers taking gruel or soup to him on the job, and watching how hard it was for him to swallow even that food. Soon Kalle Murto's condition weakened. He had to be taken to the Chelyabinsk hospital. There was no money for the trip, and Rauni went through all the barracks with a slip: "Can you help me, my father is sick." She also went to the station to buy the tickets for her father and his escort—no one else was able.

In November of 1937 a wire arrived in Chelyabinsk "Kalle Murto died and the hospital took charge of the burial." Rauni remembers how her mother squeezed her to her breast in anguish and kept repeating, "How will you get along without me, you're still so little."

Aino Kantonen from Haukipudas, the mother of two children, sent this word to Finland: "Kamensk 21 October. We've moved again, and we're all still alive." In March 1937 Kantonen wrote to the foreign ministry:

> Honorable Sir Minister: is there any knowledge there of our getting out; will we ever get out of here to our homeland; what way is there for us to get out; can you give us advice about a way; will the minister please write us what news there is about our getting out.

Aino Kantonen added that she was writing to her sister in Finland asking her to send the money for postage to the minister since there was no way she could repay the minister for his postal expenses from Kamensk.

Isak "Ilkka" Tervonen, fifty-two and a worker, wrote what was perhaps the last letter in his life on 6 October 1937. He too had come from Haukipudas with his wife, Liisa, and his children, Annikki, Antti, Elsa, Helvi, and Tauno; Tauno was a baby when they crossed the border in 1932, and he soon died. The children heard their mother threaten in the heat of a quarrel: "When we get to Finland, I'm going to divorce you!" Their hope of returning home was still alive, although they never spoke of it to their children.

Isak and Liisa Tervonen had five children. The three who survived have now returned to Finland.

In his letters, Tervonen complained that his relatives had not written to him at all. (Letters were often intercepted along the way.) He wrote that they had not yet wound up in the mud (earth?) of Ural. Writing from Kamensk, it was "very hard" to tell them anything, but nevertheless

Tervonen wrote that the family was trying to get to Finland. "I think we'll still get out of here some day."

As if in passing, he gave a despairing picture of the family's situation.

> Elsa and Annikki are at an evening entertainment. Helvi is frying pota-
> toes. Antti is sleeping already. Mother Liisa is scrubbing the hallway of
> this barrack or house where we live; there are [thirty-two] families; all
> have a little room so the hallway is pretty long. Liisa keeps it clean and
> gets [fifty] rubles a month pay for it. Now even people like us get pota-
> toes to eat during potato digging time they cost only [two] rubles a pail,
> in the winter they cost six, seven, and eight rubles a pail. I earn only
> four and a half rubles a day. I get 110 rubles a month [ninety] rubles
> go for bread. [Twenty] rubles [are] left for other food. I'm just writing
> this down and it's true.

A week after her previous letter, Gerda Saari again wrote to her sister in Porvoo. She had better news:

> . . . now I must tell you the news that we are coming there soon, maybe
> next month; a hundred people who already have passports are leaving
> here . . .

Reportedly the Saaris had not yet received a passport, but it would come soon. The family was so ill clothed that Gerda didn't really know who they would dare go to in Finland. They would take whatever work they could get. Daughter Lea was already big enough to go to work. They could tell the grandparents that the Saaris were coming to Finland for Christmas and they should bake so much coffee bread that there would be enough for everyone.

> The world is big enough so that there surely must be a place in it some-
> where for us too.

The children were still going to the Finnish school in Kamensk. Etel Saari was in the second grade now and was the best pupil in her grade. She was given awards and was praised at the meetings.

The papers were moving slowly but surely. Hopes rose when more and more Kamensk Finns received passports and travel money from the Moscow embassy plus visas from the militia during the course of the year. It was said that some were even on their way. The local officials in Kamensk were even

Teachers with their pupils in Kamensk in the fall of 1937. Center, Jalmari Kosonen; top right, Hellä Viuhko; top left, probably Aili Eloranta. Middle row, from left: Rakel Saari, Eeva Markkanen, Eila Wahlstén, Kosonen, Helli Hämäläinen, Elsi Juntunen, Helvi Tervonen. Behind Eila Wahlstén, Mauno Alhonen and Veikko Juntunen; in front of Kosonen, Anni Kantonen. Probably also in the picture, Dagmar Kurko and Margit Vuorio.

reported to have questioned the border-hoppers in the fall of 1937 as to who wanted to go to Finland. Apparently nearly everyone announced that they did, and thus branded themselves fatally.

There were few who left without permission now that the rumors of being able to go legally were spreading. In November the Moscow embassy notified Helsinki regarding many of the Kamensk Finns in this manner:

> *Border-hopper Juuso Vilhelm Israelinpoika Juntunen and family, return case.*
>
> *The embassy respectfully informs you that it has received notice from Kamensk that the border-hopper mentioned above and his family have been granted permission to leave the country.*

Elsi Juntunen (at left) wound up in a children's home. Picture taken in December 1939. Ida Vilkman's passport photo (bottom) in the Jekaterinburg archives. Ida was executed, and her daughter died in the Karaganda camp.

Juuso Vilhelm Israelinpoika Juntunen, his wife Anna Sofia nee Kalliola and their minor sons Veikko Vilho and Heimo Jalmari have group passport No II:663 granted by the embassy on August 7, 1937; the older child Elsi Irene passport number II:664 granted on the same day. The embassy has helped the family with a travel grant of 100 rubles.

Getting permission was one thing, but actually going was another. The Juntunens' passport was never used. Their case was assigned the number 4855/34 in the foreign ministry card file, from which it can be seen that they were the 4,855th to have requested a Finnish passport.

Vilkman, Ida Elina, widow (her husband had just died), received word that the Finnish embassy had extended her passport, issued on 15 November, for a half year. To a hasty secret letter of inquiry about her from the militia, Second Lieutenant Fomkin replied two weeks later: "We advise that with regard to Finnish border-hopper Vilkman, Ida Simontytär, we have no compromising material. There is no barrier to her traveling outside the USSR's border." In addition to these letters, Vilkman's passport and the receipt for her visa payment are still in her file.

The following excerpts are from letters dated in Kamensk at the beginning of November, 1937:

. . . if you can only wait, we will get home to our country some day. Everyone will get to go. They are leaving little by little. A hundred people are leaving tomorrow. . . . School may be cut short since they say that everyone has to be out of here by the end of the year. . . I'm a little worried because others get to go, but there's no news about my getting out, but mother's group is sure to get there this winter. . . . When I get to Finland, I will never go to another country, not ever in my life. . . . It's so exciting to wait for them to tell us this is the payoff, as they say to those who are leaving. They just jump for joy.

On the other hand, Ellen Närvänen gave a different picture of the number who had actually left. Närvänen wrote to Finland in March of 1938: "Last fall [four] women and their children left here; their men were sentenced."

In November 1937 Juho and Olga Liljeroos paid eight rubles and twenty-five kopecks to register a visa for leaving the country and received a receipt for it. In addition to the receipt, their file contains Finland passport number 676, a certificate of their dismissal from work, and two photographs, along with the notation: "He can come for his papers on 10 November 1937." Yrjö Lahtinen paid seven and a half rubles; he was to pick up his visa on 5 November.

The following entry states that the Liljeroos couple was imprisoned 2 January 1938. Lahtinen was imprisoned on the same day.

The Wahlstén girls relate that their parents too had received passports from Moscow by mail in the summer of 1937, and apparently their permit to leave was also taken care of. Their father had to go and talk to Fomkin, who wanted to know why the family wanted to go to Finland. During the autumn, their father and mother talked of leaving as soon as they had gotten together enough money for the trip.

On her last Mothers' Day, Kirsti Wahlstén sent her mother a poem. She also wrote to Finland in this vein:

Sometimes it seems very sad to think that life passes, is wasted to no avail. Ours and millions of others. . . . Sometimes the old fire flares up within me and the beauty we dreamt of is not completely lost. Humanity will have achieved happiness when we no longer exist. Perhaps our children will find what we have sought when we direct them to the proper path. The world is large and beautiful, and life could be so sweet! The bloodthirsty fascists are fanning the flames of war more hotly than before. . . . But there is the huge and mighty Soviet Union, there is the Red Army, the world's most powerful, and there are many millions of workers who will not retreat before the bloodstained hounds of fascism.

Viljo Wahlstén had learned the mason's trade, where he made better money. His thirty-four-year-old wife had had a stroke and could no longer work as a master seamstress but tried to do sewing at home. Her place at the shop was taken by a German, "who was not her equal."

They sold the sewing machine that autumn. Since they were waiting to leave, the children did not have to go to school, where they had been doing well. Irma had complete tens in conduct, diligence, carefulness, neatness, arithmetic, social studies, natural science, drawing, and physical education. A small fir tree was brought into the house for the New Year.

A small group of Christmas visitors, parents of the barracks dwellers, had come on Finnish passports, bringing with them an abundance of gifts. One of the visitors related that "things were so bad in Finland that one needed a *roopuska* (document) to find work, and there were families without bread and food."

The mood leading up to the holidays was uneasy. A number of men were arrested at night in December, among them mason Otto Paldan. His wife, Tyyne, had written to her sister in Finland that she often dreamed that they were together again. "At any rate we won't die here."

Tyyne Paldan had also written that they already felt like moving to another place since they had lived in Kamensk so long. She did not know "when they'll tell us to pack up our rags again, you get used to it, since it happens so often." Had Olga already returned to Finland from Kamensk and had Tyyne's sister gone to talk to her? "But of course you won't believe what she tells you since you haven't experienced it."

On Christmas Day, old communist Juho Hämäläinen was taken. According to the recollections of young Erkki Kuusinen and Hämäläinen's daughter, some twenty others were also taken. They did not return. Among the group was Niilo Puonti; exactly three years earlier, on Christmas Day of 1934, his family, which had returned to Kotka, had crossed the Finnish border. Before his arrest, Puonti had received a passport, but not a visa.

There were rumors in the Finnish village that the whole group would soon be sent to a new job site. The Wahlstén girls heard their mother say to their father at the dining table: "A story is going around that the Finns are being taken away." Their father would not admit that there was any reason to worry, but the children began to cry. "Will they take us to a children's home?" Weeping, their mother tried to console them, and tears came to their father's eyes as well.

Otto, Tyyne, and Else Paldan in Kamensk in 1937. None of the family survived.

A New Year's fir tree had been brought into the school, and the same kind of tree festival was arranged for the children as the preceding year. So wrote the Kantonen girl, Anni, to her relatives in Finland. In the letter she sent a last memento from Kamensk: an outline drawing of her hand.

In December some of the Finns still kept trotting to the Kamensk militia with their papers. They were promised that they could return for their visas in two weeks. When the two weeks were up, something quite different happened.

The last, or one of the last, applications was written by Meeri Salonen. She managed to send the form to Moscow, enclosing her own and her baby's picture; the end for both was near. The applicant was 161 centimeters tall, with blonde hair and gray eyes. The application was dated: Kamensk, 27 December 1937.

Chapter Seven

The Rise and Destruction of Nizhni Tagil

Many border-hoppers surreptitiously left Kamensk for Revda (west of Sverdlovsk) believing that the Finns would be left alone there. In Revda the Finns were employed in woods work. There were also dozens of them living at the Annensk "forest point," in relative freedom, at first. Kyllikki Nikula (now Suvano) recalls that in the common barracks at Katav-Ivanovski the family's only "private quarters" was a double-decker bunk in the middle of the barracks, and her job was to watch what little the family owned during the day when her parents were in the woods. The possessions had been thrust under the bed for safekeeping.

Dozens of border-hoppers appeared in Zlatoust, west of Chelyabinsk, where a steel smelter was being built. At Asbest, where the rich Alapajevski asbestos deposits were mined, the head man at one time was a Finn, Edvin Svedberg, (the great-grandfather of the well-known, present-day Finnish politician, Eva Biaudet). He was executed shortly before the border-hoppers arrived. In Bereznik, far to the north, a chemical combine was being erected, and in Nadezhdinski there was a big steel plant. In the factories, power plants, and mines around Perm, there were hundreds of Finns at work.

An even larger concentration was developing in the city of Nizhni Tagil on the banks of the Tagil River in the northern part of the Ural industrial area. The cities of Nadezhdinski (Serov) and Alapajevski also belonged to the Tagil zone, according to the border-hoppers. "Tagilstroi" employed some

40,000 workers. The population of Nizhni Tagil multiplied many times over within a short period, and it became the second largest city in the Sverdlovsk area (oblast), with 160,000 inhabitants in 1939. War industry was also built up there later.

Finns were employed in the brick-making plant and the railway car factory in Nizhni Tagil, on which construction was begun in 1931, and which needed the bricks, which were made from, among other things, straw and dung. The factory also made ceramic molds for shot. The most enthusiastic Finns went to work at the *kolkhoz* on the outskirts of the city. Tagil also had a power plant and a large iron and steel plant.

Young Finnish women in their rag footwear at work in Nizhni Tagil 1938. Left to right: Eeva Jordan, Signe Viitanen, Aino Saarela, Tyyne Sivula, and Elli Närväen. The secretly taken photo was torn up, and Sivula brought the pieces to Finland hidden in the lining of her clothing.

The brick plant and a wood-parts factory had been built earlier in record time by American Finns who had come from Nizhni Novgorod with their machines. For that feat, they had won praise and all kinds of awards. The railway-car factory was also said to be American. The work tempo of the border-hoppers, too, amazed the Russians, and their names were posted on an honor roll, but the Russian workers did not like to have the norms exceeded, for that led to the quotas being raised: "Why did you come here when our own people are dying of hunger?" they asked. The Finnish women's brigade was considered "work-crazy."

"Our life is no better here; it's worse than before," Eeva Jordan wrote to Finland from Tagil. "Alas, I don't even dare think of having to spend another winter here," Sointu Lindroos wrote later.

In the summer of 1933 a letter with this comment arrived in Finland from Zlatoust: "I've come to realize that we border-hoppers have made a little mistake. The fact is that these Russians and the GPU don't trust us at all. . . . All the border-hoppers have been moved away from areas near the border." The writer went on to say that the return of the border-hoppers might hinder the cause of revolution in capitalist countries. "If we get back, it will be propaganda of a kind that will damage the Soviet Union's prospects."

We will not be believed if we write the truth from here. I can assure you that I have seen a person die of hunger with my own eyes.

Some people had it better. Mikko Tuominen, who had skipped across the border with his sweetheart, wrote to his sister in Kangasala: I was in the Urals for more than five years, in Zlatoust most of the time, in the city of Perm for a month last winter for ski training and all we did was ski five to sixty kilometers every day. . . . It was a nice trip, now I'm 500 kilometers west of Ural doing construction work in the city of Ufa.

The family had two small, healthy children, and the father had learned Russian. According to the letter, the only concern was that for all those years they had received nothing to read in Finnish.

Somewhere along the line, Ellen Närvänen had sold her sewing machine and her other valuables, and the Närvänens moved to Nizhni Tagil, inviting the Laurilas to follow them. Life in Kamensk had not been easy for the solitary widow, who had lost three children. She had been injured in a fall from a sixth-story scaffolding at the factory, and a new family was already being sought for little Raili. But the mother recovered. She had also survived a fall from a truck platform onto a road.

Finnish children in a nursery in Kamensk or Nizhni Tagil. Raili Närvänen sits at the center with a spoon near her mouth.

Among the first Finnish residents in Tagil were Aino Saarela from Kemi and her daughter, Sirkka. Aino had married in 1930 as soon as she reached the age of seventeen. Her husband, who had been forced to take relief work in Finland, decided two years after the marriage that the family would skip to the east; his plan was to earn money for a small house by driving a bus in Leningrad for a year. He believed, in spite of warnings, that an honorable worker would always get along.

The Saarela family walked the same route over the hills as deep-sea diver Juho Vuorio, whose "apparatus operator" Artturi Saarela had been in Petsamo. Aino nursed Sirkka, who was only five months old, on the trip. The baby's father carried her in the sleeve of his warm fur coat. The Finnish border guards turned them back, but they circled through the hills and tried again. They got lost and walked for two weeks before reaching their goal.

Aino Saarela found a new companion and separated from her husband, who returned to Kamensk in 1937. There Artturi Saarela received a return permit, but the officials noted that he had not come into the country alone. "Where is your family?" Saarela went to visit his former wife, but she would not agree to leave, and soon Saarela was arrested.

Aino Saarela recalls that one day in 1934 a girl dressed in ragged clothing and completely black with dirt walked into Tagil and asked for a carpenter from Kemi named Matti Eskola. Eskola fainted from shock when he saw that his sixteen-year-old daughter Tyyne had come to the Soviet Union. In Kemi, Finland, she had been brought up on charges of being a member of the Young Communist League. A little after that she fled the country. Later the Vaasa Court cleared her of the charges.

Because the family was going hungry in Finland, Tyyne's mother sent the girl on her way in 1933, even though she did not know the father's address. In the Soviet Union, Tyyne and ten other under-age boys and girls from Kemi had been dropped off a train in the woods near Omsk, Siberia. Even the matches they had been given were in short supply. They built a sod hut and stole food; once they brought an ox to their hut, putting birch bark shoes on its feet so that it would leave no tracks in the snow. But the ox's head was found in the spring, and the boys were arrested.

"Special housing" had been set up for the workers brought to Nizhni Tagil. Here too there was a Finnish section in the city, Posjolok Finnov or Fingorodok, a village clustered around huge water tanks. There were at least forty barracks in it, for Eino Hanhela lived in Number 36 and Kalle Rosenström in Number 39. We were able to certify 203 names of Finns there, but according to Aino Saarela, there were many more, over 600. Three hundred had come by train from Nadezhdinski in the fall of 1934. According to another report the number of Finns was 430.

The 600 number seems too high, if there had actually been 700 Finns in Kamensk, so that Saarela was perhaps thinking of Kamensk. On the other hand, one must remember that people shifted from place to place and that many border-hoppers who had been sentenced to Siberia found their way to Ural. One should also take into account the fact that there were Finns in the vicinity of Nizhni Tagil.

The barracks in Tagil were quite good; the Finns themselves had built them. There were several dozen children here, and they had their own nursery. There were many young people too, and Irja and Alfa Pekala, along with Aino Saarela organized dances for them, where Reijo Nivel played the fiddle.

Nizhni Tagil was one of the places in which the "specially banished," Finns among them, were crowded into common rooms in wretched barracks.

In the summer a meeting was held, at which the chairman asked questions about the kind of life the Finns had. Machinist Eero Härmä answered: "Things are well otherwise, but the pay isn't enough to buy oils." The chairman's refutation ("one can get oils from cabbage") evoked a roar of laughter, and the meeting broke up.

In another meeting in 1936, interpreter Väino Tyykyläinen and an NKVD *politruk* were present. The people were asked to state honestly what life was like and whether things were better in Finland or the Soviet Union. Saarela gave her own version of the arrest of Palmén mentioned above:

> *Dressed in his ragged quilted coat, Thure Palmén rose from the bench, holding in his hand a photograph of his family. He said: "Look, my friends, at what it was like in Finland. I had a wife and three children. I was a carpenter. We lived in a rental apartment, but I was able to support my family. And look at me now when I'm in the Soviet state." He looked like a scarecrow. "I don't drink or smoke, but I can't even take care of myself here."*

Eino Aho and Eino Järvelä also said that the standard of living was higher in Finland. They were told to sit down. The NKVD man appropriated the picture and said that Palmén would be sentenced for anti-revolutionary activities for what he had said. Two weeks later a court session was held in the same red corner. Palmén was said to have incited others to acts of sabotage. There were shouts of denial from the room, which were silenced by the banging of the chairman's gavel. The accused was finally given the floor and expressed a hope of "getting to his beloved homeland." There was an uproar in the room when the sentence, eight years of forced labor, was announced. Heikki Lehikoinen was sentenced to prison and disappeared, and that after he had whinnied like a horse in the line for meat stew. Lehikoinen had earlier come to Tagil thin and ragged after suffering through a three-year term for having tried to escape.

Niilo Inki, a former Red Guard member who had slipped away from Aura, leaving behind a Model T Ford among other things, sent his last message to his parents at the end of 1936. The telegram read: "Your son is alive!" He had been sent money repeatedly, money which he had received. After that telegram nothing more was heard from him. Now it is known that he was arrested in the spring of 1937 near the Leningrad railway station while attempting to flee, and was executed early the next year in Ural. (Lahti-Argutina, *We Were Only Outsiders*, 2001, p. 159, Jorma Inki.)

From letters and from interrogations of those returning, VALPO eked out information about the grim lot of the Finns. One of its reports stated that people were "banished by the group from Nizhni Tagil in 1937."

Beginning in 1936 "centers of rebellion were uncovered" in Tagil. On the night before Christmas Eve 1936, the NKVD arrested L.M. Marjasin, the manager of the Ural railway-car plant. He was accused of sabotage and of planning the murder of Sergo Ordzhonikidze (the folk commissar for heavy industry). In January a party meeting was held in Tagil at which the first secretary of the area's party, central committee member I.D. Kabakov, and the city's party leader S. Okudzhava revealed the existence of "Marjasin's Trotskyite clique." Soon Okudzhava confessed to his own Trotskyite errors. A committee from the chief governing agency of the construction industry arrived in Tagil to investigate sabotage in the plant. The committee issued a surprising final statement: "Acquaintance with the Ural railway car plant led us to the positive conclusion that . . . there is no extensive sabotage on the construction site."

That did not satisfy Moscow. Molotov himself said at the RKP(b) central committee's plenary session in February 1937 that "we still suffer from lack of skill in recognizing our enemies." He accused the committee of political nearsightedness and ineptitude and condemned Okudzhava and Marjasin.

Late that winter, party leader Kabakov, Marjasin, Okudzhava, and the leader of the local mine-governing agency were executed. The dragnet was so fine that, among others, a worker—Kabakov had happened to drop in on his mother during an inspection trip five years earlier—was now arrested. The wave of arrests spread over Ural, sweeping thousands along with it. In the Sverdlovsk area, 29,724 people were arrested in 1937, while in Tagil alone over 2,000 individual deportees were imprisoned.

In December of 1937, the Nizhni Tagil NKVD got a new head, V. Kotkov, who was himself sentenced to execution in 1939. Already in 1936 men had begun to disappear at night occasionally, and on the night of 16 and 17 December, Finns in Nizhni Tagil were arrested as a group. At least fifty-two Finns were taken from the city alone that night. Sointu Lindroos wrote from Tagil in the summer of 1938 that "some [sixty] Finns were arrested here."

NKVD men marching in Nizhni Tagil. They arrested the city's Finns just before Christmas 1937.

If we include the Finns arrested that same night (and the night before and after) in the nearby area, we end up with the number 115. These are positive cases for which there is information. Probably more than that were arrested. On December 26th another quite large group was arrested—just after the NKVD's twentieth anniversary had been ostentatiously celebrated.

The first time, the night of December 16, NKVD riflemen with dogs surrounded the Finnish quarter. Lights were burning in the whole village as night-shift workers returned home. The men making the arrests went from door to door and ordered the people—men and women who did not have little children—onto the platforms of trucks. A house-search was made of the rooms. It was considered an aggravating circumstance that Lenin's picture was found on the floor in one room; the family's child had been playing with it.

A little less than a week earlier Aino Saarela had listened as eight men, including her neighbor Aatami Nuutinen, were taken at night. In the morning, Nuutinen's pregnant wife warned her that it would be wise to destroy photographs brought from Finland. Saarela burned the picture of her home, but not that of her mother, and that got her in trouble: the NKVD believed her to be lying about her working-class background because her mother had a hat, pocketbook, and fur collar in the picture. In addition, Saarela's features in her childhood picture were not "those of a typical working-class child."

Saarela recalls that one of the married couples liquidated was a Helsinki mason, Isaak Heikkilä, and his wife, Inkeri. "Inkeri once told me that she would not eat the crusts of bread in Russia, having seen how the bread was transported. The day came when they were good enough for her."

Saarela was allowed to remain "temporarily" because of her children, but her husband, Eino Hirvonen, a house painter from Mikkeli, was taken. His last words were a vow to escape from the prison camp and to meet his wife in Finland some day. He had only a month and a half left to live; he did not make it to the prison camp.

The people arrested were moved to a nearby village which had been fenced in as a prison. The seven mothers with their children and the two young boys left after the arrests were allowed to visit the prisoners a few times. Then the latter disappeared.

The oldest of the women arrested were released soon, and they returned to the Finnish village. Saarela reported that in January 1938 the "grannies" were fetched again, and that they did not return.

In 1938 the women left in the village made a group inquiry about their husbands. According to the reply they received, the men had been sentenced to twenty-five years without the right to appeal. Later there were rumors that many of them had been shot at Chelyabinsk.

During these years, the Ural areas largest concentration of prison camps was developed in Nizhni Tagil. Hundreds of camps had already been built in the Urals, from Vorkuta to Orsk, and in the summer of 1937 the NKVD began construction on the Ivdel camp in the Tagil area. The basic tasks of its inmates were to be woods work and railway construction. By early February 1939 the number of prisoners there was already nearly 21,000.

In February 1938 the NKVD established the huge Sevurallag camp organization in the area around Nizhni Tagil. It covered twelve administrative districts and comprised an area of 110,000 square kilometers. The work force was about 50,000 prisoners. In 1939 there were nearly 200,000 people in the labor camps and the prison transfer centers of the Sverdlovsk area, eight percent of the area's entire population. In Nizhni Tagil itself, the wartime camp, Tagillag, was established, where there were initially 65,000 prisoners. The Tagil prison camp is still in operation today.

To judge by the KGB archives, the slaughter was not quite as total in Nizhni Tagil and Revda as in Kamensk. Perhaps the difference was local or perhaps it resulted from differences in the time of arrests. At any rate, some men here received "only" long prison sentences, which was not the case in Kamensk, and a number of Tagil Finns were evidently released in 1938 and 1939. Nearly ninety of those arrested died or were executed. It may take years to arrive at an accurate figure.

Researcher Viktor Kirilov writes that in 1935-1936, those arrested in Tagil were merely scolded or punished lightly: they were dismissed from the party, subjected to surveillance, or sent to reformatory labor camps. Rarely were any executed. But, according to Kirilov, in 1937 nearly half of the victims were shot. The wave of arrests rose sharply that year and crested in January 1938.

One apparent cause of the differing results was that the prosecutors in Revda and Tagil did not always write spying down as the charge but sometimes called it illegal border-crossing. An example is, Arvo Lampi, born in Valkeala in 1900, about whose case the Russian security ministry released information to his family in 1993.

Lampi had belonged to the Red Guard and taken part in the 1922 meat rebellion in Finland. He had been arrested three times in Finland, had skipped to the Soviet Union, married a Russian woman, and requested

Soviet citizenship. Before his arrest 16 December 1937 Lampi worked as a sawmill setter in the Revda logging area and the Pervouralski region. The night of the arrest was the same as in Nizhni Tagil, and four Finnish men in all were taken from the village. His wife, Natalia, went to ask about Lampi, but she was told nothing and her packages were refused.

The charge was set down as illegal border-crossing, although Lampi had been arrested as a Finnish spy who had collected information about "war-production plants and people's opinions." An NKVD trio is seen first (October 1938) to have condemned him to a reformatory labor camp for spying, to which he confessed his guilt. In January 1939 Lampi retracted his confession and declared that he had signed a false statement in the proceedings because of the interrogator's lies and recommendations.

The charge of spying was thrown out, and in January of 1940 Lampi was sentenced to three years for crossing the border illegally. This sentence was not carried out because Lampi wound up in the hospital "on account of a swelling on his upper lip." He died on 19 February in the Nizhni Turinski prison hospital of meningitis and blood poisoning.

> The case of Arvo Lampi was closed because of the death of the accused. Now the case has again been investigated, and closed for lack of a crime description. We extend our sincerest sympathy for your father's tragic death.

Until 1993, Arvo Lampi's daughter knew nothing about her father, not even his right name. It was known only that he was a Finn, and she had heard from other prisoners that he had died in prison.

The charges against Jaakko Olkkonen, a teacher, were changed in the same way; he too had been sentenced in January 1940, and he too died in the hospital right after Lampi.

Jaakko Olkkonen had been born in Oulainen in 1908, had been active in the workers' movement, and had skipped across the border 9 July 1930. To be more specific, he was driven to the border by members of the Lapua movement via Sotkamo, the most northern route in the district. According to his escorts, he had "mocked the symbols of White Finland." The sheriff and judge considered the matter of little consequence and did not summon a special session of the court to deal with it. In November the district court gave five of the men involved brief probations and rejected Olkkonen's claim for compensation. This is the story Olkkonen told on being interrogated as soon as he crossed the Russian border:

When they took me to the border, one of the fascists whose name I don't know, said the following words to me: "There is the border between Finland and the Soviet Union, but it is not a natural border, for it divides the Finnish nation in two. On that side of the border live the Karelians, who are also Finns, and are under the bolshevik yoke. Karelia is going to be ours, but you are helping the bolsheviks, you are betraying your native country, you are a traitor to your state. There is no longer any room for you in Finland. We will destroy all the communists, and if you come back in less than two years, we will shoot you. Now you can go and eat sour cabbage and Russian bread, and when you start to go hungry, remember Finland." That was the end of the discussion. After that he just pointed to the trail and told me to go.

Olkkonen worked as a teacher in Karelia, studied in the Petroskoi Teachers College, and was granted Soviet citizenship. He stopped writing to members of his family in 1935 out of fear, he said, that they would be persecuted. In 1937 he was dismissed from the college, after which he worked in the woods at Komi and Nizhni Tagil. He was arrested in 1938 and accused

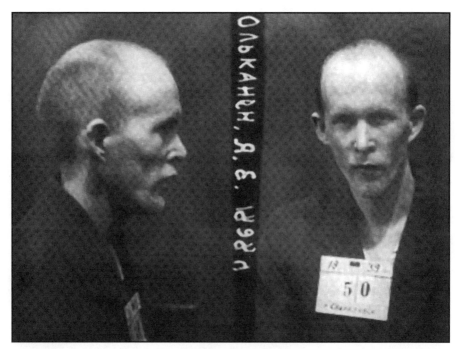

Men in the Lapua movement drove Jaakko Olkkonen across the border in 1930. The NKVD arrested and photographed him in 1938.

of spying, but during the interrogations the charge was changed to illegal border-crossing. Olkkonen was given three years in a reformatory labor camp and died of tuberculosis in Sverdlovsk on 24 March 1940 at the age of thirty-two.

Veikko Miettinen, a young man from Leppävirta, was a carpenter who worked on the housing for the brick plant. The NKVD arrested him for the first time in September 1934 on the charge of leaving his residence area. The consequences were not serious: in November the people's court decided to free him and assign him to a group of border-hoppers that was under the supervision of the NKVD.

But when Miettinen was again arrested on 16 December 1938, the result was entirely different. He was sentenced to death for spying, sabotage, and anti-revolutionary activities.

The American Finnish workers' turn was coming, but not until the summer of 1938, and their fate was different from that of the Finland Finns. From the records, one can see that before Midsummer, they were arrested and charged with spying and sabotage, among others, Matti Kuusisto, Viljo Käkelä, Edvard Laakso, and Felix Lankila, who had lived in Canada. All of their cases were finally dropped "because of unclear specification of the crimes" and the accused were freed, but Käkelä is seen to have died in the work army in April 1943.

Chapter Eight

Escapees and Embassy Prisoners

SOME OF THE BORDER-HOPPERS SUCCEEDED in fleeing the thousands of kilometers from Ural to the Finnish border, where they attracted considerable attention. There were even some who made it from Siberia.

In the opinion of the Terijoki sub-district of the EK, "it seems incredible that one can get back from Siberia—is that a way of sending in agents?" According to that police unit, there "was quite suspicious material" among those returning. VALPO declared in their 1938 summary document that the Soviet Union was sending spies to Finland, who were recruited while arrangements for their passports were being made. "They seem to be trying to recruit as spies practically every Finn with whom they have any dealings." VALPO appears to have calculated that about twenty percent of those who had skipped back were of the type sent by the SKP for party work or by the GPU for spying.

On the eastern border there were six quarantine stations for the returning border-hoppers. "Damned filthy," an EK representative reported to Helsinki of the twenty escapees who had just been locked in at the Petsamo and Salla stations. "You need a gas mask."

"I'm so happy here that I can't say it in words," a woman who had returned to Finland wrote to her friend in the spring of 1940, according to VALPO. She had received more than enough food during the interrogations at Kotka, and "everyone was so polite and friendly there."

According to the letter there was a card ration system in Finland too, but people got their quotas regularly. "I tell you straight, it's much better here than there. Everyone here has such fine and up-to-date clothes, you can't believe how ashamed I was when I walked home from the station, everyone stared at me. Yesterday I went to buy myself a black woolen dress for 550 markkas."

EK took pictures for publication of those returning and directed suitably repentant border-hoppers to newspaper editorial offices. The result was a series of articles along this line: "We Finns were in a worse state than domestic animals . . . I prefer ten years in a Finnish prison to one day free in Russia. . . . A warning from a worker who has experienced the horrors across the border. Hunger, thirst, illness, brutal treatment, and steam closets . . ." In 1937, EK had collected "border-hoppers' stories for a certain writer to use in a patriotic drama."

The Finnish chargé d'affaires protested in October 1937 against the Finnish newspapers' habit of printing pictures of thin and dirty border-hoppers in ragged clothing.

> In my opinion this type of "hyena journalism" tends to slow down the already slow pace of handling the border-hoppers' cases in Soviet offices and leads to a tighter watch being kept on the border.

Three friends, Urho Karttunen, Veikko Nieminen, and Allan Vuorio, who were only eighteen years old, judged that things were only getting worse in Kamensk, and decided to flee to Finland while they were still able. There was no point in even thinking of fleeing during the winter. They picked 18 June 1936 as the day to leave, as soon as they had gotten their pay. The boys did not breathe a word of their plans to anyone, either to their parents or to their Russian girlfriends. Accompanied by these girls, the boys cleared the first barrier: past the guards to the Kamensk station.

The boys got money for the trip by breaking into the linen storehouse in the barracks village and selling their haul to the Tatars. They now had 300 rubles. They had no compass or map. They had earlier practiced swimming across the river with their clothes in a bundle on their heads.

The boys answered all questions by saying they were on their way to study in the forestry teknikum in Petroskoi. Allan, who knew Russian best, did the talking. Students were respected, and in the station at Perm, the militia helped them get to the head of the line to buy their tickets.

The trip to Leningrad lasted weeks, for the boys walked through the woods past those stations where they knew their papers would be checked.

Veikko Nieminen—here ill at Chelyabinsk—was successful in fleeing from Kamensk to Finland in 1936. Many border-hoppers who had been interrogated and tortured later mentioned him as being recruited by spies.

Soon they were barefoot, the last shreds of their footwear having fallen by the wayside.

They started on foot from Leningrad toward the Finnish border on July 18, guided by the sun during the day and by the stars at night. A large part of the trip was made creeping on all fours; once they crept and crawled for an entire night when they ran into a Red Army training area where the troops were using live ammunition. Once a man guarding a grainfield fired at them, and they crawled away through the grain. The boys swam and waded through rivers and brooks, and climbed over or crawled through barbed wire fences. In the end, their clothes were hanging from them in shreds; they had no underwear. Often soldiers and border guards walked right by them.

In a hut near the border, the boys bound and gagged an old woman who had seen them stealing. They tried to give the impression that they were Russian criminals heading toward Leningrad, and soon they saw the guards rushing away from the border. During the last phases of their journey, the boys were mentally and physically exhausted and had considered giving themselves up. "They'll at least give us bread and water before shooting us or sending us to Siberia."

With the last obstacle behind them, the boys heard the voices of hay-makers speaking Finnish who were talking about smoking Club cigarettes. They knew they had reached the border. Somehow they made it through the barbed-wire barrier and crossed a river by wading underneath an old wood-en bridge, badly frightening some Finnish women who were swimming naked in the river. The Finnish border guard had been watching their arrival through field glasses and at first suspected that they had been sent by the Russians, for they had crossed the border at a point where "no one could pos-sibly get through"—right under the noses of the border guard at a place where there were known to be dogs trained for war.

The boys enjoyed coffee and coffee bread at the border post. It was Saturday July 25th, and the radio was broadcasting a song request program. When the new hit song "Little White Sister," began to play, the boys could not hold back their tears.

Allan's interrogation by the EK at Terijoki lasted a week. The police showed the most interest in the names and personal data of Finns still in the Soviet Union. The log book begins thus:

> At the Somerikko post on the Isthmus, on [July 25, 1936], the guard detained laborers Allan Johannes Juhonp. Vuorio, Urho Kullervo Eliaksenp. Karttunen, and Veikko Lauri Otonp. Nieminen, who had on that day come secretly from Soviet Russia at Haapala village.

According to the log, Allan Vuorio's chances of getting by "depended on his brother who lived in Finland and on his chances of getting work here." The pictures Allan had brought along were taken from him, and he was set free. On his train trip to Helsinki, no one who saw him could help staring; he was still wearing the same rags and his feet were bare, bruised, and swollen. "EK probably sent me off this way as an advertisement." In Helsinki, Allan found an information office, and begged on the street until he collected the fifty pennies needed to learn his brother's address.

Allan wrote a letter to his father, Juho Vuorio, in Kamensk, telling him that he had succeeded in getting to Finland. In spite of the censorship, his father received the letter and was even able to write once to his son. In it he asked for a package. The boy sent him mittens and 200 markkas. After that, he heard no more from Kamensk.

In the fall of 1936 three men, Kalle Aalto, Aleksi Kortelainen, and Eino Metsämäki, plus two others left Kamensk on a long journey of escape. They headed first for Tashkent, from where Aalto and Metsämäki started out on their effort to reach Finland. They traveled to White Russia via Moscow, but did not dare attempt to get into the Finnish embassy. The Polish border seemed impenetrable, so they turned north and wound up in Kantalahti. On the way they found out that Kortelainen had made it as far as Leningrad.

In June of 1937 the men appeared on the border at Salla in miserable condition. There had been some kind of encounter on the Russian side: they had been spotted and an attempt made to stop them, but they had "forced" their way though.

Eino Metsämäki swore that he had revealed no military information (he had been a corporal) nor had he been a GPU agent. He took part in the Winter War, at which time Finnish officials investigated him as potentially unreliable, and in the Continuation War as well. He became a buck sergeant and was decorated for leading a patrol behind enemy lines. (T. Metsämäki, EK/Kemi interrogation records 47/1937)

When Aalto, Kortelainen, and Metsämäki had already reached their destination, mason Tahvo Kakkinen and his son, Viljo, left Kamensk in an attempt to get to Finland. The mother, Anna, had come to Kamensk on a Finnish passport and soon returned home. Neighbors recall how shocked and exhausted she was on her return: her baggage had been stolen on the trip, and the first thing she asked for was food. Horrified she told of seeing sellers in Russia scoop out clabbered milk with their hands into a buyer's dish.

The men of the Kakkinen family left Kamensk without permission with a group of men going to work on the power plant for a liquor distillery. From there they decamped to work at a copper combine near Sverdlovsk. Their passports were not checked, for good workers were needed, and they earned well. Drinking away their earnings in a restaurant, the two men came up with the idea of leaving for Finland.

Väinö Nieminen and Jaakko Åberg, and Viljo Kakkinen's Polish girlfriend, went with them. Åberg, a pipe-fitter from Pietarsaari, took his pincers along to deal with barbed wire. They traveled together the entire time. They made it all the way to Leningrad by train, but on Nevsky Prospect the girl fell into the hands of militia who were checking papers. The others ran away.

Creeping through woods and swamps and swimming across rivers, they reached the border in three days. Their food supplies were a bottle of vodka and a piece of sausage. Near Valkeasaari, the Helsinki man, Niemelä, left to make a short reconnaissance. Soon the others heard a shot. No one saw Niemelä after that.

All the rest of the troop of refugees succeeded in crossing the border into Finland on 17 July. The father, Tahvo, had a different notion about the route to take, and finished the last part of the journey by himself. A guard dog at the border had sniffed at him as he lay in a ditch but had not barked. On his part, Viljo had lain under a pile of brush the last night and seen a mounted man who stayed near him for a half hour.

The pincers broke as they were cutting the last wires on the border fence, and the rubber soles of their shoes fell off as Viljo and Jaakko ran across the last field. They realized that they were on the Finnish side only when they saw a bicycle rack in the yard of the border guard barracks on which these words were printed: "Lean on Nokia; it's a firm support." Reportedly no one else had come through at this point in three years.

After being interrogated, Viljo wound up in the Viipuri jail to answer a summons issued earlier. He was asked to give his word of honor that he would not try to escape again. Then came service in the army, and soon after that, the war, where he once more met Åberg, his comrade on the flight. The latter died at the front.

Many other attempts to escape from Russia did not end as well as the Kakkinens'. Two of the first to try fleeing from Kamensk were Alfons Höglund and Teodor Kunnas. Both were bachelors from the Jyväskylä area. Höglund had worked as a saw filer in Chelyabinsk, and Kunnas as a stone-cutter, but they did not go to work in Kamensk. Arriving there 27 September 1935 they fled three days later. They got to Petroskoi by train, and from there they went by foot along the road toward Säämäjärvi. On 8 October 1935 they were captured.

Höglund and Kunnas had joined a group of border-hoppers from Kotka who had purchased a boat for 4,750 markkas in November 1931. During his interrogation by the Russians, Höglund said he had been "content with the work at first, but dissatisfied with living conditions" in the Soviet Union. He had even suffered hunger. Later on, even the living conditions had been satisfactory. Kunnas, on the other hand, complained that the wages were low and said there was no chance of living well in Ural.

The men were sentenced to three years' banishment beginning 8 October and were sent to Siberia.

In the summer of 1935, Kalle, the father of the Murto family, and one of the boys, Väinö, had tried to get out of Ural and back to Finland. At the time of the flight, the father was sixty-five years old. The men lived for weeks by stealing and traveled long distances hidden on vehicles. They managed to reach Leningrad by way of Moscow.

Both of them were captured in the border zone on the Isthmus while they were hiking toward Finland. The punishments were not yet too severe: the Murtos were freed and allowed to return to Ural. Kalle Murto moved with his family to Kamensk, but Väinö refused to give up. He fled again in the company of two other Finns. In August 1936 he appeared on the Finnish side of the border and was immediately given two months in jail. Väinö Murto served in the U. S. Navy during the war and moved back to Finland again when it was over.

One of a kind among the men who fled was Tauno Flinkman from Kotka, the Murto children's uncle. He had gone on the same boat with them in the summer of 1932, having been caught on a previous attempt to sneak across the border at Suojärvi in the summer of 1932.

Flinkman had made four previous attempts to escape from the Soviet Union, at times getting close to the border, but he was always caught and sentenced to a new punishment. He must have sat in dozens of jails and had often gone on strike, once even on a hunger strike. He even made the acquaintance of a new generation of border-hoppers, when Finnish men who had crossed the border without permission after 1945 were brought to the same camp at Mordva where he was held.

Flinkman's fate was revealed to the world when released Norwegian prisoners of war revealed it in Berlin in 1953. He arrived home in the company of a number of prisoners of war in 1954 after a round trip lasting a total of twenty-two years.

Veli Hyrsky underwent a truly extraordinary escape adventure. First he fled with two other Finns in 1933, but was returned to work in Magnitogorsk. He made a second attempt in 1935, when the punishment for flight was still not particularly severe. He left Chelyabinsk with his twenty-year-old wife, who was pregnant, and with Arthur Nyman in April. They headed for Afghanistan. The direct route to Finland seemed too difficult.

The fugitives went south by train to Tashkent and crossed the border on foot. They were held in the Bashkira police station for nearly a week. Although they explained that they were Finns, the police took them for Russians, seemingly not knowing there was such a country as Finland. The travelers, for their part, thought they were in Persia. At length the Hyrskys and Nyman were turned over to the Soviet Union.

In Chelyabinsk his wife was soon freed, but Hyrsky said that he was left in a basement cell of a GPU jail into which a half-meter of water flowed when it rained. Fomkin interrogated him, accusing him of sabotage, in addition to fleeing: as a locomotive engineer he was supposed to have caused a train crash, an assignment given him by the Finnish secret police. Hyrsky had, in fact, been involved in a train wreck, but according to him, the fault lay with the train dispatcher. Hyrsky was finally given six months of forced labor by the people's court, Nyman three months, and Anna Hyrsky a month's probation. The time they had spent under arrest was counted toward their sentence.

Nyman later ran away from Nizhni Tagil to Revda. Hyrsky promised to apply for citizenship and was freed from surveillance. In June 1937 the Hyrskys returned to Finland legally with their small child, having lived in Kamensk among other places. Rarely was a whole family allowed to return home from Ural.

Veli Hyrsky joined the Finnish and Soviet Peace and Friendship Society (SNS) in 1940. He sometimes visited the Soviet embassy and acted as a part-time interpreter there. For that reason he was kept under observation, and military counter-intelligence headquarters barred him from work in war industry. Hyrsky undertook to organize a "battle group" from among the remaining SNS members, and promoted such a radical line, which included taking up arms, that even the communists suspected him of being an agent provocateur. VALPO received tips about him and suspected him of spying and sabotage.

In January 1941 two of Hyrsky's representatives appeared in the Soviet embassy to ask for money to buy weapons. They also requested to be put in contact with the Comintern and with Toivo Antikainen, a well-known Finnish revolutionary. When the requests were rejected, Hyrsky himself arrived at the embassy. In a letter which was forwarded to Moscow, he declared that he represented "Finland's secret communist party" and declared that the old party "had disbanded or become incapable of action." While the letter was being considered in other agencies, the NKVD ascertained what sort of man the sender was. It became clear that Hyrsky had tried to escape from the Soviet Union, and furthermore that he had gotten permission to go to Finland in 1936. The NKVD was forced to come up with the explanation that only later, in 1938, had they come to know that he was a provocateur sent by the Finnish secret police.

In 1941, Hyrsky was sentenced to jail in Finland. During the Continuation War, he wrote repentant letters to VALPO, which viewed his change of heart with skepticism. Hyrsky offered to work with them and said he was now ready to give his life for his country. He hoped that VALPO would support his plea for mercy.

I've come to realize how happy I was here in Finland with my wife and child. In the Soviet Union I did not even have clothing to wear, and although I worked every day, my family often had to go to bed with empty stomachs. On my return to Finland I was able to build a beautiful home in six months . . .

Veli Hyrsky was arrested in Ural, made it to Finland and was arrested again.

Nor was Helsinki musician Pauli Valkama a particularly delightful returnee. He was classified in VALPO records as a communist, and he reappeared in Finland in 1935. Valkama had run away from Siberia, was caught, banished east again, and escaped from Tara by ship to Omsk and by train to Moscow, where he and his comrades sought help at the embassy. Train tickets to Kantalahti were purchased for the group, and they were given a compass, a map of the Murmansk area, and rubles to spend. Another man, one Veikko Huotari, who returned later, must surely have aroused interest. According to SUPO, a GPU operative had recruited him in 1932 to observe railway traffic in the Oulu area. Huotari had skipped across the border while the court was considering his case.

Hilda Lappalainen, whose husband had been executed, also escaped in an unusual way. She rode to Ural from a stone quarry near the Chinese border lying down on the roof of a train. The journey took seventeen days, and

Lappalainen reportedly did not once leave her hiding place for any reason whatsoever. Many such riders were said to have fallen off along the way.

Väinö Alatalo, who had fled from Kamensk, was arrested on a train in Karelia 25 August 1937. He had no identification papers. He had crossed the border in the north in 1932 and had wound up in Ural and Kamensk, where he had worked as a driver.

During the interrogation Alatalo admitted knowing that men without papers were not allowed to leave Kamensk without permission, and asked that he be sent back there. A wire was sent from Petroskoi to Kamensk, and the NKVD district chief for that area, Lieutenant Bykov, and deputy chief Fomkin sent Alatalo's personal data and fingerprints to Petroskoi.

In November 1937 Alatalo was sentenced to confinement for two years (without being deprived of his rights). He appealed the sentence and the supreme court overthrew the verdict. However, Alatalo remained in jail in the winter of 1938, for the case had not been concluded. He had only a half year left to live.

Only those border-hoppers who had requested and received a Soviet passport were allowed to travel within the country. Others were forbidden under penalty of punishment to leave the area to which they had been assigned. The punishment was a few years in prison and about five years banishment. Some hundreds of fugitives tried over the years to get into the Finnish embassy in Moscow and into the chief consulate in Leningrad. If the militia succeeded in stopping them at the gate, the result was banishment to Siberia. It could happen otherwise, however. One day in 1937 the militia stopped six Finnish men at the embassy gate. They were held for a year and a half at the NKVD and in jail and then in 1939 they were suddenly rushed to the border and turned over to Finland.

Those who managed to get into the embassy or consulate often had to wait for a long time in the shelter of the Finnish establishment. With the permission of the foreign office, they, along with American Finns waiting for passports, were employed on the new embassy building in Moscow, under construction in 1936 to 1938. In 1938 the Soviet Union demanded the eviction and surrender of five border-hoppers living "illegally" in the embassy. Finland did not give in, but the border-hoppers who dared go into the city disappeared without a trace. Toward the end, whenever an automobile left the embassy it was trailed by another, and those who left on foot were followed by a foot patrol. Arvo Katajisto, the building superintendent, relates:

Every morning a few of the workers failed to appear. One morning, when a funereal atmosphere prevailed at the building site, a man named Laine spoke out: "Comrade Stalin's party is always right. Stalin knows what he is doing, saboteurs must be annihilated." The next morning Laine did not show up for work, and apparently never did return.

Among those waiting in the embassy was Aili Nikula, who had worked in the Kamensk sewing shop under Kirsti Wahlstén. It took three months for her to get a passport and visa. Eemeli Nikula had been run over by, or been pushed under, a train in Ural. It had taken the widow and her daughter a long time to get permission to travel to Moscow. In the embassy, Aili became acquainted with border-hopper Toivo Kivistö, who had fled many times and reportedly had even crossed the Siberian border into China. Kivistö had left Kazan at the last moment and was saved from imprisonment there in 1937. His name was on the list when the NKVD arrested the "agents who had spied for the Finnish embassy."

The reception of the widowed woman in Finland was so harsh that she suffered a nervous breakdown after she returned to her home neighborhood. Kivistö married her when he got back to Finland, and both joined the Finnish communist party.

Edit Ahonen, the Siberian Finn who was Ambassador Yrjö-Koskinen's chambermaid, recalls that some of the border-hoppers lived on the embassy grounds for years. According to her, Yrjö-Koskinen sometimes lied outright to the Soviet officials, telling them that he knew nothing of men he was questioned about. If the border-hoppers tired of waiting, embassy employees might "smuggle" them past the militia in their automobiles to a point farther off and let them out there.

The embassy officials would give the fugitives 500 rubles for travel money, a compass, and advise them. They might provide a paper stamped with the lion seal which they hoped would have some effect on officials; often they could give no other help. One border-hopper reported being told confidentially by an official at the embassy in October 1934: "The only accessible road (to Finland) is the road you took to get here."

The fate of Akseli Perho, who sought shelter at the embassy in August 1939 was an exceptional one. He had skipped to the Soviet Union in 1932, where he was discovered to have been a member of the White Civil Guard. He wound up spending a long time in the Kresty jail.

Aladar Paasonen, a military attaché at the embassy, gave Perho travel money, a compass, and a knife, and the latter attempted to go secretly to

Finland. A GPU agent was said to have led him into a snare—the result was five years of forced labor in Solovetski and on Stalin's canal. Perho started off for Finland again, was caught, and wound up in Vorkuta. He tried to escape from there too. Freed in 1939, Perho "lived by robbery and caused a train to derail." Now he asked the embassy for help and got to live in the potato cellar there. At first Perho was suspected of being a provocateur because of the stories he told, but finally it was decided that he was an honest Finnish man.

Not only was the embassy unable to shelter the people seeking help—in the end it could not even protect its own employees. Many Finns and American Finns employed as maids, cooks, caretakers, construction workers, and chauffeurs in the Finnish, American, German, and British embassies who were awaiting passage home experienced that fact at the end of the 1930s and the beginning of the 1940s. They disappeared and were sent to prison camps for long terms.

For example, Stalin's scythe mowed down the father and husband, plus the brothers and sisters along with their families of the aforementioned Edit Ahonen. Allan Karenius, a friend of the Ahonens who had come from the Kazan commune, worked on the Finnish embassy and then got a job at the German embassy as a chauffeur. In 1941 he was accused of being a spy for the Germans. He was sentenced to twenty-five years and died in the Karaganda camp. Ahonen conjectured that he knew where the microphones were hidden in the walls of the Finnish embassy and thus had to be liquidated. His mother received a ten-year prison sentence.

Karenius's father, Oskari, had been the director of the "Sement Commune," which had built the automobile plant at Nizhni Novgorod and the airplane plant at Kazan. When the Kazan NKVD hauled in its net in 1937 he was one of the "Finnish embassy's agents," who could not be arrested because he was working on the embassy in Moscow. Now he disappeared into thin air in spite of his already having a visa to leave for Finland. The same thing happened to Henrik Kanerva, whom they were too late to catch in Kazan.

According to Ahonen a group of young border-hoppers who had been working on the embassy along with some American Finns succeeded in fleeing to Finland sometime around 1937. They had asked his brother to go with them too. He later perished in the Soviet Union.

A member of the same circle of friends, an American Finn, Suoma Lahti, (nee Laine) had come for a second time to the Soviet Union with her parents. Suoma worked in the Finnish embassy and her young husband was the caretaker at the U.S. emissary's residence; him the Russians reportedly tried in vain to recruit as an informer. Suoma and her husband had automatically been given Soviet passports when they turned sixteen, but nevertheless they had not given up their American citizenship. Both fathers were taken and disappeared without a trace. Then Suoma's husband was arrested and two weeks later, her mother, Anna Laine.

In the camp in Siberia Anna Laine became acquainted with Hilma Kilkkinen, a teacher who had been seized in Petsamo at the start of the Winter War. The foreign ministry had inquired after her in vain—the answer was always that there was no information about any such person in the Soviet Union. On the basis of Anna Laine's information, Kilkkinen was finally freed. She had already been lodged in a barrack for the terminally ill. Arvo Katajisto says that when in Moscow the teacher looked into a mirror for the first time in eight years, she fell to her knees from the shock. Tauno Flinkman became acquainted with Kilkkinen in the Krasnopolj repatriation camp. An ambulance was waiting for her when they arrived in Finland in 1954.

Suoma was arrested in December 1941 at the office where she had gone to get her bread coupons. She was told that her whole family were spies. On Christmas Eve her mother-in-law was brought to the same prison in Moscow; she had come to the city to look for her lost daughter-in-law. Suoma was sentenced to ten years in the Karaganda camp. An effort was made to take her son to an orphans' home, and only the perseverance of a Finnish-American embassy official brought the child safely to Helsinki after a five-year battle.

Many embassy officials, the U.S. ambassador for example, responded more coldly to their own emigres and border-hoppers. The embassy turned down Americans asking for help—sending many to almost certain death—merely because they lacked a recent passport photo or a couple of dollars for a new passport. (AP 9.11.97)

When the Winter War broke out in 1939, Yrjö-Koskinen searched hastily for safe places in other embassies for those workers who did not have diplomatic immunity. Not all of them were saved. When the Continuation War began in June of 1941, the diplomats and employees of the Finnish embassy along with their families were loaded on trains guarded by soldiers. Their journey by the southern route to Turkey lasted, with all the waits along the way, for three months.

Toivo Laine, who had left Kamensk, served a ten-year sentence in Komi, as has already been said, the Kazan NKVD having listed him as a Finnish agent in the same note along with Kanerva, Karenius, and Kivistö. In the prison camp Laine met unfortunate Finns whom the militia had captured in

Moscow in 1936 when they had had to leave the Finnish embassy. After the war, Laine traveled secretly and without permission from Kazakhstan to Moscow and succeeded in turn in taking shelter in the embassy.

Laine, Erkki Jalo, and another young man, all of them border-hoppers, hid in the embassy for twelve days with the help of the building superintendent—he had no permission to do this. Perhaps it was their good fortune that the envoy, Cay Sundström, was on sick leave. Laine received a Finnish passport. He was not, however, able to get permission to live in Moscow, and went back to Kazakhstan to wait for a visa. He got it on the second application in 1948, and was able to return to Finland.

Even at the beginning of the 1950s, when Taisto Huuskonen, who had skipped across the border and been released from a labor camp, tried to get into the Finnish embassy with his wife, the two were seized and put quickly into a militia automobile. The couple was banished to Ural.

Chapter Nine

Operation Finns

LENINGRAD PARTY LEADER SERGEI KIROV WAS MURDERED 1 December 1934. In a report written immediately after the event, the Finnish envoy expressed doubts that "any White-Guard terrorist organization" was in back of the murder, as had been claimed. In January he reported that a Sinovjev-Kamenev opposition group had been accused of the killing.

Kirov's murder signaled the start of a great wave of terror. Large numbers were arrested, and new directives issued for the investigation of political crimes. Investigations were speeded up, court cases could be carried out without a prosecutor or a lawyer, even "without the accused parties taking part, and death sentences were to be executed immediately." The opportunities for appeal and petitions for mercy were limited. A little later the death penalty was extended to children as well. During the height of the craze, children were also imprisoned as spies.

In the summer of 1934 a section was added to the criminal law having to do with punishment for those without passports. (The use of passports within the country had gone into effect in 1930). The section limited, for example, the border-hoppers' freedom of movement outside the place to which they had been assigned. Without a pass, they were instant criminals if they were caught attempting to flee.

As early as the spring of 1933 the Finnish consul in Leningrad was aware that "Gylling, that Greater Finland advocate" and his program were running

Unknown border-hoppers in Kamensk, of whom at least the two marked with crosses may have been executed.

into problems and that Moscow was regarding him with suspicion. "International anti-communist seditious organizations" were mentioned for the first time that year in connection with Karelia. In 1934, "local nationalism" was declared to be the chief danger in Soviet Karelia, and for the first time the people who had come from North America were bitterly criticized.

Beginning with the summer of 1935, disturbing symptoms, especially with regard to foreigners, were in the air. The Finnish embassy then first reported on the arrests of Germans and on the tighter surveillance of the embassies. They did not yet notice any particular signs of anti-Finnish sentiment. The opening notes of it were heard in the fall, when anti-Finnish propaganda prevailed in the plenary session of the Karelia district committee. According to the resolution passed at that session: "The district committee leadership under Rovio has come to be controlled by nationalistic elements leaning toward bourgeois Finland's attitudes." The new party chairman, P.A. Irklis, criticized bringing in labor from America and regarding the arrivals as some kind of "higher class and quality of workers."

In March 1935 the Leningrad and Karelia NKVD authorities had received from Genrich Jagoda top secret Order No. 55709 for an operation whose chief objective was "to purge the Leningrad area and Karelia of kulaks and anti-Soviet elements." A twenty-two-kilometer-wide border zone was to be cleansed immediately and all "extraneous class elements" deported from Petroskoi. In the second phase a 100-kilometer-wide zone was to be cleared, which meant the deportation of the Ingrian Finnish population to Ural, Siberia, and elsewhere.

In the fall of 1935 it was the turn of the Finnish Red officers. The Leningrad military district fobbed up a court case about a "secret league organized by Finnish military headquarters for intelligence purposes." The purge swept through the military units and schools, and the Karelia brigade was disbanded.

Viacheslav Molotov was brusque when questioned later and did not ever "remember" that he and Stalin had approved the formation of the SKP (Finnish Communist Party) support groups. The support groups became the hook with which to catch and hang the Finns. Gylling and Rovio were dismissed in 1935 as nationalists and arrested in 1937. The press labeled Gylling a fascist spy, an enemy of the people, and a traitor to the country. It didn't help that Gylling signed a self-critical article according to which "continually, and especially after 1930, Finnish secret service agents . . . [and] even armed gangs were sent across the border. . . . This fascist Finnish maneuver we did not succeed in uncovering immediately." A certain Finnish-American wrote in the newspaper *Vapaus* that even though in the spring of 1933 "more than two thousand agents of White Finland were arrested in Soviet Karelia," the local government did not learn a lesson from it. Gylling and Rovio were accused of spying and conspiracy and were executed in Moscow in 1938.

The first multiple arrests of Finns involved those who were politically active and those in positions of leadership. Thereafter, Finns were no longer desired as citizens; according to VALPO, after the fall of 1937, no Karelian Finn was granted Soviet citizenship, and border-hoppers' residence permits were renewed for only two months at a time.

Seventeen hundred nineteen persons were arrested in Karelia between 1932 and 1936, of whom seventy-five percent were border-hoppers. Families requesting return to Finland were transported by boat across Lake Ääninen. The area within which they were permitted to move was marked on their passports.

Foreign Minister Rudolf Holsti had already received letters containing heartbreaking pleas for help from the relatives of Finns who were in the Soviet Union. He took up the border-hoppers' issue in his visit to Moscow in 1937, a visit which roused ill will in Finland and led in part to his dismissal. Later he described the negotiations he had conducted with Maxim Litvinov. He, Holsti, had raised the issue of:

> the fate of those thousands of Finns who during the depression had gone to the Soviet Union to find work. I mentioned at the outset that these men were still Finnish citizens according to the law and that they must have the right to return to their homeland if they want to. For years their relatives had been asking for help from the Finnish government. . . .

Litvinov had an answer ready. According to Holsti, he said that:

> he took quite the opposite view of the matter, since according to the Soviet conception, the question of war and peace between Finland and the Soviet Union was an integral part of the issue. The Soviet Union was of the opinion that these men had not come voluntarily to seek work in the Soviet Union but had been sent there by Finnish officials for the purposes of espionage, so that in case of war, their knowledge of local geography and other expertise could be used against the Soviet Union.

Finnish officials did not believe the charge of espionage. Their opinion was that the border-hoppers were "totally unfit" (Nykopp) for spying and that the majority of them had left Finland misled by Soviet propaganda.

Holsti repeated that the border-hoppers must be allowed to return home "even though our own officials for their part believe that while in the Soviet Union they had been made into purveyors of communist propaganda for the purpose of increasing communist agitation in Finland." (Holsti had discussed the matter with Riekki before his trip.) He requested that the Soviet Union undertake all possible measures for the return of the border-hoppers.

In early 1937, increasing numbers of Germans were arrested in the Soviet Union; at the same time Trotskyites and the aides to the dismissed NKVD head Jagoda were hunted down. In June Yrjö-Koskinen reported great numbers of imprisonments, death sentences, and suicides. "It is difficult to find a rational explanation for the wave of terror." A "nightmare atmosphere" prevailed in the Soviet Union.

On 9 June 1937, the state newspaper *Izvestia* published a lead article that reeked of xenophobia and spy hysteria. According to it, "spies and enemies of the people" were jotting down state secrets in their notebooks. In his report, Yrjö-Koskinen continues:

> *Further on the newspaper quotes these words of Stalin: "Is it not clear that as long as we live surrounded by capitalist countries, we will have behind our backs saboteurs, spies, and obstructionists sent from abroad." And further on, in his words: "As long as the power to rule is in the hands of the bourgeois beyond our borders, their counter-espionage and their high commands will forever keep devising new means of espionage and vandalism."*

Where there's smoke there's fire. The *politburo* of VKP(b)'s central committee passed a resolution on 2 July 1937 which obligated folk commissar Nikolai Jezhov to put into effect a campaign of mass terrorism. The order was signed by Stalin. Antagonistic elements were to be arrested immediately and shot, less activist ones were to be listed and moved to "appropriate areas," that is, sent to construct the Gulags' prison camps. There was great haste: the central committee was to receive a report on the number to be executed and deported within five days.

Advance preparations had begun in the prisons: cots had been removed from the cells and common one- or two-decker platforms built in their place. The prosecutors signed blank forms on which the NKVD officials could write in the names of those to be arrested. In the fall of 1937, Stalin added fifteen-

and twenty-year sentences to criminal law. "Troikas,"* or special judgment courts, got the right to issue sentences of up to ten years ("administrative punishments") and later even death sentences behind closed doors without seeing or hearing the accused. There was no appeal of the decisions.

In July 1937 according to the Finnish embassy, "Jews, Baltic peoples, Poles, and other foreign nationals were among those being purged." The persecution of the Germans continued: all Germans employed in war industries were to be imprisoned. The newspapers warned about foreign spies and "diversants."

With the permission of the *politburo*, on July 30th, Jezhov signed operational Order No. 00447, which commanded the smashing "without any mercy" of anti-Soviet groups. Security agencies were ordered "to begin on the date of August 5, 1937, an operation to repress former kulaks, activist anti-Soviet elements, and criminals in all republics, areas, and districts." The order demanded that the investigations be carried out in the "simplified and expedited manner."

The order laid down the criteria for enemies of the people and listed eight groups which belonged to that category. Finns could probably be included in the fifth: "5) The most inimical and activist members of anti-revolutionary organizations now being liquidated who have been uncovered by investigation and trustworthy operational materials."

According to the degree of danger they posed, the people in the first group, or "the most anti-Soviet material" were to be arrested immediately and executed once a *troika* had considered their case. The second group would be sent to camps and prisons for eight to ten years. In all, 259,450 people were to be arrested and 72,950 executed by firing squad.

Order No. 00447 was to have been carried out within four months, but the time dragged on to over a year. In the middle of everything (August 11, 1937) another order arrived (No. 00485), for the liquidation of "the Polish sabotage and spy group and the disbanding of the Polish military organization." Border-hoppers and those who had entered the country for political reasons were to be imprisoned. From the papers of the Finns arrested in Ural, it can be seen that they too were charged on the basis of Order No. 00485.

In January 1938 the *politburo* approved a motion to "increase the number of preventive arrests." Permission went out to several areas, and also to

---

*In 1935, the "troikas" or "triads" were formed in the republics, areas, and districts in connection with the NKVD. They were made up of the local communist party's chief secretary, the NKVD head, and the chief prosecutor. Later the cases came to be handled by a "dvoika" or dyad (the interior ministry's folk commissar and the Soviet Union's chief prosecutor). In the fall of 1938, "special triads" were formed everywhere.

the autonomous republic of Karelia, to continue the activity and imprison and execute more people. The Karelian NKVD also asked to speed up decisions, complaining that the prisons were completely full.

Whether one can speak of a separate "Operation Finns" is a question of interpretation, for neither in Ural nor in Karelia can one find a governmental order specifying only Finns as the target of persecution. There is indeed a rough draft of the resolution according to which the punishments would be extended to Finns and "to Karelians and in general to the Finno-Ugric part of the population."

Even the interpretations of local officials may lie in back of the persecution of the Finns. For example, in December 1937 the head of the Karelia NKVD wrote about the "Operation Finns" in a letter to the area commander in Leningrad urging haste in decisions regarding those to be sentenced. In December 1937 Moscow ordered the Ural NKVD to expedite the arrests of "Poles and other Baltic peoples." It was also then that the order to arrest the border-hoppers from Finland arrived in Chelyabinsk, as we shall see later. At the end of January the NKVD received permission "to continue until 15 April 1938 the operation for smashing the spy and sabotage activities of the Poles, Latvians, Germans, Estonians, Finns," and many other nationalities. A dyad sitting in Moscow levied punishments on spies from bordering countries—all the way from Finland to Japan. According to NKVD statistics, 172,830 people were condemned to death on the basis of nationality.

A secret circular from Jagoda in 1936 prohibited the use of "threats, torture, and similar illegal methods" in the interrogations, which may well be taken as a hint that one could and should use such methods. The following year the NKVD received permission to extort confessions by torture—the fact was revealed to the world by Nikita Kruschev in his speech to the party meeting in 1956. He cited the words in Stalin's secret wire to party and NKVD agencies:

> The central committee of the communist party declares that the use of bodily pressure in NKVD activities is approved from 1937 on with the permission and support of the communist party.

According to the wire, it was known that "all bourgeois intelligence agencies used techniques of bodily pressure against the representatives of the socialist proletariat."

> *The question arises as to why the socialist intelligence service should be more humane than the mad agents of the bourgeoisie who threaten death to the working class and the kolkhoz. The central committee of the communist party is of the opinion that the use of bodily pressure must absolutely be continued as an exceptionally fitting and just, as well as a practical, procedure against known and avowed enemies.*

Aleksander Solzhenitzyn writes that before 1937-1938 the use of torture required separate permission in every case, but in those years investigative officials were given unlimited permission to use violence as they saw fit. The permission was rescinded temporarily in 1939.

Intimidation, deprivation of sleep, and physical abuse began in the early phases of the imprisonment. Crowded cells, where it was difficult to rest or even to breathe, beatings, sitting or standing in an uncomfortable position, and sleep deprivation were a part of the interrogation procedure.

At the end of the autumn of 1937 the Finnish embassy reported that in a number of states and autonomous republics, including Karelia, "bourgeois agitators" had been uncovered, who were to be quickly put out of action. According to the Finnish chargé d'affaires, Stalin's line "has changed greatly of late and is now reminiscent of Great Russian patriotism, which is only one step away from Czarist nationalism and imperialism." In October Yrjö-Koskinen reported that the chaos and radical purging of the party and the governing machinery begun in the summer were continuing. Officials were terrorized, nearly prostrate. The terror and the "Great Russian purge" were now directed at the minority nationalities.

In November the Finnish chargé d'affaires pointed out that the purge was not directed at the Karelian and Leningrad Finns alone, but, with a few exceptions, at all foreign communists in the Soviet Union. They were branded as agents of the fascist countries' spy organizations.

One of the border-hoppers sentenced in 1937 sent the chief consul a copy of the decision in his case and an explanation of the proceedings. The NKVD had imprisoned him in 1936 specifically because he had been corresponding with the consulate—he had applied for return to Finland. Another accusation was that he had praised conditions in Finland to other Finns—he did not know Russian. In a closed session, the court had condemned him to four years in a "concentration camp" according to Section 58, Paragraph 10. The highest court verified the sentence. He was judged to have spread "anti-revolutionary and libelous anti-Soviet talk about the workers' conditions and their livelihood in the USSR." Some Finn may have informed on him.

According to the court's decision, "several Finnish runaways" had testified against him.

At least in 1937, quotas were in effect. The NKVD offices in the various republics, areas, and localities had to fill a certain quota in a given time, "according to the calendar plan." The numbers to be destroyed from each segment of the population—the educated, the workers, and the farmers—were assigned. Under the Jezhov order, 268,950 men and women were to be imprisoned in the entire Soviet Union and 75,956 executed.

In the Leningrad area, according to the same order, 4,000 were to be shot and 10,000 sent to camps. In Karelia the corresponding numbers were 300 and 700. "Well-grounded requests" for larger numbers could be presented if "the situation warranted." At least in Leningrad the goal was clearly and quickly exceeded: over 18,000 people had been shot by the end of the year. In the Levashov forest alone nearly 40,000 people are buried, 13,000 of them Ingrians and Finns.

Suoma Lahti, who was imprisoned in Moscow, relates:

> They told me: if you're a prisoner here, there is no way you can escape sentencing. If we jail a hundred people and if only one of them is guilty, we are doing well. I understood then that it was their mission to send as many people to prison as they possibly could.

Kerttu Eurén (Kirsti Huurre) wrote in her memoirs of the time she spent in prison:

> Even one of the judges said he had received an order to get such and such a percentage of saboteurs, "diversants," and anti-revolutionaries from his district. He was horrified and objected, asking where he could find so many unless he "baked" them himself. He refused, and for that good deed he was taken along with us.

In 1937 the quotas were so high that the local NKVD leaders had to comb through the old card files and order those who had been under suspicion long before or had already served their terms to be arrested again. It is clear that a group such as the border-hoppers formed a tempting target. Paid informers supplied endless tips about people to arrest. If the quota was not filled, the secret police officials themselves became suspect.

As the number of prisoners swelled, the second and third five-year plans were supplied with cheap labor. In 1929 the GPU had already been given the right to develop economic activity in remote areas that were rich in natural resources "putting to good use the labor of socially dangerous isolated elements and colonizing sparsely inhabited areas." All reformatory labor camps and places of banishment were under control of the NKVD from November 1934 on. Their main governing body was known as the Gulag. It developed into the country's largest construction organization: in 1940 there were 1,672,438 prisoners in the Gulag camps.

A secret directive of July 1935 ordered that all those convicted under Section 58 of the criminal law (political crimes) would be banished to distant areas of Siberia on their release. Another secret directive in 1937 lengthened the prisoners' workday to eleven and a half hours.

After the Poles in the fall of 1937, it was the Finns' turn. With the disappearance of their leaders and the rise of Jezhov to leadership in the NKVD, ordinary Finns were arrested in bunches. First the border-hoppers and the American Finns were put away, and Finnish culture was exterminated in Karelia, Leningrad, and Ingria. Even VALPO reported "many mass arrests."

Apparently the NKVD just picked an area to be purged on the map and set out at night to fill its quota of arrests there. Whoever happened to be traveling or hiding or had moved elsewhere might be saved. On the other hand, whoever happened to be around would serve the purpose. The wave swept by, and those who were left after it had passed resumed their lives.

Spy and sabotage activity had been uncovered in "all the Finnish colonies" in the Soviet Union. The Karelia NKVD leadership reported to Jezhov that in early 1938 it had "destroyed 387 (rebellious) groups and organizations and jailed 5,340 of their members." These organizations "had been established in Karelia by Finland's counter-intelligence" which had "recruited most of the border-hoppers before they were sent to the Soviet Union." Of the 874 Finns imprisoned, 805 had confessed.

The NKVD report, "Finnish border-hoppers in Karelia" related that from the fall of 1937 to the spring of 1938 there had been "arrested and revealed to be agents of Finland's spy apparatus and participants in anti-revolutionary organizations: 1.) Finnish border-hoppers—1,357 persons. 2.) Political immigrants—fifty-four persons. 3.) Legal arrivals in the Soviet Union from Finland—115 persons. 4.) Legal arrivals in the Soviet Union from Canada and the United States of America—342 persons. Total—1,868." According to researcher Ivan Tshuhin, a total of 2,869 Finns were arrested in Karelia during 1937 and 1938.

There were many other victims, but proportionally the heaviest blow was directed at the area's Finns: of those arrested from that group, seventy percent were executed. Population statistics indicate that calculations for the year 1939 show a decrease of 5,700 people of Finnish stock in Soviet Karelia.

During this time the prison in Petroskoi was filled to the brim with inmates. It is claimed that at one time there were up to 3,000 in it. The place for interrogation and torture was at first the Hiekkaranta rest home, then it was a wooden barracks on Kivimäki, and from 1941 on, the new four-story NKVD stone building. Interrogations of the "spies" lasted from a few days up to as long as months.

It was said that on the worst day, 450 Finns were taken from the Kontupohja cellulose and paper plant. The NKVD arrested so many engineers and technicians in 1937 that the plant was shut down for two weeks. The prisoners were tortured in the cellar of the plant's cultural building. From the Petroskoi ski factory 120 workers were taken on trucks in the middle of a workday. Finns also disappeared from the Onega tractor plant.

Most of those arrested in 1937 and 1938 vanished into the unknown. To inquiries from relatives, the NKVD usually answered, "sentenced to ten years in a distant camp without correspondence privileges." In actuality, that meant they had been executed.

The families of the people arrested were evicted from their dwellings and taken away from the city. They were again pressured to tell why they had once come to the Soviet Union and were accused of being lackeys of Finland. For example, wives and children from Petroskoi were hauled on a barge to Olenia Island in Lake Ääninen, where a stone quarry, a lime pit, and an incinerator were located. There they were lodged in a stable and an old prison barracks.

Karelia was cleared of border-hoppers. Among the places to which they were shipped were Ural and Karaganda, whence there arrived in 1938 "a long list of names of people to whom it was no longer necessary to send food packages." They had died of hunger and the heat. From the Sverdlovsk area, letters arrived in which the hungry exiles asked that dried black bread be sent and also old clothing.

The summer of 1938 was still a bad time in Karelia. Some kind of turnabout took place that fall; the local party leadership changed again, and the terror subsided. Jezhov's star faded during the year, and in December he was dismissed. In 1939 some of the exiles were already returning, prison conditions were eased, and those who had not yet confessed were freed—in Ural as well. The restoration of reputations to those who had been condemned without cause was begun.

After the Winter War in 1940, the arrests and the deportations of people with Finnish blood in their veins from Leningrad and Karelia began again. Some of them were sentenced to forced labor for anti-Soviet activity and wound up in Siberia. When war broke out in 1941, the release of the "Section 58" people was suspended everywhere, and the political prisoners who had served out their terms were slapped with new and longer sentences. Food rations were reduced, and nourishment deteriorated in the camps, except in those where vital war production was being done, or which received United States aid.

In 1936 the Sverdlovsk NKVD exposed a so-called Ural rebellion headquarters, an organization of "deviationists, eserries, and priests." The wave of persecution which followed affected, among others, the Finnish concentration in Nizhni Tagil. The resolution "to repress former kulaks, activist anti-Soviet elements, and criminals," involved the arrest of 10,000 people in the Sverdlovsk area within four months.

In August 1937, the command came from above to begin the operation with regard to the "border-hoppers"; in actuality, the Poles and Finns. That fall the NKVD area chief informed Jezhov that he had put an end to a secret military organization and had uncovered entire "rebellious rings" in Nizhni Tagil and Nadezhdinski, for example.

In 1937 a group of Soviet leaders were sent to various areas to supervise the purge. For example, Lazar Kaganovitch, one of the men closest to Stalin, was made responsible for Chelyabinsk, the Donets Basin, and a number of other areas.

Fomkin and the vice-commander of the Chelyabinsk NKVD investigative branch gave corroborative testimony at later hearings that NKVD Order No. 52623 arrived by wire in this Ural area in December 1937. The same wire came to Sverdlovsk. It commanded that all border-hoppers from Finland were to be arrested and investigated and that information about them sent to the Soviet NKVD in Moscow for the purpose of "handling by an outside court." The arrests could be made without any particular reason.

The wire was signed and sent on 6 December. On the following night the NKVD surrounded the building trust's Finnish lodgings, which were almost completely emptied.

According to a secret wire from Chelyabinsk, "repression of Polish border-hoppers continued 20 December" by order of NKVD chief commissar Jezhov.

Based on this order we recommend: Existence of Polish border-hoppers in your district to be thoroughly investigated and any others found to be arrested immediately and sent under special guard to the NKVD-command's security district 3. . . . The charge to fall under criminal law statutes section 58-6 and to follow this form: "Is the agent of a foreign country and carried out espionage activities in the territory of the Soviet Union."

A careful home search is to be carried out during the arrest and a log book made of the search. The prisoner is allowed to take with him a change of underwear, a towel, soap, and a maximum of [fifty] rubles in money.

The wire regarding the Polish border-hoppers was found years later in the KGB file of one of the men arrested. An NKVD official sent to that area said during a hearing that in 1937 there was investigated "the anti-revolutionary activity carried out by Poles and other Baltic nationals" which extended as far as Ural, and at the end of the summer an order was given to begin "the arrest of Poles, White Russians, and others."

Next, in December-January, it was Kamensk's turn, where according to NKVD statistics, "over 200" Finnish border-hoppers were arrested on one night in January 1938.

The Ural "Operation Finns" with its interrogations and sentencing was carried out very quickly. By January-February 1938, the Chelyabinsk NKVD had already begun a new "group-type foreign operation" and by March, another new one. This time the targets were Germans and Austrians, among others.

In Ural it was at first a question, as explained later, of a "normal investigation," but then a command came from Moscow to speed things up. District chiefs were ordered to expedite the liquidation of the "foreign base." A daily summary was to be made of all the arrests and sentences. According to the admissions of NKVD men, the judgments in the Urals were harsh at this time. Of a hundred arrested, on the average one was freed—the rest were shot.

Suharev, the assistant head of the area's NKVD investigative branch says that in the middle of the "Operation Finns," at the end of January or the beginning of February 1938, his chief held a talk session with his men and complained that the "disclosure of inimical elements" in their area was proceeding too slowly and feebly. He underscored the fact that in the Sverdlovsk area (which included Nizhni Tagil, Asbest, and Revda), 22,000

Eino Saarelainen was executed, and his wife and son died in Kamensk in the 1980s.

had already been arrested. The Chelyabinsk area (which included Kamensk and Magnitogorsk) was lagging behind, although there were in it "any number of White Guardsmen, rebels, border-hoppers, kulaks, mensheviks, eserries, Germans, and other nationalities."

The chief also emphasized the need for increased arrests. He told of Jezhov's saying in his explication of the class struggle and of the rooting out of enemies that the purges must be speeded up and the repression strengthened. Immediately after the counseling session, a directive was sent to area districts to make lists of foreigners and prisoners and send the lists to Chelyabinsk.

According to Suharev, the lists arrived at the NKVD third district's statistical branch. The chief and his deputy ran through the list and wrote on them: "To Be Arrested!" The order went out to the districts. The prisoners were to be taken to the Chelyabinsk, Magnitogorsk, and Zlatoust prisons.

The NKVD officials were forced to speed up their investigations and sentences were handed out by conveyer belt. The interrogations were carried out following "the simplified form." There were investigators in the operation who managed to interrogate twenty prisoners and draw up their trial papers in one day. They were, according to the records, "the most able and conscientious workers in fulfilling their bolshevik duties."

According to Suharev, division heads' attention was now concentrated solely on how many reports they could send to NKVD headquarters and how often. "The number of such communications was the criterion for competi-

Ville Viita phtographed in the Revda prison, 1937.

tion among the branches. The NKVD administration and the division heads demanded of the operational branches, which were compiling so-called 'albums,' that the reports be sent in by the hundreds at five-day intervals."

When Beria purged the "Jezhovites" from the NKVD in 1939, including those in Ural, a witness named Knjazev testified at the war tribunal session how he had functioned up to 1938 in the Nizhni Tagil NKVD.

Knjazev had conducted many "investigations of provocateurs," in which mainly Finns had been sentenced. "I, like the others, tried to get signatures into the records, considering it indispensable for the Soviet nation." It was reportedly easy to get confessions of spying from the prisoners. Many of them were nearly illiterate. He went on to say that people were arrested without a warrant, which was sought only after the trial was over and the prisoners had been sent to the NKVD.

> With regard to some of the prisoners, there was no compromising material. In such cases, when the prisoner had already been shot without having signed a confession, an entry was made saying that he had refused to sign.

According to official and admittedly incomplete information, the NKVD's "Operation Finns" liquidated 11,346 Finns (Ingrian Finns included) from the fall of 1937 to the fall of 1938. This statistic gives us the following figures for Ural: 450 disappeared from the Chelyabinsk area and 322 from the Sverdlovsk area, a total of 772.

Salli Lappalainen and Vasili Genov had only a few weeks of marriage. They met for the last time in the exercise yard of the Chelyabinsk prison in 1938. The picture is from 1937.

Chapter Ten

That New Year's Night

T<small>HERE WERE SMALL FIR TREES IN THE FAMILY DWELLINGS</small>, and Finnish Christmas songs were sung. The regular New Year's celebration had been held in the red corner—not a very happy one, since a noteworthy number of men had already disappeared from the Finnish village in Kamensk.

One person who had not enjoyed the club's celebration was twenty-year-old Salli Lappalainen. A week earlier her husband, Vasili Genov, and five other Bulgarians had disappeared. The couple had been married for only three months and worked in the same auto repair shop. When they came for him, Vasili thought he was only going to be questioned and did not even take a clean pair of underwear or a toothbrush with him, merely changing from his work clothes into a suit. He did not return.

Salli began to cry and left the club party for home. Henrik Kaukonen, who worked as a construction foreman, consoled her: "Don't cry. They don't send the innocent to prison here."

"Be careful, Henry. You may have to eat your words some day," Salli replied.

The young people could not be burdened with the their parents' worries; they wanted to dance and sing. On Sunday January 2, 1938, a group of boys and girls decided to go to a dance at the Russian club a couple of kilometers away. The dance was held in a building with an earth floor located on the shore of a brook in Krasnaja Gorka. When friends came to get twenty-year-

165

old Sylvi Ollikainen, her father told her not to go—the barracks floor needed cleaning. The delicate girl had fainted from the heavy work at the factory, and her father had taken her away from it. Her new task was to clean the barrack.

"I'll clean it tomorrow. I want to go with the girls to see the Russian Christmas tree," Sylvi said. She loved to sing and dance. Her father's last words were blunt: "If they take me too, you can run around to your heart's content. Just go and stay."

By midday it was already apparent that Red Army men were moving around near the *Finski posjolok*, many of them very young soldiers. The soldiers were checking any vehicles that drove by them. That evening there were many soldiers with dogs near every barrack. No one paid very much attention to them—"It has nothing to do with us," someone said.

In the evening, when it was already dark, someone rushed through the barracks' corridors shouting that there was a general meeting at the factory dining hall. Everyone was urged to come and hear an important announcement. Fomkin's wife came into Salli Lappalainen's room just when she had come back from skiing. Salli was still wearing her ski pants. "Salli, go to the meeting!"

Warmly dressed border-hoppers in the winter of 1933. The woman in back is Anna Fomkina. In front are Esteri Lepokorpi, Esteri Lintunen, and Kukka Laine. On the right is probably Tauno Hytönen.

Salli refused to go; she had other plans for the evening.

"Goddamned activist, won't go to a meeting," snorted the woman.

Many from the barracks did go to the meeting, among them Salli's younger sister's husband, Reino Orell. "I'll go if my neighbor goes," said Viljo Wahlstén. After her father left, Eila, whose temperature was a little high, lay down and read a story called, "The Empty Chair" in a paper that had come in a letter from Finland.

The men put on only their suit coats and the women locked the children into the rooms, as they hurried to the dining hall with their coats over their shoulders. It was thirty degrees below zero Centigrade. Many boys went along with their parents out of curiosity. The Murto twins, Reino and Veikko, left together without their mother's even knowing where they had vanished to.

There were soon hundreds of Finns in the place. The wooden benches in the dining hall were filled. They waited for what was to come. Salli Lappalainen relates that men came back to the barrack from time to time. "It's not a regular meeting; it's best to have a supply of tobacco in our pockets."

Seamstress Ida Sinkkonen returned home and said to her daughter Hilkka, who had been left washing the family's evening dishes: "There is a meeting there, but it seems very strange. I said to Father that this isn't a

Modern appearance of the dining hall, now an auto repair shop, to which Kamensk Finns were coaxed for a "meeting" on the night of the mass arrest in January 1938.

proper meeting and we should go home. Father said no, I want to see what will come of it." Ida anticipated the worst; she took her husband's pack and put into it clean underwear, shoes, tobacco, and dry foods so that he would be prepared for anything.

At this point the barracks were surrounded and no one could go outside. Siiri Hämäläinen did a test—she went to carry out a slop pail—but the soldiers stopped her. Elsa Tervonen, who had been out visiting, was not allowed to return to her own barrack without a soldier escort. Ida Sinkkonen was not allowed to go to the outhouse. On his part, one of the Finnish men hid in the outhouse and watched the proceedings from there.

Siiri Hämäläinen, who had been in the dining hall, explained what happened there:

> A man in civilian clothes got up on the stage and said: "Comrades! You who are the best Stakhanovites in the factory! Near Kurgan (a city 260 kilometers southwest of Kamensk-JR), there has been a railway accident, a train has slipped off the rails. Since you are the best Stakhanovites, you cannot stand on the sidelines. We ask you to come and help!" The young men stood up immediately and shouted: "We're ready, we just have to get more clothes and take some of our tools with us!" Then the man said: "Comrades, you don't need to take anything with you, you'll be given everything there." At that moment the doors opened at the four corners of the room and Red Army men with rifles came in.

A command was heard: "Outside, one by one!" The Finns were ordered from the building with their hands behind their backs, and then were forced to get down on their knees in four long files on the snowy road. It was now about nine in the evening.

Close by was the factory railroad, a side spur along which building materials were brought to the site. In the railway yard there now stood a long row of cattle cars, white with frost. After a two-hour wait, the men taken prisoner in the dining room were marched to the train. "A step to the right or left will be considered an attempt to escape, and you will be shot!" The men were stuffed into the cars. They were not allowed to go home to get anything to take with them.

Then a roundup began of those who had not attended the meeting. There was a hammering at the doors, and into every room walked two or three riflemen to conduct a search. They soon had everything topsy-turvy, and then they ordered: "Let's go now!" They answered questions by saying,

"You'll see when you get there." Families were hurried along with shouts of
"*Davai, davai*" and were told to take the necessary goods with them.

Salli Lappalainen noticed too late, when she was outside, that she had
left her winter hat in the barrack. One of the soldiers threw a fur coat hanging on a nail over Hilkka Sinkkonen's shoulders as she was walking out with
only her ski pants, blouse, and ski boots on. The soldiers asked the age of the
slight-looking Hilkka. "Eighteen," her mother answered. They were ordered
to leave. "Where?" asked the mother. To the "red corner." Ida Sinkkonen
took with her the pack she had prepared for her husband.

Erkki and Rauni Murto had fallen asleep waiting for their mother. A
thumping in the hallway awakened them. According to Rauni, there was a
heavy pounding at the door, and someone in back of it shouted, "Arrest!"
They were given five minutes to get ready.

The Wahlstén sisters awoke to the sound of a woman weeping loudly
outside the door. Their mother peeked out into the hallway—it was full of
NKVD soldiers. Soon there was a knock, and they were ordered outside.
"Bring the children, and you can take a little stuff with you." Panic-stricken,
they dressed and took with them whatever was at hand. Eila noticed that her

Kamensk-Uralski, 1958: Stroke victim Hilja Jelonen, front, second from left, made a living as a fortune
teller. Kerttu Jelonen with baby in her lap. Standing at left is Aune Jelonen.

mother's hands were trembling a little as she packed some clothes for her daughters into a small suitcase. Soon there was another knock at the door, and they had to leave.

Only two women were left in the barracks. One was Hellä Viuhko, whom the soldiers found sitting by the body of her child. The girl had just died and the mother was allowed to stay and bury her. Later she too died of pneumonia. Her husband was an interpreter at the hearings.

Another was Hilja Jelonen, who had returned to Kamensk from the hospital after suffering a stroke. She packed food into the others' bags since she could not carry anything, and sat waiting for someone to get her. "I can't go by myself, carry me if you want to," she said to them. They did not carry her.

One Finnish man who was on the night shift at the factory was left, apparently overlooked; the others on the night shift were fetched in automobiles.

When the women and children with their bundles were out in the barracks hallways, they were marched in a column of twos to wait in the red corner, where they sat on the bundles of clothing. Some conjectured that they were starting a journey to the Volga canal job site. Or was it a question of some kind of inspection? They could think of nothing else, for the Finns were not guilty of any crime.

Mothers were brought back from the train to the barracks village, and told to bring out their children. Then trucks drove up, and they were all ordered into them to be taken to the train.

The Russian wives of Finnish men were separated from the group, some by force. They were not allowed to go along. On the other hand, at least two women who had come from Finland on a Christmas visit, one of them very old, were taken along. One of them was, as some recalled, either Oskari Stenman's or Laina Stenman's mother.

The dining hall and the barracks were already dark when the boys and girls returned from the Russian cultural building before midnight. Boys had come to the dance saying that there was a big meeting at the Finnish village. Many riflemen were in evidence and the young people returning to the village guessed that they were guarding the factory for some reason. They saw the trucks and the large crowd of people near the building which housed the red corner, the office, and the children's nursery. "Why are the Russians swarming around there?" someone asked. Then they noticed that they were indeed Finns.

"Hey, Hilkka, what are you doing here?" Sylvi Ollikainen asked Hilkka Sinkkonen, who was a little younger than she was. She was on her way back from the dance. Hilkka waved to her from the truck. "They're taking us to a new job site."

"Where?"

"I don't know. They already took Father from that meeting," Hilkka replied. "They took your brother Oiva too." Hilkka's father, a fifty-two-year-old cabinet maker, was among those arrested at the meeting.

The young people returning from the dance tried to enter the barracks to get their clothing and things, but the riflemen stopped them. Thus Salli Lappalainen, Sylvi Ollikainen, and Irja Pekala, for example, were forced to start on the long trip wearing only slippers, and Salli had only a small hat on her head. They were held temporarily in the entry to the children's nursery with Mrs. Fomkin standing guard and interpreting for them.

The men were ordered into different cars than the women and children. The cars were not heated, but they were so full that the people leaned against each other and stayed warm after a fashion.

"It was an awful night," Siiri Hämäläinen says. "Everywhere there was shouting and cursing and weeping." Shocked, Aili Markkanen said that she would go nowhere without her daughter. Eeva was just on her way back to Kamensk from the children's home. One of the militia promised to get the child, and drove off somewhere in an automobile. Apparently they only wanted to deceive the mother, for the driver did not return.

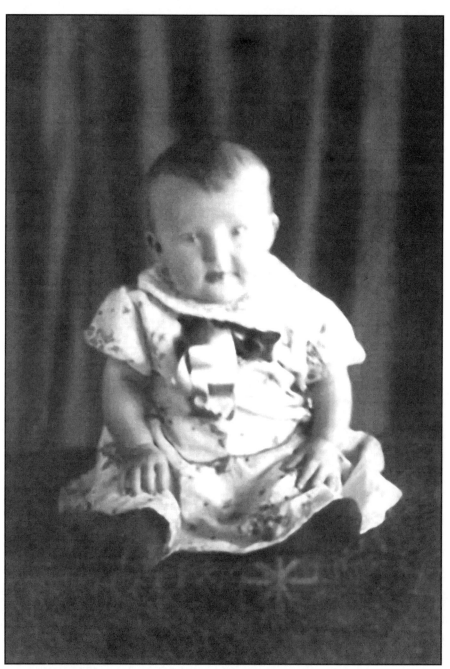

Tamara Orell was less than a year old when her father was arrested.

Chapter Eleven

"Where Does This Road Lead?"

IN THE MORNING A NEW TUMULT AROSE—before the train left the factory yard, all mothers with children under four and all pregnant women were
ordered to remain in Kamensk. They were to be taken back to the barracks.

Sanni Orell was carrying her daughter Tamara, who had been born in
Kamensk and was not yet a year old. A young soldier tried to take Tamara
away from her when she did not immediately obey the order to leave. Salli
Lappalainen, who had fallen into a restless doze, awoke when the mother
called out to her for help.

"You leave that child alone; you're not going to lay your dirty hands on
her!" Salli shouted.

"I wasn't going to . . ." stammered the soldier.

When Sanni was forced to get off the train, Salli kept shouting to her sister, "Don't let them take your child away from you!" She was afraid the child
would be gone forever.

It is said that during this time Akuliina Vaittinen succeeded in pushing
her seventeen-year-old stepdaughter Hilma off the train. The girl lived in
Kamensk for the rest of her life. Lauri Vaittinen went with his mother and
wound up in a children's home.

The first stage of the journey was short. The train puffed away from the
factory rails to the main line and on to the Sinarskaja station in Kamensk.
On arrival, the names of the prisoners were recorded. Mothers traveling with

children were ordered to move into warmer coaches. There was weeping then too: the mothers were afraid that preparations were being made to steal the children from them.

Now all the boys and girls over sixteen and under eighteen were ordered off the train. Hilkka Sinkkonen remembers that the Katvala brothers were in the same coach with her. As seventeen-year-old Veikko Katvala was being taken away, his mother, Anna, looked out from the train window and wailed loudly: "What have I done, what did I bring my child into, what have I done . . ." Veikko left the death train, but he did not get to live for long.

Panic-stricken Vilhelmiina Murto, who was journeying toward her death with her two sons, Ilmari and Urho, did not know where her twins Reino and Veikko had disappeared. Since leaving the factory yard, she had kept shouting in vain: "Reino! Veikko!" The NKVD bookkeeping was accurate. Since the boys would not be eighteen until later that month, both of them were taken back to the barracks village. Those Murto children who wound up in a children's home later heard by chance that Reino and Veikko were "safe" in Kamensk. The two would also be arrested.

One of the young people who was ordered off the train at the Sinarskaja Station was Siiri Hämäläinen, who had just turned seventeen. She noticed some kind of command group sitting in the cold railway station, and then she recognized one of the soldiers who had given orders to the people in her barrack the evening before. She went up to the man and said she wanted to stay with her mother.

"You'll be worse off there; just stay home," the man said. In tears, Siiri repeated her plea, whereupon the man went over to the command group. First there was the sound of talk and then a

Seventeen-year-old Siiri Hämäläinen.

loud roar of laughter. The man returned and waved a hand. The girl was allowed to go along with her mother.

Siiri returned to the train, much to the astonishment of the others. She was the youngest of the prisoners to set out on the long journey.

When the young people got back to the village from the train, thieves driving horses had already emptied their rooms, although their occupants had been absent for only a day. The doors and windows were broken. Sanni and Tamara Orell returned to a room that had been stripped of everything. Only the tree was left standing on the floor, with a few decorations hanging from it.

Having just been separated from their brother, little sister, and parents, Annikki and Elsa Tervonen went home together. The room was empty. The strain was too much for the nerves of seventeen-year-old Elsa, who fainted when they entered the door.

Any goods that had been left were heaped up in one room, and there Annikki retrieved the family's cooking pot and washboard. Later, quarreling Russians informed on each other regarding the thefts, and Tyyne Pynnönen went to a house on the basis of one such tip. There she found her ring, her cookbook, and a watchband of hair she had made for her husband as a wedding gift.

When the residents had been evacuated, the Finnish village in Kamensk was given another name. From then on, *Finski Posjolok* was called Posjolok TETS, after the power plant, but even today some of the residents speak of

TETS (heating and power plant), built by Finns. The Finnish village was known by the name of the plant after the Finns were moved to Kamensk.

the "Finnish quarter." The barracks were taken over by other workers. The Finnish women and children were crowded into one barrack.

The trip from Kamensk to Chelyabinsk lasted three days. The Finns arrived in the evening. Fanni Pyykkö, who was living in that city, related:

> When I was going to work one morning in early January 1938, I saw a long line of cattle cars, with a guard with a rifle and dog standing at the end of each car. Only freight trains used this railroad near Stangostroi (Stankostroi). I wondered about the sight. Were there people in the cars? I had been transported in that way too. I kept on going to work, and when I came back in the evening, the cars were standing there empty.

What had happened? When the car doors were opened, the officers had announced to the parents: "You can say goodbye now." Children under sixteen were to be taken away. When nothing happened, the soldiers began pushing them out.

Again there was weeping. Children and mothers wailed loudly. "It was awful," Salli Lappalainen recalls. "The whole coach was a mess. Officers and other bosses were shouting curses." Listening in shock to the uproar, Siiri Hämäläinen vowed that she would never have a child. She kept her word. For decades, to the very end of her life, Siiri had nightmares about that evening, and would wake up nights in a cold sweat.

When Irja Salo's daughter, Sinikka, was pulled from her mother's arms, she cried out: "Mommy, don't let me go. Don't give me to the bad man!"

The soldier slung his rifle over his shoulder but still could not pry the child loose. Then he tried to lure her with candy and cookies. That didn't work, and finally the screaming child had to be torn by force from her mother's neck.

Etel Saari, who was nine years old, remembered that the men had clubs and whips, and that they used them. Etel assumes that she fainted. Others say that her mother, Gerda, clung to Etel's feet as she was carried away.

Sturdy Antti Tervonen, eleven, said to his weeping mother, who was losing the last two of her five children, "Stop sniveling, Mother. I'll send you bread from the children's home."

Kirsti Wahlstén made a hasty little speech to her daughters Eila and Irma: "Study hard in school, pray that we will soon be together, and remember that you are Finns." She supposed that it was an inspection of some sort, and that the separation might last a couple of months. Eila Wahlstén recalls:

Mother put into both of our bags a pair of woolen socks knitted by Granny, scissors, a comb, a scarf, [thirty-five] rubles, and all the family photos. Father had asked a soldier in the other car to get one of the family photos for him. When we went, Mother was left sitting on the upper bunk in the coach.

Eila has guarded the photos like a treasure to this day. In the children's home she cut a slit in her mattress, put the pictures inside, and sewed it shut again. On the other hand, the slip of paper on which her mother had written the children's birth dates and their grandmother's address in Helsinki was lost in life's turmoil.

The NKVD took the children in a column of twos to the Chelyabinsk station, but their cries of "Mother, mother" could still be heard from far off. The smallest were taken directly on from the station, but those of school age were interviewed there. They were asked their own and their father's and family names, and were immediately given Russian names, which were later confirmed on passports issued to them at the age of sixteen.

For example, Olavi Kemppainen became Vladimir Kompanjon and Oiva Ronkainen—Juri Rongaljoff. Etel Saari became Lidija, Dagmar Kurko— Tamara, and Siiri and Helli Hämäläinen—Sima and Valentina; Helvi Tervonen also became Valentina. Her name change led to her being separated from her sisters later. When she returned to Kamensk, she was given a passport on which she was "Valentina Tervonena, Russian." Elsa and Annikki were Tervonens, and Finns. Helvi was afraid that someone would inform

Finnish pioneers in a summer camp at Chelyabinsk, persumably in 1935. In the picture at least Helli Hämäläinen can be seen, and Annikki Tervonen in the center opposite the boy.

Kirsti Wahlstén managed to give this family picture to her husband by means of a friendly soldier on their last trip on a prison train. It was found decades later in Viljo Wahlstén's KGB file.

on them to the militia and moved away. For decades she did not communicate with her sisters for fear of causing them trouble.

They wanted to change Erkki Murto to Erik Ivanov. When Eila Wahlstén told them that her father's name was Viljo, they came up with Elja Vasiljevna Valstena; her sister Irma became Iraida Vasiljevna. Rauni Murto herself decided later to take the name of Ljuba. Anja Hansen was allowed to be Anja—the name suited the Russians fine.

Trucks were already waiting nearby. All the children cried when they were ordered to climb up on the platforms. When the NKVD man tried to console them, they burst out weeping even louder.

As they drove away, the open tarp at the rear of the truck flapped in the cold wind. On the bad road one of the children fell off a truck and ran weeping after it until she was picked up again. The journey ended in the Chelyabinsk children's reception center, which was guarded and also fenced in with barbed wire. The children were fed pea soup and then all their heads, including the girls', were shaved bare. The were told they could see their parents again, "soon."

Eila and Irma Wahlstén wound up in a children's home.

They spent two months in this children's home, the inhabitants of which were mainly picked up from the streets of Chelyabinsk. The children's bags were put under the beds, and immediately young thieves began to take a toll of them. The orphans slashed one of the Russian girls with a knife.

Then the children's eastward journey was resumed.

The Chelyabinsk prison would not agree to accept a group of hundreds of Finnish prisoners since there were no written charges against them. Hilkka Sinkkonen, who was brought into the prison with her parents, says that the Finns were kept in holding cells for two days until all the charges were written up. What the charges were they were not yet informed.

One morning the women were taken to the sauna at seven o'clock. They walked through a lighted yard just as a hundred men prisoners were out for their fifteen-minute "walking hour." Even in the yard there were many guards. "Just think, Mother, what if Vasja is there," said Salli Lappalainen.

"Don't be silly," her mother replied.

Just then Salli saw her husband in the circle of walking men and called out his name. He caught sight of her, and the next time the circle came around, he had moved to the outer edge. Whenever he reached the spot where Salli stood, the circle would slow down. The couple looked at each other for the last time, afraid to speak. The other women went on their way. Salli stood as if stricken until she heard her mother's voice calling her. A guard said softly to her: "Listen girl, they're waiting for you, go to the sauna!"

When Salli entered, the guard there was astonished. Did she really belong to the Finnish group? A count had been taken, and no one had appeared to be missing.

The women had to wait one night longer than the men. Once Sylvi Ollikainen stood in the corridor and shouted into the men's cell, asking if Ollikainen was there. Her father came to the door and asked how she was doing, and she asked his forgiveness for her behavior on the last night in Kamensk.

Then Hilkka and Sylvi were put into a thirteen- or fourteen-person cell into which eighty people had been jammed. The men were even more crowded than the women. Svetlana Mironova, the chairperson of the Chelyabinsk Memorial Society, says that during the hot summer of 1937, there were from 280 and 290 in cells meant for thirty, and that people died in them from heat and lack of oxygen. At that time the Butyrka prison in Moscow had a bad reputation and was said to be chock-full, but prisoners brought there from Chelyabinsk or Sverdlovsk reportedly said that it was a "vacation camp" compared to what they had earlier experienced.

Sylvi found a place to lie down under a bed; there was no room elsewhere. There was no room for a person to lie down on her back, and those who were lying on the floor all had to had to turn over at the same time. The women took turns sitting on the iron beds and sleeping on them at night. There were no mattresses.

Soon they were moved into larger cells where there were double-decker platforms for sleeping. There too Sylvi, being one of the youngest, had to sleep on the floor. The women had only one change of clothing for the waiting period, which stretched into three months; they washed their clothing in the toilet and put it back on still wet. Women had a turn in the toilet in the morning and afternoon, but it was so brief that not all of them had a time to go there. They had to relieve themselves over a smelly bucket in the cell.

The Chelyabinsk area NKVD had "disclosed and liquidated," as it informed Moscow, "a Finnish fascist anti-revolutionary spy and sabotage organization which functioned in the Kamensk district." This litany is also recorded in the justification for the sentencing of the prisoners arrested on 2 January 1938.

Now only the confessions were lacking.

The interrogations began after a couple of weeks. The investigators found it easy to get confessions from the Finns. A rumor was spread among them that they would be sent to Finland if only they would confess to being guilty of spying. According to Svetlana Mironova of the Chelyabinsk Memorial Society, the procedure was first for the NKVD men to interrogate a few prisoners and then hold a conference to decide who would be designated as the "leader of the group of spies." The proceedings were written up accordingly, and those interrogated signed them, either voluntarily or after torture.

The first interrogations were the harshest, and that alone frightened many. Physical violence such as beating was not generally required. In the headquarters building of the Chelyabinsk NKVD, in cells known as the incubator, men and women were "ripened" by having them stand for two or three days until their legs swelled up. The treatment was called "*stoika*."

The *stoika* did not always work. A young border-hopper named Arvo Rajala stated that a chief interrogator said of him: "Rajala is an athlete—he can stand longer than we can sit." So they began immediately to beat him.

There might be twenty to thirty people in the incubator at the same time, among them some who had confessed and some who hadn't. The former advised the latter exactly as the NKVD hoped they would: "You'll have to confess in the end anyway, so go ahead and sign!"

The men even managed to get word to the women's cells that they should not let themselves be tortured and ruin their nerves and health—the result, a ten-year-sentence—was predetermined in any case.

According to NKVD directions the person being interrogated could be made to sit for 180 hours on a backless footstool with his legs out straight in front of him. Many fell to the floor before the limit was reached. The next "degree" was that he had to sit on the very edge of a chair on his tailbone, or the last vertebra of the spine. His limbs were to be kept straight. This position, according to the reports of those interrogated, quickly became extremely painful. The "last degree" for some was that they were forced to kneel on the edge of a bench in a painful, tortuous position.

When Siiri Hämäläinen had to endure the *stoika*, a man standing next to her said it was nothing—he'd had to sit an entire day on one leg of a stool turned upside down.

The people being interrogated were also threatened with a cold-tub treatment and some were subjected to it. Fanni Pyykkö relates that a Finnish man she knew, who had a heart condition, died when he was sat down in a tub of ice at Chelyabinsk.

Pjotr Suharev, the assistant head of the area's NKVD investigative branch, admitted later that in 1938, "investigations were conducted in this building which flagrantly broke rules of law and court procedures"—for example, prisoners were kept standing or on their knees.

Jussi Kuikka, forty, a smith from Rautu offered stiff resistance to his interrogators. He was tortured for a long time before he agreed to sign the record. He was forced to stand for fifteen days, then he had to sit in a tub of cold water, then he was shut up in a cell where he could only stand, with water dripping constantly on his head.

In the end he was so confused that he already had a pen in hand and was beginning to sign his name. When he realized what he was doing, he rubbed his hand across his name, reducing it to a smear of ink. Then he was put into a room with a blindingly bright light shining directly into his eyes. That ripened him, and he signed his name—his nerves shattered. "Don't be a fool like me, you'll just waste your nerves and health in vain," he told the others. "I saw everything in front of that big lamp," he reportedly managed to tell his wife in a corridor.

A full thirty years later in his book, *The Gulag Archipelago*, Aleksandr Solzhenitsyn wrote of the same familiar methods of torture which the Finns experienced in Chelyabinsk. He mentioned, for example, the standing, the sleep deprivation, the filthy cold or hot cells, cubicles in which one could only stand, interrogations at night with a pistol lying on the desk, sitting on a stool and on the edge of a chair, being forced to kneel, being tortured with hunger and thirst, coaxing with food, bright lights, and dripping water on one's head.

According to Solzhenitsyn, the water torture could reduce a man to such a state in one day that it would take him weeks to recover. Aimo Kuusinen tells of a woman subjected to the water-drop torture who lost consciousness on the second day. Aimo Salminen relates that he was in the Tara jail with 180 other Finns, and that every one interrogated confessed to being a spy. The interrogations might last over a week, and when a confession had been obtained, the prisoner got a decent meal and water. In Tara too the interrogations began with the prisoner sitting on the sharp edge of a chair.

The Finns who were arrested in Soviet Karelia in 1938 also said that the same torture method was used there as in Chelyabinsk—standing for days on end in chock-full rooms.

Aimo Salminen, a border-hopper from Kotka, tells in his book of how the Finns were interrogated in Tara; they had to sit on the edge of a chair with their arms and legs out straight.

Now it was time for Siiri Hämäläinen, in her cell in Chelyabinsk, to regret having insisted on accompanying her mother that evening at the station. She and Hanna Hölsä, a tall, slender woman, were taken in a black automobile for a nighttime interrogation in the NKVD building—the reverse Soviet alphabetization was being used, and they had begun with the letter H. Thus the only volunteer in the group of prisoners was the first into the fire.

Two interrogators sat behind a desk. Juho Hämäläinen stood facing the wall. He had already been standing for many days on end and, according to Siiri, his legs were "swollen like barrels." Her father was forty-eight years old when he was imprisoned and had thick black hair; now a scant month later it was gray, as far as one could tell from his closely cropped head.

"Oho, why is Hämäläinen here? His case has already been settled," said one of the interrogators. "We'll let Siiri say goodbye to her father," the other replied.

Siiri sat with her father the whole night. When she fretted about having half-forced her way onto the train that night, he consoled her that she should not reproach herself; she had not even been twelve years old when she was brought to this country. He told her that after they were arrested in December, they had been forced to stand for ten days. His legs had swelled up and water oozed from them when they were touched. For a week the whole group had been given only two loaves of bread.

With Mrs. Fomkin as interpreter, Siiri was asked who had sent her to the Soviet Union and who had recruited her as a spy. She wondered why they had wanted her to leave the train at the beginning of January if she was such a big criminal that she had begun spying at the age of twelve. The interrogator sighed, and said it would have been better for her to have stayed in Kamensk.

There were questions galore, and they were "really crazy," Siiri recalled later. According to the interrogator, it was useless to resist: "Everyone signs sooner or later, we have ways to get you to sign."

Siiri was made to stand too—three days with her face to the wall. During that time many Finns came, signed the papers, and left. At night shouts and moans could be heard from somewhere. If one went to the bathroom, there would immediately be a knock on the door. "You can't sit for so long, out of there, right now!"

When she finally had to start walking away, Siiri fell over. She was thrust into a dark room, into which an interrogator without an interpreter strode. He turned on a light and said that her father had confessed everything and signed and that Siiri should do the same. Siiri signed everything they asked her to. She didn't want to stand anymore.

Sleep deprivation was an effective means of making someone yield. The interrogations were held at night, and cold water was poured on the person being interrogated if he dozed.

An interrogator named Tomunov said later that he had come straight out of school to work at Chelyabinsk in the fall of 1937. It was the practice then to have men stand in the "incubators" until they confessed. According to him, the men were to be kept standing for five days straight, and given only bread and salt; even the amount of water was regulated. He who lasted out the five days was forced to his knees on the edge of a chair. If that didn't help, there were "special rooms" where those interrogated confessed to everything. It was sometimes reported to have happened that a Finn being interrogated lost his temper and tried to strangle his interrogator.

Siiri Hämäläinen's friend, Sylvi Ollikainen, who was a couple of years older, demanded an interpreter and got one, Pauli Viuhko. First Sylvi was asked what she had done. When she was unable to answer, the interrogator refreshed her memory: "You have agitated. You have said that things are bad here and good in Finland."

Sylvi blurted out: "Well, that's true. All I said was that there are goods in the stores there, and that here the shelves are empty."

Sylvi was urged to say that her father, fifty-five-year old Albin Ollikainen was a spy.

"Never! Father came here to work, not to spy. And I was just a kid when we came here."

The interrogator banged the table with his fist. "You're going to say it yet, believe me!"

Sylvi was lying in her cell hungry and with a splitting headache when they came again to get "Silva" Ollikainen for interrogation.

"You should be ashamed to torture a hungry child," the women shouted.

"This won't last long," said the guards and led Silvi into the room.

The interrogator wrote something down. Sylvi was brought a cup of tea and a sandwich. She was urged to eat, but refused. Then the man began to read the proceedings: "I have denounced conditions here . . . and my father is a spy, although I didn't know it."

"How can I say that about my father since I don't know it?" Finally, however, she signed the paper because the other women had asked her not to get herself tortured for nothing.

"Do I get a ten-year sentence now?" she asked.

"No, we don't give them to the young. Sylvi will go to school," the interrogator consoled her.

In the KGB file of her father, Albin Ollikainen, is a Finnish passport and a confession according to which he had been recruited as a spy by a man named Nieminen, who had already returned to Finland. The confession went on in this way: "I informed on three members of the SKP [Finnish Communist Party], who ran an underground press. They produced communist propaganda and distributed fliers. As a result of my information, the following communists were imprisoned: Kalle Pasanen, Liisa Lindqvist, Matti Heikkilä . . . I received 2000 markkas in 1931 . . ."

Hilkka Sinkkonen reports that she was interrogated once and that it was done very peacefully. The charge was her failure to disclose that her father was a spy. She went for another interrogation at the beginning of March when the name Sinkkonen was shouted out at the door of the women's cell. Her father, Aleksander Sinkkonen, happened to be sitting in the waiting room at the same time. His hair and beard had grown long and his face and legs were swollen.

"Mother sent you these shoes too," Hilkka said to her father, handing him some bread and a piece of sugar.

"No, my poor girl, they won't fit on me," said her father, showing her his swollen feet, sheathed in felt slippers.

In the interrogation room they asked for her name and date of birth, and then it became clear that it was her mother they were expecting. Hilkka was taken to an isolation room and returned to the women's cell only after her mother had left it.

All the men signed the interrogation record book—and their death warrants—except one. He was a welder from Lapland named Veikko Huotari. He had been caught attempting to escape from the country and was already sitting in jail when the others were arrested. According to his account, among other things they had conducted a mock hanging for him three times, but he had vowed to die rather than sign.

Huotari returned to Kamensk with the women and set to work as a house painter. He was alive, but his nerves were shot, and his hands shook. "I won't stand it if I wind up in their claws again," he is reported to have said.

When the war broke out he was taken into the work army, where he is said to have walked up and down behind the barbed wire like a crazy man.

There was no evidence for the guilt of the Finns. As confirmation there were the interrogations they had been subjected to years ago when they had first entered the country and tales they had told about others or which others had told about them. No accusation by informers was necessary, for the order had come from above and the fact that they were Finnish border-hoppers was reason enough to arrest. They were easy to round up, for they lived together and were under surveillance by the NKVD.

The confessions were obtained by wearing them out and torturing them and were entered in the records. Immediately afterward the prisoner was told that the investigation was concluded and then a report was made on the interrogation proceedings and sent to the national NKVD for "extrajudicial handling of the case." Then the prisoner's file, which contained the investigation folder, with the decision to arrest, the explanation of the charges, personal data form, and the records of the investigation and its conclusion, was put into a cabinet.

The directions were to use Section 58* against the Finns and to write up the records accordingly. The interrogators were given a ready-made list of questions. According to Section 58-1, any activity the object of which was "to overthrow, shake, or weaken" the workers' and farmers' soviets or the ruling agencies chosen by them is considered anti-revolutionary. Anyone at all could be sentenced; according to chief prosecutor Vyshinski, direct involvement in a crime was not necessary, merely activity which might lead to such results made one an accessory to the crime. Several subsections were added to this clause in 1934, and the punishment was specified as execution by shooting. A ten-year sentence was possible for civilians in the event of mitigating circumstances.

Section 58-2 mentions, among others, armed uprising and coup d'état. The sentence for them was shooting or being publicly declared an enemy of the working class; in the mildest cases, three years in prison.

Section 58-2 (also 58-9 and 58-11) was generally applied to the Karelian and Ural Finns: "Espionage, or in other words, gathering, obtaining by stealth, and passing on information containing state secrets, with the intention of

---

*The notorious Section 58 (crimes against the state) was contained in the RSFSR's (Russian Federation's) compendium of criminal laws from the year 1926, which were in effect from 1926 to 1961. Anti-revolutionary activity was threatened with death in twelve separate cases, and shooting was mentioned forty-eight times in that section. This criminal statute also extended to children: twelve was the minimum age for being subject to punishment. From 1935 on, "all types of punishment" could be applied to them, thus including shooting.

transmitting it to foreign powers or anti-revolutionary organizations will lead to . . . the loss of freedom for at least three years, the partial or total confiscation of property, and in cases where the espionage might lead to very dangerous consequences for the USSR . . . execution by shooting or being declared an enemy of the working class, deprivation of citizenship in a soviet republic or in the USSR and banishment for life from the USSR along with the confiscation of property." Likewise it is declared that prying into economic data will lead to the loss of freedom for three years and notice is given that types of information which involve state secrets are listed in government publications. Sentence will also be imposed for suspicion of spying, unproved allegations of spying, and even for circumstances leading to suspicion of spying.

Section 58-7 (sabotage activity) relates that those who damage industry, trade, or other such will be shot to death. 58-8 covers terrorist actions against representatives of the soviet state (most likely punishment, shooting to death), and 58-9 blowing up or burning railways, pipelines, warehouses, and other such state property with anti-revolutionary intent (same punishment). 58-10 anti-soviet or anti-revolutionary propaganda or agitation or the "dissemination or production or possession of such literature." (minimum six months, maximum same as in 58-2). 58-11: belonging to an organization planning or carrying out the crimes listed in this section of the criminal law, 58-12: not reporting information one has about such crimes (fateful for many wives) and 58-14: anti-revolutionary sabotage or "consciously leaving assigned duties undone" or fulfilling them carelessly (maximum punishment, execution).

All the prisoners were asked the same questions in the same order. For example, they were asked to give the names of all of their friends.

The Finns generally tried to avoid mentioning the names of men who were still free. Purely imaginary names were also invented, which were accepted as genuine by the interrogators, who did not speak Finnish or know anything about Finland. Since everyone had to tell who had recruited him as a spy, they gave such names as Crooked Carl, Woodenhead Pete (a popular Finnish comic-strip figure), or Cracked Abel. The names were recorded. One border-hopper interrogated in Petroskoi said that a man named J.L. Runeberg (Finland's national poet 1804 to 1877) had recruited him. Where had it happened? On the Esplanade in Helsinki, where Runeberg had been standing when the man had gone there (Runeberg's statue is there).

Some of the confessions went too far even for the interrogators. One of the Kamensk Finns confessed to having killed Stalin. Another confessed through an interpreter that he had "blown up a factory."

"Where did you get the explosive?"

"I made an arrangement with a dynamiter."

"But you don't know Russian."

"I did it with gestures."

A man named Huppunen said, when he had to describe his sabotage activities, that he had blown up a certain Ural railway station. The interrogator objected to this; he had lived in the city and knew that no station had been blown up there.

When they were forced to give names, the people being interrogated could often recall only those who were "safely" dead, sentenced, or had gotten across the border into Finland. For example, Salli Juhontytär Lappalainen—Finnish border-hopper, born 1907, arc welder—answered the questions in the following way:

"The investigating agency has information that you are a foreign intelligence agent. Do you admit that?"

"Yes, I admit that I am an agent of the Finnish espionage organization, whose mission was to carry out sabotage activities on Soviet territory for the good of Finland."

"Who recruited you for these sabotage activities?"

"Finnish espionage agent Veikko Nieminen recruited me for this work in Kamensk on 7 November 1935."

Before things had come to this point, Salli had been "softened up" for a long time. Fomkin kept her standing during the interrogation, reportedly telling her at the very start: "Listen, Salli, if you sign first, the other women will follow suit." Sally refused. When the interrogation had gone on for four or five nights, she said: "I'll sign everything if I can see my husband."

That was not possible; Genov's whereabouts were unknown. Salli was even able to give the number of the cell where her husband had been held. She had been driven to the interrogation in the same automobile as Impi Quintus, to whom Genov had mentioned his cell number. It was also reported that Salli's name had been frequently shouted from that cell when Finnish-speaking prisoners passed by it.

When Fomkin could make no progress with Salli, he turned her over to Russian interrogators, who, impatient at her refusals, struck her in the face. Once when an effort was made to cajole the hungry girl with tea and sausage and cheese sandwiches, she brushed them angrily off the desk and demanded an interpreter. They said there were none. Salli suggested another prisoner, Henrik Kaukonen, who spoke Russian.

When Salli saw Kaukonen, she recalled what he had said at the New Year's celebration. "Do you still say that they don't arrest the innocent here, Henry?" She began to administer a sound tongue-lashing to the man, which the interrogators cut short.

"You can't speak Finnish!" Kaukonen said to her: "I knew you had guts, but I didn't think you had that much."

Salli finally gave in at her mother's plea. Thus began the record of "espionage agent" Veikko Nieminen, whose acquaintance Salli had made in the trade school at Magnitogorsk in 1934. In Kamensk the boy had often visited the Lappalainens, "praised the fascists and talked of Finland's wanting to get into a war against the Soviet Union and said that with German help, the fascists would soon raise the blue and white flag over Ural." The new order would be supported by former White officers, trotskyites and kulaks, as well as by the many foreigners in the country.

Salli said that she had carried out her espionage tasks by becoming a good welder. In Kamensk in November 1937 she had welded an auto body without the proper preparation, "as a result of which the auto was soon in a garage for repairs." That wasn't all: as a crane operator at the factory she had dropped "a bucket with its load from a height of [eighteen] meters, with the result that it broke and the cement workers missed two shifts for lack of materials."

Furthermore she had carried out "regular anti-Soviet agitation among the border-hoppers, and "praised the fascist order" and said to young people that "fascist youth is better educated than soviet youth." She had "spoken every day of her dissatisfaction with the Russians and said that in the Soviet Union only the Russians lived well."

"Where is your mother?"

"My mother, Lappalainen, Anna Tuomaant. was arrested January 2, 1938, and is in the Chelyabinsk prison."

"Do you know why?"

"No I don't."

"Court organs have disclosed that you knew of your mother's anti-revolutionary activities in Soviet territory."

"I can say nothing about my mother's anti-revolutionary activities."

"Where is your husband?"

And so on. Finally it was affirmed that Salli had given false information about her husband and mother. According to the report of the proceedings, she denied the charge.

Salli Lappalainen's imprisonment order (number 2816), which we found in the records, is signed and dated 2 January. The signature of the NKVD official has been blacked out in the copy we obtained.

According to the records, the interrogation involved only one session on 19 January, described as a preliminary interrogation, in which Fomkin and two other men participated. One of them was presumably named Samsonov, since NKVD representative Samsonov has signed the "report for the record of the conclusion of the preliminary investigation" along with Salli.

Salli testified that the drawing up of the report was "partially correct" and signed it. Samsonov announced that the case would be sent to the court for handling under Section 206 of the criminal law.

To judge by the records of the proceedings, Salli's fifty-three-year-old mother, Anna, "informed on" her own daughter and her husband, who had died long ago when crossing the border.

> My husband Juho Lappalainen recruited me. He was sent for by the Finnish espionage organization, and there it was suggested that he move to the Soviet Union and get himself a job at a big factory, the Kemi (Viena) sawmill or the Kontupohja paper combine, and establish espionage groups there.

Through these groups, Lappalainen would gather data for Finland's espionage agency, the account continues. "Finland's secret police left the whole family in Soviet territory for the purposes of espionage and sabotage activity." Aino Lappalainen also mentioned a man named Eino Metsämäki who had returned to Finland from Ural. During the phase when reputations were being restored, there is mention of the fact that an Eino Metsämäki had lived in Magnitogorsk and had returned illegally to Finland in 1937. The account in the records continues:

> The members of the espionage group held anti-revolutionary meetings in our lodgings in Kamensk. My daughter Salli and her husband Vasili Genov were also members of the espionage group.

From Genov's file it can be seen that after his arrest he listed his own Bulgarian countrymen as members of an espionage group. Similarly the acquaintances of Finns and the people who had come into the country with them were put down as members of the same spy group.

Anna Lappalainen also mentioned the names of Laitinen, Lindstedt, Vuorio and Nieminen—all had returned to Finland in 1936 or 1937 without leave, as the investigators recorded, so that the arm of the NKVD could no longer reach them.

In Lappalainen's personal file there are also two copies of applications placed there on 13 August 1938. From them it can be seen that Anna Lappalainen's daughters had sought to leave the Soviet Union in 1938. Apparently the applications had not been forwarded.

Urho Murto, a painter in an aluminum factory, born in Pyhtää in 1908, residing in Barrack 9, Room 26, Kamensk, arrested 2 January 1938, was, according to the papers in his file, first interrogated in December 1932. Then he had carefully related how the Murto family had come from Kotka along with a boatload of fifteen, and sworn that he and his father had crossed the border in search of work. Another interrogation seems to have been held (or concluded) 17 January 1938 in Chelyabinsk after "Murto had been arrested as a member of a Finnish espionage and sabotage group."

"You are accused of sabotage on Russian territory. Do you confess?"

"I confess."

A man named Räkä (snot), Toivo was said to have recruited Urho Murto in Kotka in 1932. He was a close friend and served in the Finnish secret police. As the story went, Räkä took Toivo to a beer joint where they discussed the possibilities of employment in the Soviet Union: if Murto would go there, he would be paid well for certain tasks and information, which he would send back with people who were returning to Finland. Räkä promised him 300 markkas to begin with. "Since I was in a bind, I promised to accept the assigned tasks."

What sabotage had he done?

The Finns had frozen the water in water pipes and boilers, and the aluminum plant had to be shut down, causing a work stoppage. They had also broken rails, causing cars used for transport in the plant to derail. "The result had been hundreds of rubles worth of damage to the factory." Murto said he had informed Erik Kallio about these deeds.

The final official decision on the case begins:

> District 3 of the NKVD Chelyabinsk area command has uncovered and liquidated a Finnish fascist espionage and sabotage organization functioning in the Kamensk sector of the Chelyabinsk area. The organization's leader, Murto Urho Kaarlenpoika, has been arrested and held accountable. A court investigation of the case has ascertained that Murto Urho Kaarlenpoika is a member of Finland's intelligence apparatus, who was recruited for this task in 1932 by Finland's secret police . . .

It goes on to tell how Murto had come to the Soviet Union to carry out sabotage and espionage, had accordingly rendered three locomotives unusable at the Pervouralski pipe factory and had caused the derailment of a freight train. He had also disseminated nationalist and terrorist opinions in opposition to the RKP(b) leaders of the Soviet state.

On these grounds, "Murto Urho Kaarlonpoika. b. Pyhtää, Province of Viipuri, Finnish border-hopper, without citizenship, a painter at the Kamensk aluminum plant prior to his arrest," according to Section 58, Clauses 6, 8, 9, and 11 (espionage, terrorism, sabotage, membership in an anti-revolutionary organization) is sentenced to death. "Has confessed his guilt." His wife, Ebba, remained alive only because she was pregnant. ·

Ebba Murto was told that the court organ knew that Urho Murto was a Finnish agent, and "you yourself know it. Do you admit that you are guilty?" "I do. I did know about it." When had she found out? Her husband had told her in a "family discussion" in 1932 that he was a Finnish agent. What did she know about her husband's activities? "Nothing." Ebba Murto had carried on fascist anti-revolutionary agitation. Did she admit it? "I do." Under whose direction? "Out of my own hatred for the soviet state." Did she have anything to add? "I have nothing more to say," Ebba Murto stated.

Before pronouncing the death sentence, the interrogator asked Sylvi Laukkarinen, "What form did your nationalist activity take?"

"I did not inform on my husband or tell anyone that he was performing espionage tasks for the good of Finland, and in addition I myself carried out anti-soviet tasks every day, taking advantage of every opportunity to do so, wherever there was a group of people gathered, especially in lines in stores." How much money had the spy Fabian Laukkarinen gotten? "He didn't tell me, but I saw the money in his wallet, which the Russians took."

Viljo Jamarovitch Wahlstén's interrogations and confession followed approximately the same line. He had truly, according to the records of the interrogation, done a great deal more than many others.

Wahlstén was recruited by Honkamäki, Metsämäki, Aalto, and Kari; Aalto's arrest is recorded on the same day as Wahlstén's. "We committed sabotage on the job site, we made poor quality concrete forms for the pilings. We ruined the iron reinforcements for the concrete. We held drunken parties where we arranged how to continue the espionage and sabotage. At one of the discussions Metsämäki, Aalto and I approved of Kirov's murder. We continued our sabotage and decided that if war came, we would blow up the tool factory."

The prisoner was also reported to have told Kallio on the job site that the Soviet Union betrayed the workers, that the pay was small, the bread expensive, and that the workers went hungry. "We also said that although there is unemployment in Finland, the pay is good, bread is cheap, and we recommended that border-hoppers leave their jobs and go back to Finland." "The court's investigation revealed" that Wahlstén had been a member of a Finnish espionage and sabotage organization, who had been recruited in 1934 and sent to the Soviet Union. On assignment by the group's leader, Saarinen, Wahlstén "planned to blow up the Svirstroi dam. In Magnitogorsk, his assignment called for him to arrange to blow up a bridge lift, to ruin construction materials at Factory No. 78, and to arrange explosions." Also on his sin list was the invented notion that Wahlstén and company had poured a faulty foundation at the Kamensk heating plant.

Wahlstén acknowledged his guilt and was condemned on the basis of Section 58-6, 9, and 11. According to order 00485 the case was sent to Moscow for checking. The record of NKVD proceedings No. 33 arrived in Chelyabinsk 11 February 1938. In it Kirsti Wahlstén was also condemned to death by decision of the NKVD procurator.

Bruno Aalto and the aforementioned Kari—apparently Aarne Kari— were, according to the records, arrested in Kamensk on the same day as the rest. They had engaged in agitation. "I said that the Soviet Union betrayed the workers, that the pay was small, bread expensive, and life difficult," Aalto related. "I also said that life is good in Finland, bread is cheap, and the pay is good."

Border-hoppers in Nevdubstroi in 1933. Rear, from left: Onni Eskolin, Bruno Aalto, and Toivo Laine.

Their sentence was the same as Wahlstén's.

Sawmill filer Hugo Katvala, born in Haapajärvi got the following for his list of sins. "Son of a kulak, border-hopper. Informer reported Katvala's saying that the Soviet Union would become capitalistic." In addition he was a "spy" and "had confessed his guilt." The sentence was death.

Katvala had sent word to his wife that the women should confess everything they were asked to, and accuse their husbands. Anna Katvala and her son Reino seem to have "told on him." Katvala himself named Viljamaa, who had died the year before, as the spy with whom he had had contact.

According to the first information in his file, Katvala had crossed the border in 1932 to find work and improve his family's living conditions. "I was born into a prosperous farm family. Father had 130 hectares of land, [twelve] cows, and one horse." After a year had gone by, in the fall of 1933, Katvala had written a request in lead pencil that he be granted a hearing at last, since he had been in a camp for so long. An informer had reported of him that

> border-hopper Katvala (I don't know his first name) has said in the presence of other border-hoppers that the Soviet Union will become a capitalist land because the building phase now going on will soon end and there will be unemployment here as in the capitalist countries.

The informer's name is not on the paper. Underneath there is only the word Los (Moose).

In 1936 Hugo Katvala had written to the NKVD area command stating that he had made application to the Finnish consulate to return home. He was, however, still "positive" that he wanted to work among the Russian people. "For this reason I ask permission to remain here and to destroy the application I sent in for my return to Finland. I ask that you consent to my request."

The Katvalas' file indicates that, with the help of Partanen as interpreter, he had requested Soviet citizenship in 1934. He reported having worked and studied conscientiously. "I have always participated in polit-education and group cultural work by attending the soviet party's school." The boy reported having joined the pioneers and the Tenho athletic club in Kemi as a ten-year old. His aim was to be a "knowledgeable builder of socialism."

In the interrogation of January 1938, his father confessed: "I admit that I was left on the Soviet side of the border for special espionage and sabotage activities . . . I was recruited for this work by Puhakka Jaakko in the city of Kemi in August 1932." It is recorded that Puhakka had praised the fascist organization and slandered the soviet government, which he viewed as "the rule of loafers and swindlers."

According to the proceedings, Puhakka had given Katvala 400 markkas and urged him to spy on factories across the border and find out their weak spots so that "a '*diversio*' could be carried out and this production facility destroyed." When war came, he had to carry out sabotage in the factories and on the farms by "causing accidents and possibly derailing trains." To Viljamaa and Hyrsky, Katvala had then passed on espionage information from his job sites, the last one being Kamensk.

"On 19 December 1937 I caused great damage by freezing the water pipes, so that the power plant did not function for a day."

The final decision on the charges, which resulted in a death sentence is in a class by itself: in a few lines the names of Katvala and the others named in the case are changed many times. First Katvala is "Hugo Arturinpoika" Katvala, then he is "Hugo Tanelinpoika," then "Hugo Artur" (his right name), and finally his last name has been changed to "Hatkavala." Haapajärvi becomes "Hanajärdi." Puhakka is now "Muhanen" and Hyrsky is "Herkin."

Anna Katvala is recorded as saying that her husband told her as early as 1933 that the family had not come to Russia to escape the unemployment in Finland but to spy. The wife had helped her husband to spy and had recruited, among others, Vuorio, who had already returned to Finland.

Anna Katvala was also condemned to death, along with her son Reino, who had joined the spies recruited by his father at the age of eighteen. As a filer on duty at Kamensk in the summer of 1937, he had "deliberately ruined two electric motors by sprinkling sand in the bearings of one, and rubbing the other with a sandy oil rag." In addition, "to weaken the might of the Soviet Union," he had tried to organize insurrectionary groups, and his father had ordered him to burn some of the factory buildings too, but that he reportedly had not dared to do. He said of his parents:

> They totally discredited the leaders of the soviet state and the communist party in every possible way, and they always praised fascist organization as better. They praised Germany as the best possible kind of political organization for ruling a country. . . . Father said that when war with some capitalist country begins, all the border-hoppers are to intensify their espionage work, and if possible are to fight with weapons in hand against the soviet state.

Reino had "influenced" Pentti Kurko, and Reino and Veikko Murto in an "anti-revolutionary way." He had also meant to get into the Red Army with the intention of spying—and so he had slyly requested Soviet citizenship!

Ida Vilkman, who was condemned to death, described planning to set the aluminum factory on fire by gathering up paint, rags, and oil and heaping barrels on top of them. "The result would be the burning of the workshop, then the power plant and the factory." In September 1937 the fire reportedly started by itself, but the workers noticed the smoke and called the fire department.

The Alhonen couple, also condemned to death, left four underage boys. Mrs. Mari Alhonen born in Säkkijärvi, had gone to work as a maid at the age of ten. In Sarov in 1933 she had made the mistake of writing: "I don't want to stay in the Soviet Union. I thought we would have a better life here, but there is a shortage of food and we go around half-hungry all the time. I ask to be sent back to Finland."

A little later her husband, Viktori Alhonen, had said at a hearing: "I don't want to stay in the Soviet Union, it's hard to get by here, there's no food, only lice." He demanded to get back to Finland with his family. From Chelyabinsk, Alhonen wrote a letter to Finland, which was found in his court file:

> If I write the truth, this letter won't get there. I can tell you about this life only when I get there. The children often go hungry for days. We can't get any butter, meat, or coffee bread. All the Finns get money from Finland. The wages are so small that a single man can hardly get by on them. I go to work and have only bread to eat. It makes me sad to look at the children, who are living in misery.
> Chelyabinsk, in the machine tool planning office, May 4
> Viktori Alhonen.
> This letter won't get there either, I wrote too much.

In the 1938 interrogation, Alhonen stated that his mission was to "decrease the number of machines, to burn factories, tear up railroad tracks so the trains would derail." At Svirstroi he had ruined a saw, so that boards could not be had and construction was delayed. "In Magnitogorsk in 1934, I dismantled a railway by loosening the screws, which resulted in the derailment of a freight train." In Chelyabinsk in 1935 with Antti Roiha (he had returned to Finland) Alhonen poured cement steps that were ten centimeters too long. In Kamensk in 1937, "we broke [sixty] large electrical insulators."

The proceedings of the Saari couple's interrogations both contain about 150 pages. Everything from the time the Saaris decided to leave Porvoo is carefully recorded: where they lived and worked, their wages, their work performance, their friends, the names of those they had crossed the border with. . . . The file also includes the informers' reports on the family. In their personal possessions envelope there is only the aforementioned brief handwritten request by Aleksis Saari to return to Finland.

Saari was asked: "Were you a member of the fascist group?" The answer was "No," and underneath it is Saari's signature. The interrogator continued in the same vein. According to him, it was useless to deny it: he mentioned the name of the border-hopper who had informed on Saari, who finally "understood" and admitted that it was "useless to deny it."

"I am a member of such a group." His signature is at the end.

According to his confession, Saari had gone deep-sea fishing and met a Swede-Finn recruiter to whom he was related. Every time they met, Saari had gotten fifty markkas from the man. The group to which Saari belonged had been given the task of blowing up the Kamensk railroad so that the aluminum factory could not get coal. During the "rehabilitation" phase it was ascertained that the man Saari supposedly met with on the Gulf of Finland did not exist. The fact was recorded in Saari's papers later.

In February 1938 a troika condemned Saari to death as a member of a fascist Finnish terrorist organization. His wife got the same sentence.

And so on. "Head polit teacher" Onni Sipinen or Sanin, who had gone to Ural along with the Finns and returned to Leningrad from Kamensk, also took part in the interrogations—on the side of the interrogators. When all the border-hoppers had been dealt with, he was no longer needed. He too wound up in a cell and followed the same course as the others. The old activist Jalmari Kosonen and the loyal interpreter Aleksander Partanen experienced the same fate as the rest of the border-hoppers. Interpreter Pauli Viuhko was transferred, according to Fomkin's report, to Chelyabinsk as an interpreter.

Sipinen was interrogated more thoroughly than the others about the Finnish anti-revolutionary activity, but his file cannot be found in the archives. According to the leadership of the NKVD, another group, "at most twenty to twenty-five exceptional individuals," received the same special treatment, among them Albert Höglund, who had earlier been sentenced for attempting to flee.

It is said that Fomkin tried to enter the Finnish men's cell to ask about something, but was driven away by angry shouts: "This is your fault!"

According to another account, an "honest truck driver" had gripped him by the throat and lifted him against the wall, saying: "You Judas, are you coming here to question us." The guards had rescued Fomkin.

The sentences did vary. For instance, shoemaker Robert Markkanen, "born 1902 in Kahvakkasaari, province of Mikkeli, Finland, Finnish citizen, without citizenship, not a party member, elementary education, crossed the border illegally in 1932" got "only" a five-year sentence—probably because he had been already been imprisoned in February 1937 and sentenced before the others in 1937. The charge was anti-revolutionary activity. In the end, he was to spend ten years in Siberia and die there after his release.

It was the fate of the Kamensk and Nizhni Tagil Finns to be sentenced at the very worst time. The death sentence seems to have been the rule rather than the exception for foreigners arrested in the winter of 1938. Afterwards the sentences for the same offenses gradually became a little lighter—if it is possible to say that about condemnation to a labor camp for ten years.

March 1938 witnessed the last big act of the show trials before the war. After that the "great terror" began to diminish—or to become more selective. Perhaps Stalin had achieved his end, or perhaps it is only that unpredictability is part of the nature of terror. In July Lavrenti Beria became the number two man to the hated Nikolai Jezhov in the leadership of the NKVD, and the power was in Beria's hands even before Jezhov was sidelined. Stalin made Jezhov the scapegoat, and he was blamed for the worst excesses of the terror. He and many of his assistants were condemned and executed.

In the summer of 1938 the security agencies in Karelia reopened the case of Väinö Alatalo, who had lived in Kamensk, and who had been captured at the border on his way to Finland. Given a light sentence, he appealed it. The Kamensk NKVD had informed the court that it had "no compromising information regarding Alatalo." By decision of a special procurator, the case was transferred to the NKVD in December 1937, and on 13 April 1938, a court record appeared, which began thus:

"Being then a prisoner, you concealed the fact that you belonged to a Finnish espionage organization, and it's no use to deny it. Do you admit it?"

"Yes, I concealed the fact that I was a Finnish spy, and now in this interrogation I don't want to hide the truth. I was one of the Finnish spies, and I was recruited in the fall of 1932 when I lived in the village of Pelkosenniemi. When I was working on the roads there, I often met with an agent of the

Finnish secret police Kanerva, the road commissioner, who was also an agent. . . ."

"List the assignments you got from Kanerva."

"First: to gather information about political life in the Soviet Union, about the activities of the party and the soviet state. Second: to report to Kanerva about the political and moral state of mind of the people. Third: the basic task was to gather information about the Soviet Union's largest industrial plants and their production figures. In gathering the information I was to use to my advantage Finns who were antagonistic to the Soviet Union."

According to the proceedings, among these Finns were border-hopper Matti Kilpelä, who worked in a Leningrad factory, and Ville Saaristo, with whom Alatalo had to use the password "Morjens" (Swedish for "good morning") when they met. In military espionage, the men had reportedly "taken advantage of the May Day parade," that is, they had checked the units marching in them.

In one factory they had checked its products and how many trucks it had. They had found out where the Kamensk explosives storehouse was and how it was guarded. Together they had decided that one of them would go to Karelia, where it was easier to send information to Finland. Their activity ceased in 1937, when Kilpelä had skipped back to Finland.

"That is not true, you kept up your activity until the end."

"Our contact man no longer came to us. I've told the truth about everything."

"Were you paid for the information?"

"I got 300 Finnish markkas and a thousand rubles."

"Where is Saaristo now?"

"In 1937 he was still in Kamensk working as a plasterer in the aluminum plant."

The NKVD had succeeded in extorting its confession. Alatalo admitted that the record of the proceedings was correctly drawn up, and declared that he had nothing more to add. A "special triad" condemned him to death and he was executed 28 September 1938. Later a search was instituted for Kanerva, Kilpelä, and Saaristo, along with the others whose names Alatalo had mentioned. Saaristo had actually already been imprisoned in the spring of 1937.

While Alatalo was being grilled, the border guard turned over a much larger haul to the NKVD: six young Finnish men who had made it almost to the Finnish border on skis.

In the group were Sylvi Ollikainen's eighteen-year-old brother Veikko, who apparently with an escape attempt on his mind, had left Kamensk with Kauko Reinikainen in 1936 to go and study in Karelia. Kauko had chickened out and soon gone back to Kamensk. When Finnish-language teaching was done away with, Veikko had to go to work. In 1937 he wrote from the Patojärvi logging site in Karelia that he would gladly come back to Kamensk but did not have money for a ticket to travel.

"Even if we have to go without eating, we'll send the money to Veikko," said Father Ollikainen in Kamensk. The money was never sent: Albin Ollikainen was arrested 2 January 1938.

With Veikko Ollikainen on the escape attempt were Vilho Hasala, Uuno Komsula, Eino Piispanen, Viktor Seppänen, and Toivo Terho. Viktor had a sore leg, so they were yet not able to leave during the summer of 1937. The attempt was made in the winter, when ski tracks obviously exposed the fugitives to discovery.

Two border guards arrested the boys at 23:00 hours 23 February 1938 when they were spending the night at a hut in the border zone near Veskelys. The men called for help and the young fugitives were brought to light.

Confessions were obtained in short order. The interrogators decided that Ollikainen was "an agent of Finland's secret police" who had crossed the border illegally in 1932 and whose mission it was to gather information about industrial plants in Kamensk, Magnitogorsk, Chelyabinsk, and Petroskoi. He had been recruited by Veikko Nieminen, who, according to information recorded at the interrogation, had been arrested while trying to flee across the border. Now Ollikainen had tried to take this information to Finland's secret police by crossing the border illegally. Ollikainen confessed.

A little later in the interrogation record, it states that Ollikainen had already been in regular contact with agents in 1935. He was then fifteen years old.

Hasala, Komsula, Ollikainen, Piispanen, Seppänen, and Terho were sentenced 11 April 1938 to death by shooting. They were all executed six days later.

Finnish officials could only guess at what was happening in Ural. Something was already known by January 1938. Esko Riekki wrote "respectfully" to the foreign ministry that

At the end of last year, numerous arrests were made among the so-called Finnish border-hoppers living in the city of Nizhni Tagil and elsewhere in the Ural area. According to information received by relatives living in Finland, all the men are said to have been arrested, and even those women who do not have children to care for. There is no information regarding the cause of the arrests, but it is apparent that they are related to the recent persecutory actions taken against foreigners in general. Those arrested are said to assume that if they are not condemned of being spies and saboteurs on the usual false and totally groundless charges, they ought to be deported to their homeland. On the basis of tips from various sources we may expect that the return of our citizens from Russia may take on the nature of a mass movement and that among the deported many spies sent by the NKVD will get into the country.

As the Finnish border-hoppers were already progressing toward their inevitable fate, VALPO let mercy serve as justice and would have admitted many border-hoppers whose return they had previously opposed. The foreign ministry, which was now bombarded with petitions for help, asked VALPO for a new statement, given the altered circumstances.

However, VALPO did not change its mind with regard to the Hämäläinens. The names of this pair, who had three children in their care, and who were waiting in the Chelyabinsk jail, appeared at the end of a VALPO letter dated 3 March 1938:

To return to the Ministry's written communication No. P-71 dated February 24 with enclosed minutes, touching the return to Finland of (18 names-JR) who went secretly and illegally to the Soviet Union, the state's police respectfully states that for its part it does not wish to oppose the return of any except Juho and Anna Hämäläinen.

Some individuals received skimpy news, chance letters from relatives in Ural, and from these VALPO seems to have gotten the first information about what was happening. Ellen Närvänen, the return of whose family the foreign ministry saw "no need to hasten" in 1934, wrote on 17 March 1938:

I did not dare talk about how things are in the last letter, but keeping quiet probably won't make them better. Life is just awful for us right now. Hiski has been in prison for two months, now he's been sent away and been sentenced like all the foreigners, women too who don't have small children. I was allowed to take [two] packages to him, but when I went the third time he wasn't there any more. I don't know what good this all does. . . . We don't know yet if they'll let us be with our husbands.

She had received only one note from her husband on which there were greetings to his relatives. Ellen Närvänen also wrote that she had heard that the men had been given sentences of ten or seven years—"and that's a lot." She asked her relatives to "get busy" arranging for her return and that of her daughter to Finland. Letters went so poorly now "that you can't find out anything about anything," and she complained that at times she was "all mixed up."

In the foreign ministry archives there is an undated, handwritten slip of paper pertaining to the Wahlstén family:

According to private sources, Viljo Wahlstén and wife arrested January 1938, children probably in some children's home near former residence. Mrs. Lydia Wahlstén, the grandmother, would like to have the children with her. Lydia Wahlstén, Sec. 5 Line 1. b. 82

On 12 April the ministry assigned the Moscow embassy the task of finding out, if possible, where the Wahlsténs and their daughters Eila and Irma were.

Juho Hämäläinen left four young daughters. Valpo opposed his return to Finland until the end.

Chapter Twelve

Amen!

T HE PARENTS DID NOT RETURN TO KAMENSK, nor did they ever send any indication that they were still alive. Their execution was carried out swiftly, and the children were told nothing about it; they were informed that their mothers and fathers had been sent, along with their possessions, to "far-off camps for twenty-five years without correspondence privileges." All were given the same explanation. Although in rare cases political prisoners in the camps were denied the right to correspond, no one is ever known to have met a prisoner with such a sentence in Soviet camps in the 1930s; thus the term actually meant execution.

There was no trial procedure for any of the prisoners. It is apparent that all of the Finnish men and women from Kamensk who were sentenced were shot in large groups during March 1938, about a month after the mass sentencing.

In many of the families, the men were shot first. For example, according to official records, there was a three-day interval between the execution of Aleksis Saari, 10 March 21:00 hours, and Gerda Saari, 13 March 15:00 hours.

In the same order and on the same days, Juho Hämäläinen and his more than fifty-year-old wife, Anna, the parents of three surviving children, came to their journey's end. About a week prior to their execution the Finnish VALPO announced that it still opposed the return of the two Hämäläinens.

206 / No Home for Us Here

In exactly the same order and on the same day and at the same hour Viljo and Kirsti Wahlstén also died. And many others. Decades later, in the Wahlsténs' case file at the KGB, there was found the family picture that the wife was able to hand to her husband on the train after he was arrested.

Carpenter Kalle Vartiainen from Savonlinna is seen to have applied to the foreign ministry for admission to Finland as late as 13 January 1938. VALPO opposed his return in 1938 just as EK had done in 1935. Vartiainen died on 13 March.

Hiskias Närvänen, who had been arrested in Chelyabinsk, was also executed on 13 March. His brother Fabian, who had separated from the group and wound up in Karelia, was shot a little later. Fabian's wife disappeared without a trace.

The timing of the Paldans' execution was such that as one was dying in Chelyabinsk, his brother Väinö was coming to the end of the road in Kazan.

Vilhelmiina Murto, a fifty-three-year-old Finnish "spy" who had never learned a word of Russian, went to the grave with her two sons. The records tell us that all three—mother, Ilmari, and Urho—were executed 13 March 1938. A merciful illness had killed their father four months earlier. Both the Sinkkonens, Aleksander and Ida, were shot on 13 March. And so on.

Now it was not only the group of Finns who had been transported to Kamensk who were being shot. On the same day, 13 March, Jooseppi Mutta was killed. Years earlier he had signed a letter to Otto Ville Kuusinen from the Chelyabinsk Finns asking for help.

Those sentenced by the Moscow "dyad" on 11 February were shot on 10 March; those sentenced on 13 February were shot on 13 March. So simple was the logic of the process and so insane.

From the information on the executions obtained to date, we can calculate that at least 161 Finns were executed in Chelyabinsk on that one night alone—13 March. At least ninety-one were executed three days earlier, 10 March; together it makes 252 or perhaps a third of all the Finnish Ural border-hoppers who were executed.* The others who had been sentenced were executed at the end of March.

Apparently many more were executed on those two nights, for we have

---

*Although our statistics are only indicative, it is perhaps appropriate to mention here the figures for those Finnish border-hoppers who had been in Ural and whose trails we have been able to follow to the end. We found altogether 1,989 names about which we can be sure, and of those we know that at least 628 died, mainly by execution, but also by murder, from illness, hunger, cold, and suicide either in the 1930s or in prison camps in the early 1940s. On the other hand we calculate that according to our figures forty-seven percent (346 of 739) of the Kamensk Finns died, and forty-nine percent (100 of 203) of the Nizhni Tagil Finns, and we estimate that

House painter Ilmari Murto was executed along with his mother Vilhelmiina.

received no information on many of the prisoners about whom we have inquired, and we don't even know the names of many of them.

The figure of "over 200" Finns arrested in Kamensk 2 January 1938 mentioned by the NKVD men seems to be a very elastic one, since those executed on these two nights alone already comes to 250.

The number executed on March 13 may be considered large even in terms of the entire Soviet Union. Robert Conquest writes that the execution of at most ten percent of the prisoners was normal and that in Moscow's particularly ill-reputed Lefortovo, seventy prisoners were shot daily in 1937; he estimates that the number there probably rose during the following winter. Kaarlo Hartikainen, who had earlier been in Shpalernaja, claims to have seen as many as ninety people, men along with a few women, taken to be

in both places more than half surely died. Therefore, it is not presumptuous to estimate that at least half, or 865 people perished in the manner described. Nor does that seem impossible for the further reason that the NKVD statistics mention 772 Finns liquidated in Ural. VALPO also estimated that about half of the border-hoppers died. Up to this time we have found personal data on a total of 7,785 Finns, Ingrian Finns, and American Finns arrested and sentenced in the Soviet Union. Of them, 5,193 were shot and 635 died in labor armies.

Brothers Otto and Väinö Paldan were executed, as was Otto's wife, Tyyne. This is the funeral of their daughter Else, who died in Kamensk in 1937. Another daughter had died earlier. Rauni Murto leans against the wall in the background.

executed in one night.

A still larger number is mentioned in connection with Karelia. In the Sandarmo woods near Karhumäki a mass grave was discovered in 1997, where thousands of Finns rest along with others. According to papers in the NKVD archives, up to 400 people were executed there in one night. (Karjalan Sanomat 29.10.97)

We have seen earlier that orders were given for the execution of 300 of the prisoners taken in Karelia in 1937, and that in Nizhni Tagil nearly half of the prisoners were shot. It has also been estimated that of those Finns who were charged in Karelia perhaps seventy percent were shot. And finally let us recall that, according to one witness, in the Ural foreign national operation at the beginning of 1938, on the average only one prisoner was freed out of every one hundred arrested. When the Jekaterinburg memorial was erected in 1996, the local paper reported that 200 people were executed there every night in January 1938.

In his book Aleksandr Solzhenitsyn expressed horror that "in December

Shortly before the end: Yrjö and Onni Nissilä, 1936.

1932, in the Leningrad Kresty prison alone, AT ONE AND THE SAME TIME 265 PEOPLE CONDEMNED TO DEATH were awaiting their fate." If he had been familiar with the figures for the Chelyabinsk prison in February and March of 1938, he would have found as many or perhaps more people awaiting execution at the same time—and they were all Finns. Solzhenitsyn also says that in February-March 1938, a "secret order was circulated throughout the whole NKVD that the number of prisoners was to be reduced." There was a shortage of cells, clothing, and food. The reduction was not accomplished by freeing prisoners . . .

That March 13 can be considered the fateful day for the Soviet Finns. The first and only hearing for Kustaa Rovio, the party leader in Soviet Karelia, was held on that day. He confessed to all the charges, was dismissed from his post, and was condemned to death.

Let it be mentioned that on that same day the Germans marched into Austria, and Hitler proclaimed the Anschluss, uniting Austria to Germany. The world's attention was also fixed on Moscow, where Stalin's showplace trials were being held with great fanfare. On the same night that the group of Finns was being slaughtered in Chelyabinsk, Nikolai Buharin, soon to be dead himself, was writing a plea for mercy in his cell in Moscow.

According to Tauno Flinkman, the wave of executions began in the Uhta prison camp in Komi at the same time as in Chelyabinsk—in March 1938. The NKVD men came into the tents that morning and read in alphabetical order the names of men to be shot, thirty at a time. Waiting shattered the nerves of the prisoners; one committed suicide, another went out of his mind. The executions ended in May when forty-one men were left out of 262.

Tradition has it that the shooting of the Kamensk Finns occurred in a smallish, half-underground room in the Chelyabinsk jail. Two guards escorted the prisoner into one chamber where an NKVD worker asked him his first name, last name, date of birth, and the section of the law under which he had been sentenced. In the next room a bullet was fired into the back of his head—the expression was that he was given "nine grams"—and the bodies were stacked up in the next room.

It seems impossible that up to 200 people could have been executed one after another in the one room. The bodies would have had to be carried out of the room, taken somewhere, and buried. Besides the executioners would have been unable to breathe in the room.

It is probable—and the Chelyabinsk Memorial assumes that it is so— that the condemned were taken by truck somewhere outside the city and executed directly into a mass grave by shooting them in the neck or temple

On political prisoners' day in the autumn of 1995, people from Chelyabinsk stood in line to see the room where Finns, along with others, are said to have been shot.

with a pistol. The burial places cannot be ascertained from official records of the executions nor from death certificates, but in the mass grave at Zolotaja Gora in Chelyabinsk, fur jackets, felt boots with rubbers, suitcases and even money have been found. Since the jails were full and the execution quotas had to be met, the people were taken along with their goods as if in a normal "group movement," but in this case, to the edge of a mass grave.

KGB archival information on the executions is scanty and dryly businesslike, as are the following:

Chelyabinsk Area
Procurator's Office

Vilppula Tauno Otonpoika, born 1905, by decision of the USSR NKVD special commission and the USSR procurator 13th February 1938 for anti-revolutionary activity according to RSFSR criminal law section 58-6-9-11 sentenced to the maximum penalty—to be shot.
Decision put into effect 13 March 1938
SNTL NKVD decision 13 February 1938 (register no. 37)

Wahlstén Kirsti Tuomaantytär's shooting put into effect 13 March 1938 15:00 hours.

NKVD Chelyabinsk area District 8. chief, 1st Lieutenant, national security . . .

Ebba Murto was pregnant when she was sentenced to ten years in a camp. She lost her husband, her child, as well as her father-in-law and mother-in-law.

One Finnish woman was finally saved by accident, shortly before the mass executions. She was Ebba Murto, who was in her fifth month of pregnancy. The condemned Finnish women were ordered to strip and run across the prison yard to the sauna with their clothing under their arms. Ebba saw her own husband's clothing in a heap of clothing there. When she was naked, the guards noticed that she was pregnant. She wound up in the group of girls awaiting sentencing to camps.

In March 1938 the Finnish girls were separated from their parents and moved to their own cells. After a few days, they could hear their parents being called out for "shipment." On March 19 Salli Lappalainen turned 19 in her cell, and less than a week later the name "Lappalainen" was shouted out in the corridor.

Salli prepared to leave, but they were looking for her mother, Anna Lappalainen. Shaken, Mrs. Lappalainen did not want to go anywhere by herself. She constantly blamed herself for having brought her child to the Soviet

Union. The guards led her away, talking to her soothingly, but she began to hammer at Salli's cell door, screaming, "Let the girl out, I won't go without her!"

That same day a Finnish woman was brought to the cell. She wept as she told of an oldish woman who did nothing but repeat the words: "Let the girl out, let the girl out." A doctor had even been called. Salli's mother had gone out of her mind with grief. According to the execution information, she died on 23 March.

The girls' cell window looked out on the yard, and always around midnight they could hear shouted commands and the sound of trucks starting up from outside. The trucks were not gone long. Forebodings of evil filled their minds.

At the very end of March the girls' turn came. One after another all eight were taken for sentencing: Margit Alenius (whose new, already deceased father's name was Vilkman), Siiri Hämäläinen, Tyyne Hämäläinen, Salli Lappalainen, Sylvi Ollikainen, Irja Pekala, Elma Ronkainen, and Hilkka Sinkkonen. In addition, three pregnant women were now sentenced—Aili Eloranta, Maija Melanen, and Ebba Murto. Melanen already had two children taken to a children's nursery.

Anna Lappalainen, her daughters Salli and Sanni, and her son-in-law Reino Orell in Kamensk in the summer of 1939. According to eyewitnesses, Mrs. Lappalainen went insane in prison before her execution.

All were read a brief judgment which followed the same form: "Arrested by the Chelyabinsk area NKVD District 3 command . . . by decision of the USSR NKVD special commission 13th February 1938 for anti-revolutionary activity according to Section 58-6, 10, 11 (or 6, 9, 11) sentenced to ten years in a forced labor camp . . ." The reason was that they had not informed on their parents to the officials.

"What did you get?" the curious asked when the first girl returned.

"Ten years," she answered.

"Don't lie!"

The girl told the others to go and see for themselves. The next girl to be sentenced told the doubters that she too had gotten ten years. When Salli Lappalainen heard her sentence, she laughed. "Is that all?" They explained to her that a person so young could not be sentenced to more than ten years. As the girls returned from the sentencing, they danced in the corridor: they would get to live, they would get out of the packed prison to a camp—and they could be together! One of the trustees escorting them, a man, said to them: "Girls, I got three years and I wept. Many men's nerves were shot. You got ten years and you dance!"

When the girls were ordered to be ready for shipment "with their gear" they were allowed to get their suitcases from the storeroom. Then they noticed heaps of the Finns' possessions that looked familiar, Salli Lappalainen's and Sylvi Ollikainen's father's and mother's clothing for example. That worried them, and they wondered how their parents could have left without their things. Some guessed optimistically that they had gone to Sakhalin Island.

First the girls were stuffed into a smaller prison in Chelyabinsk. The building dated from Czarist times, and the walls were full of writing. When the girls were taken to the sauna by way of the quarantine cell, they saw that someone had written in Finnish on the corridor wall in letters a half-meter high: "Where does this road lead? It leads to hell!"

Everywhere the girls went, they attracted a lot of attention. As the armed guards with dogs marched them from the jail to the station and from the station to trucks, people on the streets scolded them for treating young girls in that way. The troubled guards always tried to hide the girls among other prisoners.

The girls traveled a roundabout route to Karaganda by way of Omsk—Petropavlovsk was not able to take them in because the jails were full. For the long journey they were given herring and a piece of bread to eat. Asking for water to drink was futile, not to speak of water to wash in. The jail at

Omsk, which became their home for a month, was old, crowded, foul, and smelled of fish. It was full of political prisoners.

The girls were taken to a sauna which had icicles hanging from its roof. The cement floor was frozen. An imprisoned criminal with a large razor came in and told them he was going to shave all their hair off. The girls resisted, and after a couple of hours they were given a dull knife with which they nearly plucked each other's hair out.

Their outdoor excursions were tightly controlled. While other prisoners were marched in from the yard, the girls had to stand in the corridor with their hands behind their backs and their faces to the wall. Hilkka Sinkkonen declared that she would not go out like this and they all stayed in their cells from then on. Hilkka "celebrated" her nineteenth birthday, 6 April 1938 in a cell.

One day the girls were called out of their cells and gotten ready for a trip. For some reason only Sylvi Ollikainen was to be left alone in the jail. The guard had to tear the weeping girls, Salli and Sylvi, apart from each other. At the Petropavlovsk prison in Kazakhstan the two were reunited.

Here too they met a group of Ingrian boys who, having already served their sentences, were on their way back from the Karaganda camp. The boys told them that the time would come when they would fight over who would get to sleep on the lower bunk because "no one would be able to climb into the upper."

Time cast no light on relatives' guesses as to what had happened to those who had disappeared. VALPO stated in 1941 that women wrote in letters from Ural that they "were utterly in the dark about the fate of their husbands, brothers, and sons who had been arrested years ago and did not even know if they were still alive."

Even ten years later, in 1948, when Hilda Takalo sent a request for help to Finnish officials from Kamensk, she wrote: "I know nothing about my husband, who was arrested by the NGVT [sic] in 1938 February 2." In Finland, Vilhelm Viman's widow asked for clarification in 1939 about whether her husband was alive or not—she would get 100 markkas for her child if he were dead.

In mid-June 1938, returned migrant Veli Hyrsky, the eternal fighter, sent a stern "request" from Helsinki to the "Union of Soviet Republics' Control Committee." He conjectured that some bureaucrats had broken the law of the Soviet Union since Finnish border-hoppers had been treated with "gross injustice."

Hyrsky wrote that if the Sarov camp was meant to teach a lesson to the border-hoppers, it did not have any progressive effect on them, for the men directing it were anti-soviet. He particularly criticized the camp director and the OGPU agent Fomkin, under whom he had worked at logging.

"The work leaders and camp staff were all former kulaks." Hyrsky also mentioned deaths from starvation. He was suspicious about later shipments to Ural as well, and had more to say about Fomkin, who was "starting to imprison Finns in a persecutory way."

> Now of the 1,000 Finns I know there, [thirty percent] are dead and [sixty-nine percent] in prison and the other [one percent] waiting for when they will be purged. They are not allowed to work, so that they cannot earn a living, and if they complain about their sentences, they are immediately jailed as provocateurs.

Hyrsky offered to get testimony from Finnish labor and trade unions that the prisoners were known as honest workers. He wound up with a threat: he hoped that the commission would investigate the matter so that he would not need to tell in Finland about the fate of the refugees in the Soviet Union.

In Kamensk that July, seventeen-year-old Pentti Kosonen, who had only a short grace period left, opened a letter to Erkki Kuusinen, which had come from Turku. To the sender of the letter, Elsa Kuusinen, who was a stranger to him, the young man wrote an official-sounding, but clear and straightforward answer:

> I am informing you herewith that the letter you wrote to a person named Erkki Kuusinen has arrived and was opened by the undersigned because the aforementioned person is no longer to be found in Kamensk.
>
> I was in the same work brigade with Kuusinen and consider it my duty to inform you of his fate. Kuusinen Erkki was arrested [December 26, 1937], and Mirjam along with all the other Finns [January 2, 1938], after which there has been no further knowledge of the fate of the Finns. That is to say, everywhere in Russia all outsiders who crossed the border without permission have been arrested, for what reason no one knows. Everyone from [eighteen] years on up has been arrested, only those under age and women with small children were left, the undersigned belongs to the former group.
>
> If Erkki writes to you, I beg you to inform me at his former address in Kamensk.
>
> Respectfully Pentti Kosonen.

Erkki Kuusinen never did write. He had been executed four months earlier.

Border-hopper Sointu Lindroos, twenty-eight, who had separated from her husband on the long trip, wrote to Finland from Nizhni Tagil at the end of July, telling about herself and her boy friend, Eino Karjalainen.

> . . . can you do anything about my case from there. I'll write to Moscow again and try to ask if I can get some help from there. We can learn nothing about those who were arrested at the same time as Eino. About 800 Finns were arrested in Kamensk, about [sixty] from here. And many more from other places. And where were they all taken?

From interrogations of those who came back, VALPO got separate bits of information about the tragedy. In the first review of the situation in 1938, VALPO reported that "there was further information about the arrest of Finns in Russia." Life there was "dismal and hopeless."

The Terijoki branch reported in early 1939 that only a handful of Finns were any longer getting back from the Soviet Union by the official route, and even they with great difficulty. "The number of Finns who are free had decreased steadily because of the many mass arrests which took place last year." Those who returned via Terijoki told of what occurred in a Moscow prison:

> In early 1939 a Swedish engineer who had been a prisoner in Chelyabinsk came into the cell. He said that all the Finns had wound up in prison or in concentration camps, but he didn't say when.

At the beginning of July 1938, Väinö Voionmaa, acting foreign minister, wrote to the Moscow embassy on "the possibility of return for those who had gone secretly to the Soviet Union." He noted that from the autumn of 1937 on, fewer and fewer border-hoppers had been granted Soviet citizenship. At the same time, the extension of residence permits had been made more difficult—"from early winter on, they were often renewed for only two months"—and people were told that it was the last renewal.

> It is evident that a larger number than before of Finnish border-hoppers are gradually becoming a part of the group which only has the right to live in a place of exile assigned them by the GPU under some kind of camp certificate. Most of them already belong to that group.

In that regard, and given the fact that the above phenomenon indicates the deliberate rejection of all foreigners living there as the prevailing mode, the ministry asks the embassy to present its view about how and if it is possible to make a successful proposal to officials of the Soviet Union—taking advantage of the Soviet Union's apparent desire to rid itself of foreigners, but without making this fact explicit in the proposal—for the return to Finland of Finnish border-hoppers who have kept their citizenship.

In his reply, Minister A.S. Yrjö-Koskinen stated: "The Soviet Union's internal officials have lately begun to harass the Finnish so-called border-hoppers more and more, most recently for political reasons." Nevertheless, very few deportation orders have been issued, which according to the embassy, many are hoping to get. In addition, "repeated proposals from the embassy to the foreign commissariat" have not produced results.

Yrjö-Koskinen emphasized that foreigners were being harassed more and more and that the Soviet Union wished to get rid of them. He wondered however whether a "démarche" in the case of the border-hoppers' return was appropriate at this point. The ambassador called to mind Litvinov's reply to Holsti in 1937.

In addition, the prevailing notion in this embassy of late is that in many cases proposals to the foreign commissariat in such matters, where decisions are in practice left to the internal affairs commissariat, in this instance to the GPU, only decrease the chance of a favorable outcome. At present that office suspects all proposals from foreign representatives and searches for any possible ulterior motives concealed in them.

In Yrjö-Koskinen's opinion it was better to refrain from new initiatives in the border-hoppers' cases and wait for "soviet officials to take the initiative in deporting them."

In less than four months the Finnish diplomat reported that the border-hoppers' position had taken an appreciable turn for the worse during the current year—of how bad a turn he does not seem to have been fully aware.

Of late it seems that in practical terms all of the adult male border-hoppers, at least all those who have expressed a wish to return to Finland, have been arrested and deported to camps. All contact with them has been cut off, and the embassy now gets letters only from women and children. In many cases, children have been separated from their mothers and placed in children's homes.

Finnish children taken from Nizhni Tagil along with others in a day nursery. Among others in the picture are Raili Närvänen and Tamara Orell (left of teacher), also Rauno Karjalainen and Leo Moilanen.

The embassy had not received a single answer of any kind to proposals regarding border-hoppers during 1938. The only answers to inquiries about those who had disappeared were either the information that the person in question had died or that no information about his fate or whereabouts had been ascertained. Foreign passports sent to the border-hoppers generally seem to have remained in the militia offices awaiting a visa "for an indefinite period."

"The only result of proposals made to benefit children separated from their mothers is that contact between the embassy and the children and mothers has frequently been cut off."

The envoy assumed that the Soviet Union now viewed the border-hoppers as people without a country and at least in practice did not acknowledge that the embassy was a legitimate agency to deal with their cases. The officials did not give the border-hoppers residence permits, nor did they enter anything on the passes issued by the embassy. Residence permits were recorded only on the so-called border-hoppers' passports issued by the officials, which gave no indication of nationality, merely the designation, "*perbezhtshik*," border-hopper.

> *Things being so, it may be considered that the system for the return of the border-hoppers, which was put into effect with the soviet government in 1933, and which functioned badly the entire time, has of late become completely meaningless.*

At the end of the report, someone in the foreign ministry had written with a pen: Amen!

Chapter Thirteen

The Children of Kamensk

TOWARD THE END OF THE SUMMER OF 1938, an extraordinary cry for help arrived in Kemi for the grandmother of sixteen-year-old Elsa Tervonen. The old woman had long waited in vain for news from the Soviet Union. The card which came in the mail was completely covered with tiny handwriting.

> *Kamensk [July 15, 1938]. I'm writing this card too if the letter doesn't come. How are you, we are pretty good, we are well. Annikki and I were left in Kamensk by ourselves. Mother, Father, and Helvi and Antti were taken away. Father and Mother are in jail and Helvi and Antti are in a children's home. Helvi wrote, but we don't know anything about Father and Mother. Annikki and I are working to learn the painters' trade but the pay is so small. On the 13th a letter came from Irja Pekala to her sister, there are many young girls there, they all got a ten-year sentence to Karaganda. Father and Mother must have got a ten-year sentence, I don't know if we'll ever see Father and Mother, it's so awfully lonesome. Annikki and I have no winter clothes at all, nothing with long sleeves, we're sure to freeze in the winter. Old mother, I ask if you could send us even a little bit of old clothes if only you can then send each of us a dress, stockings, but preferably wool, shoes size [thirty-five] and woolen coats or blouses. This is asking a lot. I'll close now. Greetings . . . Elsa and Annikki*

221

In the summer of 1938, Lea Saari sent a postcard in the same vein to the Porvoo steam sawmill, apparently the only address in Finland that she could remember, telling her aunt that she had lived alone in Kamensk for a half-year.

First she asked politely about how her relatives were doing and then she said that she was working as a "'*motoriska,*' but one earns so little at it that there isn't enough for bread." She asked them to send old clothes, shoes, and woolen underwear. "And if you know Aunt Fanni's address, then send it to me so that I can ask for a coat from there." Lea knew nothing of her mother and father.

Immediately afterward, just to be sure, Lea wrote another letter in which she said the same things. She also wrote about her sisters:

> *Ester and Rakel are in a children's home I got a letter from them yesterday, and Rakel writes that they are so lonely there but they do have good clothes. Etel had been in the hospital and Rakel's eyes are sore and Rakel asks me to get them out of there . . .*

In September Lea wrote to her aunt again and said that she had gotten no mail from Finland. There was a shortage of envelopes and paper in Kamensk. Lea again asked about her relatives' health and went on:

> *Times have gotten very hard for us here. The summer has been very nice, but I can't get out of the camp since I have no clothes; no matter how much I want to go somewhere, I don't because I have nothing to put on. I don't know anything about Mother and Father, they were arrested [eight] months ago already, and Rakel and Etel are in a children's home many thousands of kilometers away, and I don't even see them so I've been left all alone. I go to work but when the cold weather comes I won't be warm enough to go to work . . .*

She asked that they send her old clothes "no matter how poor and old rags they are," and size thirty-nine shoes. "I'm in such an awful jam that I can't help begging . . ."

> *Mother really cried when they took me and brought me back to the barracks, and everyone else got left on the train. Four of us girls live in the same room and everyone gets clothes from Finland . . .*

Lea Elisabet Saari died in Kamensk the following winter when she had just turned seventeen. It is said that before her death she made clothing for herself by cutting holes in a flour sack for her arms and head. For food she had frozen potatoes. In her old age, her aunt would often sit with these letters in her hand, wondering what had finally happened to the Saari family.

Dozens of other Finns were either left in Kamensk or returned there from elsewhere. They were crowded into Barrack Number 9—later they "spread out" into Barrack Number 8. They tried to stay warm in the midwinter cold. They were not allowed to work in the factory. The children begged for bread, and, avoiding the armed watchmen, they went to pick the coal that had fallen off rail cars along the railroad tracks, which they burned in the stoves.

Besides Veikko Katvala, the Murto brothers, Lea Saari, and the Tervonen sisters, there also lived in the barracks thirty women with their children.*

In addition there were at least the Luoto boys, Kauko and Ensio, and the Markkanen and Ollikainen children, Eeva and Oiva and Alfa and Tyyne.

Hilja Jelonen was totally immobile, since her legs were paralyzed. She dragged herself around by her hands, and lived for years by telling fortunes to the Russians, who were highly intrigued by her prophecies. The Finnish girls who served as interpreters were given a pittance as pay.

The Luoto boys went out to steal food and got into a Volkovo store through the roof. They were caught and wound up in prison. Hanna Mäntylä tried to flee to Finland. She too was caught and sent to prison. Her daughter was taken to a children's home, and the mother never saw her again. Oiva Ollikainen disappeared without a trace.

In January 1938, three days after the mass arrest, eleven-year old Eeva Markkanen arrived in Kamensk on foot. Her father had been taken earlier. When she knocked at their door, a completely strange woman came to open it. Her mother had been taken "somewhere"; at the station she had missed her child terribly. Now the other women were wondering and waiting impatiently to be sent for too. Laina Stenman, who already had a three-year-old boy, took Eeva into her care. Eeva's little brother, nine-year-old Keijo had been taken to the children's home and was never heard from again.

---

*They were Hilda Arvola, Elli Eskolin, Iida Hakala, Saimi Heikkilä, Selma Helistö, Hilja Huttunen, Hilja Jelonen (two daughters), Kerttu Järvinen, Saimi Keronen, Elvi Koskinen, Hilda Kourunen, Lempi Laurila, Esteri Lepokorpi, Kerttu Moilanen, Hanna Mäntylä, Alma Niemelä, Eeva Niilonen, Ester Nikkari, Ellen Närvänen, Sanni Orell, Ester Pihlajaniemi, Tyyne Pynnönen, Tyyne Rosendahl, Eevi Räty (two children), Eeva Saarelainen, Betty Saariniemi, Selma Salonen, Laina Stenman, Hellä Viuhko (and her husband), and Lyyli Åikäs.

Hanna Mäntylä and Onni Kauppi's mother, Elli, who had been an actress in America. Hanna tried to flee from Kamensk to Finland, was imprisoned and lost her daughter.

Another young returnee was ten-year-old Sirkka Laurila, who arrived with her mother and the Moilanens. They had not heard of the mass arrest and had hoped that their life would be more peaceful here than in the Sverdlovsk area where they had been. Sirkka's father had been arrested at the end of the year at the Asbest logging site. He was not seen again. Immediately afterward, men came to fetch Sirkka to the children's nursery, but by their determined efforts, mother and daughter managed to put off the action and to move to Kamensk. Once the militia had even tried to bribe Sirkka with a collection of pretty Ural stones if she would let go of her mother.

On the way to Kamensk, Lempi Laurila, and Kerttu Moilanen had stopped to wait in line at the visitors' reception booth at the Sverdlovsk prison. They found their husbands' names in a thick register, but a guard said, "You can't see them, give us the bread if you have some." They had neither bread nor money. After this, Eino Laurila and Tauno Moilanen were never heard from again.

Gradually men who had earlier been given sentences for fighting or trying to escape and had now been freed returned to the barracks village. Among them were Uuno Saarenoja and Matti Suokas and Veikko Huotari. The latter had been tortured during his interrogation. The Kamensk children were admitted to Russian schools. The first one allowed to work in the factory was Tyyne Pynnönen, who had a Soviet passport. Gradually the men got to work until, with the outbreak of "Finland's War" (the Winter War), they were again driven out of the factory and sent to work elsewhere.

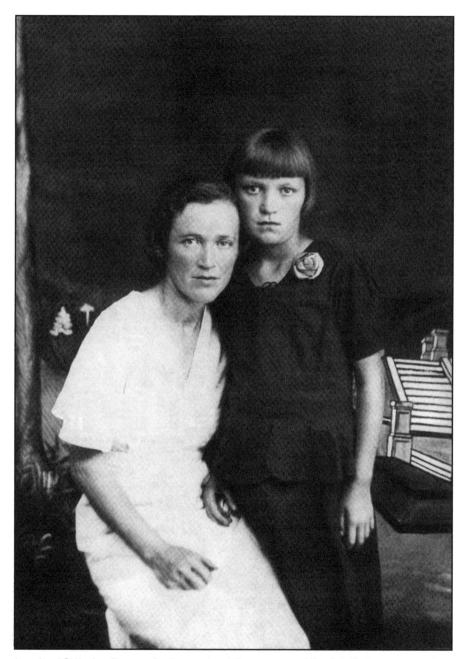

Lempi and Sirkka Laurila soon after the arrest and disappearance of Eino Laurilla.

Eino Laurila was executed a little earlier than the others, in early March 1938. His family received no information about it.

In August 1938 Onni Kauppi moved from Chelyabinsk to Kamensk with his mother and went to work there. Kauppi's father had earlier worked to build an automobile plant in Nizhni Novgorod along with 200 other American Finns (Cement commune). The previous fall the father and son had been fired from their jobs in a tractor factory even though there was a crying shortage of labor. In January 1938 the father was arrested and the family evicted from its lodging. Life in Chelyabinsk became difficult for foreigners. In Kamensk, Onni's nationality was listed as "American" on his passport. That probably saved his life.

Kauppi reports that on his arrival in Kamensk, there was still a group of Finnish mothers, probably ten to fifteen women, still living there. On their identification papers, the Finns had "*Vid na zhiteltsvo dlja lits bez grazhdanstva*" or "residence permit for individuals without nationality." The women had been taken time and again to NKVD interrogations at which Fomkin had been present. One can only guess how he interpreted what they said, for the women did not know Russian. The same interrogation carousel continued after Kauppi moved into the barrack.

The women interrogated disappeared on November 1 and wound up in prison camps. Most were given ten years, some eight. The children of these mothers were also taken to children's homes.

Kauppi was there to see as the women were take away. Selma Salonen railed at the NKVD man, who was arresting her twenty-year-old daughter Meeri, Yrjö Nissilä's wife, who had a small child. A laughing Fomkin translated what the woman was saying for the man. Selma Salonen was not taken away, however, although her records say she was tried in 1938-1939. She too had a small child.

Her daughter Meeri got "only" a five-year sentence, but even that was too much, for the place of punishment was the northern Vorkuta camp, which had a dismal reputation because of its high death rate. Meeri died in Vorkuta. Her boy, who had been born in Kamensk, perished before her.

One Finnish woman, who had gotten to work in the camp kitchen, returned later from Vorkuta. She reported that it was hopeless to wait for others to return. The prisoners had not been transported to the camp by truck or train but were forced to go on foot through the snow. Anyone who fell exhausted along the way was shot and left lying beside the trail.

Alfa Pekala was not jailed until the last day of December, but the records show that Fomkin had already written the order for her to be charged in April 1938. The order declared that Alfa was an agent of the Finnish espionage organization and carried out assigned tasks of anti-revolutionary and espionage activities. She too wound up in Vorkuta.

Otto Ville Kuusinen's wife, Aino, happened to run into the women on the way to the Vorkuta camp. Aino Kuusinen had been arrested in Moscow on the first day of 1938, and after long, drawn-out hearings, sentenced to eight years in the northern camp. In 1939 Kuusinen was first sent to the "women's area" of the Kotlas transfer camp.

> I was quite shocked to meet a few Finnish women there, who had been brought from Petroskoi to Kotlas. I remember the following names: Hilja Huttunen, Ida Kukkonen, Alfa Pekkala, Saimi Heikkinen, Elvi Koskinen, Ester Nikkari, Maire Salonen, Meeri Vellamo-Salonen, Ester Pihlajamäki, Maria Viitala, and Lyyli Åikäs. In most instances these woman had left Finland with their husbands, lured by the high wages mentioned in Soviet propaganda. The officials, however, had decided immediately upon their arrival that the Finns had not come to work but to spy, and the men were shot on the basis of this remarkable conclusion. Subsequently, the women and I shared stories of our experiences. I really don't believe that many of them are still alive.

Kuusinen's memory of some of the names is slightly wrong, nor had they come from Petroskoi; there are clearly eight women from Kamensk here. According to Alfa Pekala, Aino Kuusinen, as an older and wiser woman who knew Russian, warned and consoled the Finnish girls at Vorkuta. Kuusinen was left in the camp when the girls were moved elsewhere.

The Finnish children who were left in Kamensk—twenty-one or twenty-three boys and girls—were taken to the same children's home in Chelyabinsk, which was known to the children who had been taken there from the train the previous winter. Among this group were Kerttu Jelonen, Anni Kantonen, Eeva Markkanen, and Elli Viljamaa. The caretakers told the girls how surprised they had been "at the Finnish children there earlier, they had cried so terribly."

The rest of the children's journey was by truck, and the destination was a children's home located in the Kustanai area in Kazakhstan. There the older boys tormented the girls, even throwing stones at them, but the caretakers were humane, and one of them even began to weep when she heard the children's story.

One more letter from the Markkanen relatives in Finland came to the Kamensk barracks, and Eeva wrote to the address that she got from it: "There are [fourteen] Finnish children, [eight] boys and [six] girls, in this children's home. The small children have been taken somewhere else. . . .

Send envelopes." Later Eeva received one letter with twenty-five markkas, which the director of the children's home took away from her.

At the beginning of November, Anni Kantonen sent a letter from the children's home to her aunt in Finland.

> *[November 8, 1938]. Nice auntie. Now I will write to you since I got a letter in Kamensk from an auntie in Kamensk. She wrote that mother had already been taken from the city, and I feel that we won't be in this children's home for long.*

Anni Kantonen wrote moving letters from a children's home. Picture is from the 1940s.

So nothing more need be sent to her, wrote Anni. She said that she always cried at night out of loneliness, and if she woke up at night, she was not able to fall asleep again but cried until morning.

By early winter of 1938, the largest group of the Kamensk children had been taken from the Chelyabinsk children's home to an unknown destination. They all cried again at the time of departure, for Irma Wahlstén had a high fever, and the doctor did not want to let her go along with them. In the end it was decided that Irma and Eila Tamminen would follow the truck in an automobile. All the children kept staring intently at the car to see that it followed them to the station.

An entire railway coach was filled with the Finnish children, some fifty souls. During the journey they were tormented by being fed salt fish and sausage without tea or water. Two of the girls, one of them Margit Vuorio, in spite of its being prohibited, drank water from the train toilet and got sick. Margit died soon after they reached their destination and the other girl died later. Yrjö Dyster died of tuberculosis in the children's home, and his deaf-mute sister was left alone.

The train stopped at the Petropavlovsk station in Kazakhstan. For a month and a half, the children lived in a children's home there. All Irma Wahlstén remembers is that they lived together in one large room and that a dog cried under the floor all night. The caretakers were two NKVD men, a Russian and a Kazakhi.

Irma and Eila Wahlstén were lucky to be together because the official basic policy was that family members and friends be separated: generally brothers and sisters were not put into the same children's home. The secret edict for "arresting the wives of members of treasonous and right-wing trot-skyite organizations" (1937) decreed that the spouses be imprisoned for five to eight years and the children placed in educational and health homes for children run by the folk commissariat. Children over fifteen and those judged to be "socially dangerous children" were in the charge of the NKVD's Department 8.

Fortunately the Finnish children were well behaved, for the criminal law now in effect had lowered the age for punishment to twelve, and the prisons were full of children. There was still danger later, for by decision of the government, eleven- to sixteen-year olds who were homeless, or were hooligans, pilferers, or disruptive in the children's homes were sent to labor education colonies.

The entire group of Finnish children ran away two or three times in search of their parents but were always taken back to the home. Once the children chanced upon the Petropavlovsk militia post, near which they saw men in the same kind of uniforms as those worn on the night of the big arrest in the Kamensk barracks. Their parents must surely be there!

The children tried to get into the post. Rauni Murto, the only one who could speak Russian, was naturally in the lead. "Just a minute, kids, you can't come in here," the men said. "What do you want?"

Rauni said the children were looking for their parents.

The men promised that someone would soon come to talk to them. Indeed, the director of the children's home did come—in a very angry mood. The children were loaded onto a truck and taken away.

The final destination was a children's home, a large wooden house confiscated from a "kulak family," which was located eighteen kilometers from the city in the village of Arkhangelsk. There were some 250 children at the home. The journey there was by horse and sleigh. Rauni Murto tells about it:

*Before we got to the children's home, someone sent word to its residents
that they were bringing in children of the people's enemies. Some in our
group were no more than four or five years old. When the gate was
closed after us, faces appeared in the windows, and the other children
shouted, "Spies! Traitors!" It's hard to describe what we felt in our
hearts then.*

At first the Finnish children could do nothing but weep in chorus. Sometimes they stood holding hands in a circle and tried to sing Finnish songs—
then they would burst out weeping again.

At the table, the children had to thank Stalin for the food. Little Irma
Wahlstén refused to do so, and remained stubbornly silent. The teacher flew
into a rage, picked up a plate, and struck the girl on the head with it.

Those of school age were put into Russian schools, where at first they
understood nothing. The teacher set them to blacking out the faces of the
enemies of the people, Tuhatshevski and Blücher, from their history books.
Their schoolmates reviled them as trotskyites, and fights broke out among
the children. The Russian pupils carried tales to the teacher, who consoled
the Finns by saying that the other children did not know what they were
doing.

Citizens were given passports when they reached the age of sixteen. The
Finnish children were regularly advised to apply for a Soviet passport. At some
time in 1939 the Murto children, Rauni, thirteen, and Erkki, sixteen, were
called to the office of the home's director. There were other adults sitting in
the room whom they did not know. They were told that a request had come
from relatives in Finland to have the children returned to their homeland.

"We want to explain to you that life there is terrible, and you'll have to
work eighteen hours a day for the benefit of the capitalists," the strangers
said to them. "You'll go hungry there, and we can't permit that to happen.
We advise you all to refuse to go. Here the soviet state and the party will
take care of you, and you'll grow up to be good people."

Officials in Finland had been cool to the large Murto family's return from
the very beginning. Now after the catastrophe, they began to consider the
relatives' request to get back the Murto boys, who had been left alone in
Kamensk. But they had begun taking into account whether the returnees
might not be left dependent on the state and counties for support, and they
asked the local authorities about Reino and Veikko.

The sheriff of the Karhula district wrote that he had contacted Kaarlo
and Vilhelmiina Murto and Vilho and Väinö Murto, and "they have given

me no guarantee with respect to their possible support of their sons and brothers Reino Kalervo and Veikko Valter Murto now in the Soviet Union."

One can only wonder what kind of contact the sheriff had had with, for example, Vilhelmiina Murto, who had been executed a full year earlier. In any event, in mid-August of 1939 the ministry did ask the embassy to begin efforts for the return of Reino and Veikko to Finland.

The sixteen- to eighteen-year-old boys and girls who were left in Kamensk were allowed to go to school for a few more months, where they learned, among other things, Russian and the welder's and filer's trade. Then they were sent to work in Chelyabinsk.

The twins Reino and Veikko did not get to Finland. Both studied to be welders and became valued workers in the factory. Veikko married Tyyne Pekala and then had to go into the work army. Reino began to keep company with Annikki Tervonen, the daughter of a family from Haukipudas, and soon married her. Elsa Tervonen married Onni Kauppi. In Oulu their grandmother had fought in vain on behalf of the Tervonen children. She wrote to officials that in "Kamenskaja in Russia, a northern Asian province," they had fallen into "misery undescribable in words."

In spite of all that had happened, Annikki and Reino were still able to plan a return to Finland. Seventeen-year-old Annikki gave birth to a girl in 1940. On New Year's Eve of 1941, men came to get Reino in the night, and took him from Annikki's side. Someone had informed on him. According to one source, Reino had said at work: "Those Germans won't bomb us."

The following members of the Murto family had disappeared: the mother and father, their children Erkki, Ilmari, Rauni, Reino, Urho, and Veikko, plus Ebba and Elma, the wives of two of the brothers. Of these ten people, five remained alive in the end.

In later interrogations the NKVD demanded that Annikki Tervonen Murto sign a paper saying that her husband, Reino Murto, had planned to blow up the factory in Kamensk. "They threatened to take my children and fire me from work if I didn't agree," Annikki says.

Reino was given a ten-year sentence. Elli Eskolin saw him at a labor camp stone quarry and said on a later visit to Kamensk that he was a "mere skeleton" and had died later of a stomach ailment.

During the war a handful of Finnish women still lived in Kamensk—many with their children—at least Hilja Jelonen, the paralyzed caretaker of two children, and Emmi Kujala, Hanna Mäntylä, Tyyne Pynnönen, Eeva Saarelainen, Hilda Takalo, Annikki and Elsa Tervonen, and Hilma Vaittinen. The women were put to work as painters at the factory.

During the war, the bread lines in Kamensk increased in length. As people lined up, a number was written on each person's hand; it sometimes got as high as a thousand. At night, surprise counts were made of the people in line to see if any were missing. There was always a Finn on watch for such a count. He would run to alert the rest to get back in line. They slept with their clothes on just to be sure.

In 1941, the men, Huotari, Saarenoja, and Aarne Kari, along with the biggest boys were taken into the war army, the wartime forced labor camps. Among the boys, in addition to Veikko Murto, were Veikko Katvala, Pentti Kosonen, Ensio Luoto, Matti Suokas, and Pentti Vaittinen. A number of them died or disappeared.

Eeva Markkanen and Elli Viljamaa were sent away from the children's home to work and set out together for Kamensk, to wait there for their parents to be freed. Eeva fell asleep during the journey and woke up alone and frightened in the dark train; luckily it was in Sinarskaja, from where she could walk to her destination. There were still a few women left in the barracks. The girls were put to work on construction; the workday for fourteen-year-old Eeva, who was recorded as two years older in the children's home's books, was twelve hours.

An odd thing happened in Kamensk in 1942; three women of different ages—Lempi Laurila, Eeva Markkanen, and Eeva Saarelainen—received an order to report for service. They drew their last pay from work and went to the place where they had been summoned. The astonished officers told them they had believed them to be men and sent them back home.

The Russians who lived in Kamensk knew very little about the fate of the Finns. As late as 1989 a researcher wrote in the aluminum plant newspaper that the Finns had been banished there from Leningrad after Kirov's murder. He also related that the Finns had been taken somewhere else from Kamensk—to Russia or Finland—charged with arson at the power plant.

Onni Kauppi contacted the paper and protested the branding of the Finns. To his surprise he got a piece published about a month later in which he related who the Finns were and what had happened to them.

In the fall of 1989 the KGB vice-chairman spoke at the Memorial Society meeting, at which he explained that the cases of all the victims of the years of persecution had been investigated and a list of names of those rehabilitated would be published in the paper. Then Kauppi asked about the Finns, hundreds of whom had lived in Kamensk, and of whom only one name was in the paper. The KGB man could not answer. A former NKVD worker who was in the room suggested that the records of the Finns might have been destroyed.

An apparent misconception regarding the Kamensk Finns can be found in Arvo Poika Tuominen's book, *The Bells of the Kremlin* (1957). Tuominen recounts that he had already heard while he was in Russia what had happened to the Chelyabinsk tractor plant's American and Finland Finns, and that he had heard an eyewitness account in Finland during the Continuation War from the "only survivors," two women who had had American passports and who had inquired about their husbands in vain.

"One day in the summer of 1937 the Finns at Chelyabinsk were informed that all adults had to meet at such and such a meeting room. . . . When they were all together—three hundred people—the GPU men surrounded the building and arrested everyone." There were certainly not that many Finns in Chelyabinsk at the time, and it otherwise seems as if Tuominen has mixed the Kamensk Finns, who were brought to Chelyabinsk after they were arrested, into his account.

Gradually the children of Kamensk adjusted to life in the children's home in Kazakhstan. Before the war they were fed well, but when the war broke out in 1941 their rations were such that it was a miracle they survived. Their food was boiled beets and steamed, frozen cabbage. For weeks they went without bread. One girl, whose name the others do not recall, died, apparently of yellow fever, since her color turned yellowish.

At the age of fifteen, the girls had to leave the children's home. During the war the bigger Finnish children were sent to *kolkhozes* or to work in a meat plant and a railroad car depot in Petropavlovsk. Some twenty-five of the smaller girls had to do *kolkhoz* work. When the men went to war, the field work fell on the shoulders of the girls.

The girls were transported from one *kolkhoz* to another and offered as workers as if they were being sold at auction. Along the way, girls would be dropped off here and there. Rauni Murto recalls that at one village, their escorts asked: "Is this a rich *kolkhoz*?"

The answer was: "No, it's poor."

"Well good, we'll only leave Rauni here."

Rauni,who had grown up in a family of nine children, wept constantly at the *kolkhoz* and was allowed to move to Kamensk, where her brother Erkki lived. There she found work at the same meat-canning plant as Elsi Alhonen, Dagmar Kurko, and one of the Alhonen boys. Rauni ran off from the plant and wandered around aimlessly until a Russian family evacuated from the war zone picked her up in Sverdlovsk and gave her their name so that she could get a bread card. When the war ended, Rauni studied and became a bookkeeper at a logging site in Perm.

Thus were the dreams of the little girl, who had once written to Finland that she wanted to work in an office, fulfilled.

When the girls were distributed to the *kolkhozes*, Eila Wahlstén was left as the only Finn in a desperately poor German village; Helli Hämäläinen and Rakel Saari did not like the place and went farther on. Eila did field work and went to school. The Germans cared for her as if she were their own child, but when the war began, a new tragedy was enacted; the Germans were fired from their jobs, evicted from their houses, and the men were sent into the work army.

Eila got into a railroad trade school in the city. She studied hard, but she could not get into the *komsomol* organization like the others—she had written honestly on her vita sheet that her parents were Finns who had been arrested in 1938.

She was put to work in a locomotive depot and sent to live in a common residence. She received a token of appreciation as a "*stakhanovite*" worker. Although she had written on her vita sheet that her parents had been taken somewhere and that she was a Finn, when her passport was returned to her at the depot, she noticed that her nationality was listed on it as Russian. Eila asked that it be changed to Finnish, but the new passport still read "Russian" when she picked it up on leaving the railroad after the war.

"That won't be a problem for you," they told her in the passport office. On the contrary—as a Finn she could not live in the city or work on the railroad. "Don't tell anyone that you are a Finn. If they ask you, tell them you don't remember your parents." Only in 1992 did Eila Wahlstén become a "Finn."

Maila Laukkarinen, who graduated from the same school and became a good conductor, experienced the significance of the passport. She was supposed to become a station chief, but since her passport read "Finn," she was dismissed from her job and sent into the work army. She disappeared from among the circle of friends.

Rakel Saari and Helli Hämäläinen were also sent to a work colony when they turned fifteen. They escaped from it together, and Helli was sentenced. Many of the children in the home disappeared without a trace. One is known to have hanged himself, another threw himself under a train.

Antti Tervonen disappeared for almost half a century. He studied in the children's home and after the *kolkhoz* he learned to be an assistant engineer on a locomotive, but the conditions were so wretched that he ran away. He was last seen at the Petropavlovsk station, where he said when asked that he was going "somewhere." He destroyed his identification, changed his name completely—he became Anatoli Ivanovitsh Lotov—and completely forgot the Finnish language. During the war, he even did intelligence work at the front. If it had been revealed at the time that he was Finnish, he would surely have been shot.

Eila Wahlstén's little sister Irma remained in the children's home where she fell ill of malaria every spring. She was sent to a *kolkhoz* in 1944, and there the members of a traveling circus on the way to Siberia picked her up. They taught her to be an acrobat and a performer. She trained dogs and also appeared with two dancing bears. But she was not allowed to perform in cities.

Etel Saari had been left in the children's home with Irma Wahlstén when the others left. In the end the girls spoke Russian to each other. First Etel forgot her Swedish and then her Finnish. She still wrote to her sister and to her teacher, Eloranta, in Kamensk, not knowing that her sister was dead and her teacher taken to a camp. On 13 October 1943 Etel set off on a journey to meet her other sister at a *kolkhoz* to which the latter had been taken, and also to get her identification papers from a government farm. Etel was already fifteen, but because of a wrong entry on her passport she and everyone else thought she was thirteen.

Having no money for the journey, Etel first walked along the tracks and then clambered up to sit on the steps of a train. During the night, she apparently dozed off and fell under the speeding cars. One of her feet was completely cut off, along with the fingers of one hand. The other ankle and hip were crushed, as well as one shoulder. Besides, she had received a severe blow to her head. A man passing by found the unconscious, bleeding girl and took her to the hospital on a cart. When Etel awoke, she asked for her father and mother. The doctors managed to save her life.

Etel worked in the children's home and later in a sewing shop. With only one leg, and with a heart condition, she continued sewing in Petropavlovsk until her retirement age in 1975. She even had to work standing up without a decent prosthesis.

Etel received a passport which said that she was a Russian, born 1930, and grew up in a children's home. Her birthplace was unknown. "I agreed to it; what difference did it make, I was an invalid," Etel said. Invalids were not permitted to go abroad in the Soviet Union. "I wouldn't have accepted such a passport if I had known I could go to Finland in my old age. In those days it was dangerous even to think of such a thing."

Irma Wahlstén painted pictures from memory of her partners in fate. On her return to Finland in 1966, Etel Saari (pictured above) received this painting of herself. Below: badly crippled after having fallen under a train, Etel Saari worked in a Petropavlovsk factory until retirement.

When a birth certificate was obtained for her in Finland in 1990, she aged two years in an instant; she was born in December 1928. Her sister Rakel acknowledged on her deathbed that she had taken her little sister's birth date in order to stay in the children's home longer.

In Nizhni Tagil too, only the Finnish mothers with little children were not taken. There were six of them. When the other women were already on the truck platform, Aino Saarela, who had been ordered to go with them, and whose daughter spent nights in the nursery shouted, "I have a small child too."

She was allowed to go and get Sirkka; they would be fetched on the following day. When no one came for her, she remained in the barracks village as the seventh mother. In addition to Sirkka, the children were Liisa Härmä, Hilkka Jordan, Rauno Karjalainen, Leo Moilanen, Tamara Orell, and the Hanhela children, of whom there were two or three. The Hanhela children left for Leningrad, supposedly to go to school. Soon a letter from them arrived from Finland. They had escaped and skied over the border.

Those who were left in Nizhni Tagil moved into the same barrack. They had no bread and no money, and no work, at first. No more firewood was brought to them, since their men were prisoners; it was a cold winter.

Even afterwards when the women were doing heavy work—as hod carriers, for example—their funds did not suffice to clothe and feed their children. They ate herbs, mushrooms, berries, and rotted potatoes, and the chickens and geese they stole. Under a new law, a more stringent discipline was exercised at the factory. Their pay was cut if they were twenty minutes late for work, and for a whole day off without permission they were hit with four months in prison.

A group of young women who had made a living by stealing moved from Kamensk to the Tagil barracks village. Tyyne Pekala and Elsa Tervonen soon went back, but at least Esteri Lepokorpi, Ellen Närvänen, Kerttu Moilanen, and Tyyne Rosendahl stayed in Tagil. According to Aino Saarela, life there became completely wild. The girls had learned to live "like savages" in Kamensk. They drank, and once the girls tried to kill a billygoat in their room with an ax.

Tyyne Eskola also moved to Tagil with her daughter from a logging area after her husband and father were imprisoned and executed. The daughter, Irja, soon died, and Saarela remembers that no one was interested in burying her; the women had to get different kinds of tools and hack a hole in the rock-hard frozen ground. "Father and Sulo have been snatched away from me, my mind is at the lowest ebb," Tyyne wrote to Finland at this time.

The women wondered why a small group of men had been allowed to return to Nizhni Tagil. They decided that the men had been sent to spy on the women. Once when he was drunk, Kusti Pellikka told the women that the men's job was to listen to what they were saying.

When the war broke out in 1941, the women were forced to do men's work. The norm for hauling bricks was twelve tons a day. By the beginning of November they had already been arrested. The law was the old familiar

Section 58, which reportedly could easily entail the death penalty in wartime.

Tyyne Rosendahl was arrested at the same time, 3 November, apparently in Kamensk. She had already been arrested in 1937 for attempting to escape back to Finland. Now the charge was anti-soviet activity. After a full six months, Rosendahl was sentenced to ten years in a labor reformatory camp as an enemy of the people.

Irma Rosendahl wound up in a school-age children's home and Pentti in a pre-school children's home. After serving her sentence, Tyyne Rosendahl was again banished to Shadrinski for five years. By chance Pentti was sent to a trade school in Shadrinski and met his mother there, but Pentti could not live with her because she "had no room, no clothes, not even shoes."

The Saarelas lived in the same room with the Orells in Tagil, and Sirkka Saarela recalls how their mothers were taken after a two-hour home search. Even all photographs and Finnish books were confiscated. The girls and their mothers had to sit on opposite sides of the room without speaking to each other.

Aino Saarela wanted to go to the toilet. "Go in your pants!" she was reportedly told. When she was hesitant about taking a freshly-washed quilt with her, the captors, who were guided by a Finnish man, enlightened her; "There will be plenty of time for that quilt to dry on this trip."

Saarela was allowed to take her child into her lap for a moment, and she whispered: "Remember, don't let them change your name. You are Sirkka Saarela, you are a Finn, and I am your mother, Aino Saarela. Her captors said to her: "The girl doesn't belong to you any more. We'll make a good soviet citizen of her."

At the Nizhni Tagil NKVD there was an inspection in which Saarela had to strip in the presence of four men. Once while in her cell, she recognized a familiar voice: it was Juho Riipinen, saying: "I can't carry the pot out, I'm too weak." Someone shouted at him: "Do you think you're in a rest home!" It was learned later that Riipinen died in the jail.

The weeping girls were left in the barracks to be cared for by the remaining women, who themselves were awaiting arrest. On Revolution Day, November 7, two NKVD "uncles" came in an automobile and announced that they were taking Sirkka Saarela to a children's home. She could take clothing with her but not her doll. The first phase of the journey was a rounding up of the children in a building in Nizhni Tagil.

In the early part of 1942, dozens of Finnish mothers were deported with their children to the village of Baikalovo in eastern Ural. A few men were included in the group. On the last leg of the journey, the mothers had to drag their children after them in large baskets. One of the men, a tailor, died during the winter. There was no money to bury him. Eeva Jordan and Sanni Orell took him to the cemetery on a sled and buried him.

Funeral of a Russian boy killed by occupants of a boy's training school. Standing behind little boy in front, wearing a head scarf, is Sirkka Saarela.

The hunger in Baikalovo was brutal. Tamara Orell recalls weeping on the way to the children's home because her mother, probably out of concern for her stomach, refused to let her eat enough potato peels. Only her mother's stamina kept the family alive. Sanni Orell did not shun work of any kind. She was young and pretty, and everyone pitied and sympathized with her. She whitewashed brick ovens and ceilings, chopped ice from steps and outhouses with an ax, worked in the woods in deep snow to get firewood, was a seller in a dining hall, and worked for the village council. Tamara recalls that they always observed a Finnish Christmas. Their mother put up a tree every year.

The other children got to go to school, but Raili Närvänen was left by herself in the children's home, where everyone had to take part in working in the garden, fields, and cow barn, even at cutting wood as soon as they were big enough to cross the threshold.

Sirkka Saarela, who was in another children's home recalled that her first job—at the age of nine—was to chop the thick ice off the toilets with a shovel and an iron bar, which she was hardly able to lift. The children were thin and weak. The bread norm was constantly decreased. At the end of the war it was 150 grams a day.

There were various nationalities in Sirkka's children's home. Among the boys there were real ruffians, who stole, drove off, and teased and tortured the others. One of the children died when they threw her into an icy river. Once the boys forced the smaller children to kneel along a wall through which they had driven nails. The children's heads were slammed into the points when the boys struck them.

In school everyone had to join the pioneers and the komsomols. In a large room under pictures of Stalin and Lenin, every child who joined stood up in turn and told his life story; the young Finns had to say that their father had been imprisoned "I don't know why." They were ordered to find out the reason; children of the people's enemies were not wanted in the organization. It was a difficult hurdle with which the children coped, for they had no information about their parents. Raili Närvänen succeeded in becoming a member on her third try; Sirkka Saarela only on her sixth.

It was during their schooling at the latest location that the children had to get a passport. Raili became Raisa Ivanovna Närvänen. Sirkka related that she studied hard and was always first in her class both in school and in a teachers college, but her path was always blocked by the fact that she was revealed to be the child of a political prisoner. She was shown a paper signed by Stalin which stated that foreigners' children could not study in colleges. Nor was she allowed to teach. Finally Sirkka took a teaching degree by correspondence and got a job in an educational institute for boys.

Finding out where her mother was confined, Sirkka wrote to her and went to visit her in 1950, with her rector's permission. Shortly thereafter, the rector was dismissed and imprisoned—probably because he had allowed a pupil of his to visit a political prisoner.

Aino Saarela, who had for years inquired after her daughter in vain, fainted when she received the first letter from her. She remembers that it said, among other things: "Mother, I'm hungry. Send me a comb for lice." Her daughter arrived for their first meeting in eight years wearing a red pioneer scarf around her neck and saying the only Finnish word she remembered: "Mother."

Her mother, Aino Saarela, had been beaten during her interrogations and threatened with a sentence of death for spying. According to her, the interrogations lasted five months. Among other things she had been kept in a cell where one could not sit or lie down and in which water dripped constantly on her head. As evidence against her were photographs and letters mailed to relatives in Finland, which had been confiscated.

Saarela had been sentenced to ten years in a camp. The wake-up time at this women's political prisoners camp was 5:00 A.M. At six they went to the dining hall, where they were given hot broth and 400 grams of bread for breakfast. In the evening they got 200 grams of bread and some soup.

Aino Saarela's weight dropped to forty kilos; she lost her night vision from malnourishment and her teeth from scurvy. At one point she was unable to stand without help. The prisoners snatched up from the fields anything that was the least bit edible and stuffed it into their mouths. "Their most prized possession was a wooden spoon, which they carried with them wherever they went." Their Sunday footwear was shoes made of birch bark. A sentence could be reduced by three months and seven days for work well done. After ten years in a compulsory labor camp, Aino Saarela was sentenced to five years more of banishment to Siberia. Her daughter lived with Eeva Jordan in Baikalovo where her mother also moved.

Chapter Fourteen

Camp Inmates

So it was that the young Finnish women arrested in Kamensk and sentenced in Chelyabinsk began to serve their ten years at the labor camp in Karaganda. They were taken from the Petropavlovsk jail via the Karabas station, the transit camp and "gate" of the extensive Karlag prison-camp archipelago, established in 1931. They arrived there on May Day in 1938, and were sent off to their job sites.

There were both criminal and political prisoners in the Karlag camps—Russians, Germans, Finns, American Finns, Karelians, Ingrian Finns, and thousands of Georgians. There the women met Finnish men who had been given five years for Kirov's murder. When their day of freedom dawned, those men were given ten years more. During the war the "politicals" who had completed their terms were not freed but were given new sentences or sent to Siberia.

The youngest in the Finnish group was seventeen-year-old Siiri Hämäläinen—the others were only twenty or a little older. There was one older woman in the group—Aili Eloranta, who had just turned forty and who was pregnant. Helli Hämäläinen, who was then only fifteen, was later sent into the work army; then all three Hämäläinen girls, the only ones in the family still alive, were together in Karaganda.

All the girls in Karlag served their sentences to the very last day, except for one who died there.

Karlag was an area the size of France; it is estimated that a total of at least 800,000 prisoners were confined there. Siiri remembered to the last day of her life that she was compulsory labor prisoner number 163,402.

Ebba Murto's baby was born in the camp and died soon after, as did her next baby. Maija Melanen also gave birth, and her child lived. Aili Eloranta's baby was born on July 1938 under the most difficult conditions possible—just when they arrived at the camp. The journey by train via different prisons had lasted for months. Her birth pangs began at the very end when she was on board the truck to the camp.

Although the pregnancy was full-term, Eloranta's daughter weighed only 1.9 kilos. The guards were astonished that a mother in the last stages of pregnancy had strayed into the group contrary to orders. Eloranta had probably concealed her pregnancy because this was her first, and only, baby, and she was absolutely determined to keep it.

The babies were taken somewhere else, and during mealtimes, the mothers were ordered into a group to nurse their babies. Eloranta had a breast disease and could not nurse her Sirkka. Forced to work outdoors, she froze her hands so badly in November that they wanted to amputate them. However, a doctor who was among the prisoners saved them, and the patient got into the sewing shop to make clothes for the army.

Once when Eloranta came to see Sirkka, they told her the child had been taken to the morgue, that she had died of dysentery. When she went to look at the child's body, she noticed that its heart was still beating, and took it into her arms. Sirkka lived for ten years in the camp children's home, and is still alive today.

There were twenty children in the morgue, and Eloranta claims that some of the children's chests were still rising feebly—they had been left there to die. Later it was discovered that the Karlag archives have no record of any children born there.

A prisoner's maintenance cost eighty-two kopecks a day. In addition to meals, the expenditures included the cost of feeding watchdogs on meat and of the guards' clothing. The working day was twelve to fourteen hours, and prisoners worked seven days a week.

The women remained alive thanks to the fact that they were ordered to work in the kolkhoz fields during the summer. There were not enough guards to cover the large fields—the women were merely counted when they returned from work in the evening. Thus no one could stop them from eating raw potatoes, root vegetables, corn and other plants, although they were warned and scolded repeatedly.

The Finnish men in Karlag did not get to do this kind of work, and in addition they were always kept under guard behind barbed wire. In general they died quickly. There were 338 Finnish prisoners of war in Karaganda. Less than thirty survived.

Food seemed to be running out in all of Kazakhstan. VALPO read a letter from there to Helsinki in 1941 which told of famine and begged: "Send us more food and goods." There was said to have been no bread in months, and the starved were being buried. It was thirty below zero and the writer had no shoes.

Salli Lappalainen owed a debt of gratitude to a prisoner about to be freed, who advised her: "Salli, go to work for the dairy unit if there is any way you can. There is a lot of work and you won't get much sleep, but you'll have the cow's teat in your hand." Taking care of cows was a heavy responsibility, for packs of wolves prowled right up to the barracks' walls.

Salli was also able to help Aili Eloranta and Tyyne Hämäläinen, who were weakened by malaria. They were assigned to light work in the barracks, and were given only a 400- to 500-gram bread allowance and water. "If you don't work, you don't eat," was the camp's motto. Transfer to the barracks for those unable to work usually meant a slow death. Porridge and milk were sneaked in at night to the patients, Aili and Tyyne, and they ate it silently under the covers. When Salli herself was unable to meet her quota, some two to thirty women made a covenant to help her and give her more bread from their quotas.

During the winter, the Finnish girls hauled coal to the camp with a team of oxen from a mine so far away that a round trip took three days. For food they had herring and frozen bread. To supplement it, the girls picked the grain from the oxen's feed and gave only the chaff to the animals. The cows were fed with sunflower seeds, which the girls literally plucked from the mouths of the animals and ate.

The oxen hauled corpses to a pit at night. There were plenty of them—dozens of prisoners died every day. The nude bodies of the dead were laid in a pit in three layers of five bodies each. A metal ring with a number was fastened either to the hand or foot. Earth was thrown in after each layer. Sometimes the bodies were close to the surface, and dogs or wolves dug them up.

The girls tried in every way to stay together, but from time to time some of them were ordered elsewhere to work. During the first summer already Siiri Hämäläinen and the small and feeble Sylvi Ollikainen were forced to work on the construction of a railroad. They had heard that eating the

Russian tobacco, *mahorkka*, would induce a fever, and they ate a whole package of it in the toilet. They got sick and threw up, but still had to go out on the assignment.

Their day's quota on railway construction was to unload thirty-one cubic meters of sand, rock, and clay from a railroad car and spread it out. The working day was from sunrise to sunset. At the end of the day, the girls could make it into the coach where they lived only with someone holding them up on either side—they could no longer walk. According to Siiri, not everyone could take it. A Latvian girl named Rosa ran away and was caught with the help of dogs, which tore her up so badly that she was blood from head to foot.

When the girls were being brought back on Siiri's birthday that fall along the new track, the locomotive and many cars were derailed. No one was hurt. Once many barracks were damaged by an explosion. It was viewed as a punishment by God because conditions in the camp were so bad.

During one winter, Siiri had to chop and dig in the frozen earth without woolen mittens or felt boots. She had only socks made from old padded clothing and rubber boots of a sort to wear on her feet.

"You could count the number of grains swimming around in our gruel. I was thin, in poor shape. The wind blew me around. I don't know how I survived."

Margit Vilkman, whose sight, to top it all, was poor, wound up alone among Russian prisoners. It was too much for her—when some of the others happened to see her once, she seemed completely unbalanced. Margit died in the camp.

For ten years the women did not read a single book, did not see a single newspaper, did not receive a single letter. They had no mattresses, sheets, or pillows. Sometimes they lived in barracks where their hair froze to the wall at night.

On Christmas they gathered secretly to sing Finnish Christmas songs and to burn stubs of candles they had obtained from somewhere. Speaking Finnish was forbidden at the camp, but Salli defied the prohibition. "When the ten-year sentence was read, it did not contain a ban on using your mother tongue," she said. "I'll speak it as long as I can. If you don't know it, that's not my fault. Go and learn it!"

The summers at Karaganda were tough. The temperature was forty degrees Centigrade, and malaria spread among the prisoners like wildfire. In the winter the ground froze to a depth of two meters, and the prisoners were afflicted by the cold and by sudden and severe blizzards, especially during the winter of 1940-1941, when thirty of the guards and prisoners died in the snow. Blizzards lasting for days buried the barracks up to their roofs. For any-one caught in a snowstorm, the only thing to do was unyoke the oxen and let them lead the way to some kind of dwelling. Camels were also used as beasts of burden. Once after a snowstorm one of the prisoners, a Finnish woman they knew, was found dead outside, her arms cramped rigidly around a camel's neck.

The women met Finnish prisoners brought in from elsewhere. When they had been in Karaganda for four years, prisoner number 222,694 was brought in; between her and Siiri Hämäläinen there had thus been 60,000 prisoners. The prisoner who came in with this number was Suoma Lahti, arrested in Moscow on Christmas in 1941. Physically and mentally she was more dead than alive. Her parents, husband, son and father, and mother-in-law had disappeared, as we stated earlier. She had been tormented for seven months in Moscow jails, and a train trip thirty-eight days and thousands of kilometers long lay behind her, during which she had gotten only a little bread, salt herring, and unboiled water. The final leg of fifty kilometers she had come on foot. Even the guards pitied the group of prisoners in which she arrived and said: "They won't last long."

The women took care of Suoma, the only American Finn in the camp, and got her to revive. She survived her ten-year sentence. Suoma Lahti related that her menstruation ceased for seven years, and that her hunger pangs never let up once in all that time, although conditions improved slightly toward the end.

Aino Lotta, who worked in the sick room, told Suoma about Allan Karenius, a young man she knew. Suoma jumped at the first chance to see Allan, who had been tortured, and was suffering from tuberculosis. Soon Lotta told her that Allan had died; the last word he is reported to have said is the Finnish word for mother. He survived only one year of his twenty-five-year sentence for espionage.

One day when she had come from work, Suoma saw someone lying on her bed. Great was her surprise when she recognized her mother-in-law, Ida Lahti. She was fifty-two years old, and too sick and starved to stand the heavy work. Soon Suoma's mother-in-law was transferred to the invalid camp to die. She survived the five-year sentence, but Suoma never saw her again.

In 1948 a rumor circulated that women giving birth to children would be set free and allowed to live in "free exile" in some nearby city. Those women who sought to become pregnant, or became so, like Suoma, found out that there was no truth in the rumor. Her child was taken to the camp's orphan home for the time being.

The Finnish women learned to spout out automatically to the guards what they had been accused of: "KRD" or anti-revolutionary activities. They were considered worse than the regular criminal prisoners. The other women left in 1938 when their sentences were completely served, and Suoma Lahti was left in the camp without any Finnish-speaking companionship. Irja Pekala died after three months of freedom. She was only thirty years old.

When the women were freed, they received a small sum of money as compensation for their work, but the camp took a part of it as payment for their "support." According to the usual practice, they could choose where they would be assigned to work. The most courageous, namely Ebba Murto, Salli Lappalainen, Sylvi Ollikainen, and Hilkka Sinkkonen, chose the Leningrad area and traveled there in their ragged quilted coats. The rest remained living in Karaganda.

At the logging site near Leningrad where they went, it was soon realized that the unskilled women would get killed there. The manager at their next work camp ordered them to leave the place within twenty-four hours—released prisoners were not allowed within 101 kilometers of Leningrad or other large cities.

The women sold their scanty possessions—Hilkka a bar of soap from the camp and Ebba her children's clothing—and they begged too, but the money they collected was not enough for train fare via Leningrad to Petroskoi. They finished the journey bumming rides on train. Both Ebba's and Sylvi's suitcases were stolen, Sylvi's as soon as she left the camp area and before she had time to board the train.

They were not allowed to remain in Petroskoi; the militia sent them on to Kontupohja, where they got work.

As was previously related, the young mothers arrested in Kamensk in the fall of 1938 were sent to the ill-reputed Vorkuta camp in north Ural. In general, they too had been sentenced to ten years.

They traveled north by many stages. In early 1940 a group of some thirty women political prisoners who had been declared healthy traveled the last stretch, 150 kilometers along the icy shoreline of the Usa River to Vorkuta. Many of them were Finnish border-hoppers from Kamensk. At times they had had to cross over icy brooks in water up to their breasts.

"It was an absolute miracle that only one of us got sick on the three-week march," says Aino Kuusinen, who was with them. "She was Meeri Vellamo-Salonen, a young Finnish woman from Käkisalmi."

From the very beginning, Meeri Salonen had had a fever, but, unable to speak Russian, she had not wanted to be separated from the group of Finns. After walking a week, she collapsed helpless into a snow bank in the dark. Kuusinen stayed close to Meeri, wrapped her in her coat, and succeeded along with Hilja Huttunen in arranging for a horse to pull her. Meeri Salonen died in the crude hospital tent at Vorkuta, and soon after her Maire Salonen of Rovaniemi died of an infected appendix.

That is what Aino Kuusinen reports; according to official information, Meeri Salonen died at Vorkuta in April 1941.

Kuusinen also became acquainted at the Vorkuta camp with a large group of Finnish women border-hoppers who had most likely been brought there from Nizhni Tagil.

> *If I remember correctly there were brought into my zone in 1943 forty-eight Finnish women. They had moved into East Karelia some ten years before that to build socialism. They had come to Russia with their husbands, and many had sailed over the Gulf of Finland in their own motorboats.*

At the start, the women had with them a total of eighteen children, many of whom soon died of dysentery. According to Kuusinen, the families were first scattered into prisons and then the whole group was sent to Ural to build a brick factory. In the end, the men were shot, and the women drifted around different prisons throughout Russia.

With Aino Kuusinen acting as interpreter, the women finally found out their sentences. The camp commandant said to her: "Tell them they have been sentenced on the basis of Section 58, Article 6. That means they have come into Russia as spies. And each one of them has confirmed with her signature that the charge is true."

The women had not understood what they were signing, but had all done as they were told, believing the promise they were given, that by doing so they would get to be with their husbands. Thus they became "Espionage agents sent by Finland's state police." The women did not know what espionage meant, and in spite of their dejection could not help laughing. "Do the Russians really believe that we knew how to do that kind or work?" one of them said.

Soon after the great war had spread in 1941, the Soviet Union mobilized all "enemy nationals" into a work army or shipped them to labor camps. In practical terms, the work army men (*trudmobilizovannyje*) were prisoners and their camps were concentration camps. They were not allowed to go to the front even if they had wanted.

First the Volga Germans and others born in Germany were banished, and the men assigned to compulsory labor. In January 1942 the state's defense committee issued the order for the "advantageous use of specially banished seventeen- to fifty-year-old Germans on the labor front." In February 1942, the decree was extended to all Germans living in the country.

The forced evacuation of Finnish-inhabited areas in the western part of the Soviet Union began, and already by October-November 1942 it was the turn of all eighteen to fifty-five-year-old Finns, American Finns, Ingrian Finns, Poles, Italians, Hungarians, and Rumanians to be in the work army. They were summoned to a meeting place, loaded on trucks and trains, and taken off to an unknown destination, to the camps. The women also wound up in them. Estonians, Latvians, and Lithuanians had already been transferred from front-line service to work camps in 1941.

Many Ural, Karelian, and Siberian Finns ended up in a cluster of camps in the Chelyabinsk area a good ten kilometers from the city itself. It was probably the NKVD's largest work army camp. The large Camp Bakalstroi consisted of several "small ones," in each of which there were several thousand prisoners. The Finns wound up in Camps 15, 16, and 17. The youngsters from Kamensk, who had reached maturity after the big arrest of 1938, were also brought there.

A strict watch was kept: prisoners could not leave the area or write letters. They were threatened with death as the punishment for running away or slacking at work. Guards shot anyone without warning who attempted to get through the fence. The number of prisoners was counted morning and evening.

The task at Bakalstroi was to build a factory, a large steel smelter, which is still standing today. The first members of the work army to arrive were housed in tents. They dug pits in the ground to protect themselves from the cold, and then began to build barracks. There were no mattresses or bed clothes.

According to Onni Eskolin, hundreds of men who had just arrived were crammed so tightly into a barracks with no ventilation that the air was exhausted. The ones in the center suffocated; only those near the doorway or cracks in the wall were saved.

The food at Bakalstroi was 300 grams of bread and once a day, a watery soup made of grain and frozen potatoes. The prisoners had to have their own mess kit or dish of some kind or they did not get the soup. Those who had worked hardest and longest often went without food. Not all of them were able to get even warm water or pure drinking water. There were no toilets. Care of the sick was practically non-existent and stomach diseases raged.

The work day lasted from 7:00 A.M.. until 6:00 P.M., and there were no days off. A day's norm was to hack loose six cubic meters of frozen ground. The men were promised extra food if they exceeded the norm, but it was impossible to meet it, especially since it was so hard to sleep in the cold barracks: men lined up to stand near the stove at night.

The Finns tried to work conscientiously and were among the first to die. "Even strong men perished like cockroaches in the cold." In February 1942, according to camp statistics, 179 prisoners died in twenty days.

The records show that the barracks sections at Bakalstroi were still unfinished in April 1942. By order of Beria, the equipping of the camps was to be completed immediately, towers and guard quarters were to be erected

At the guarded Bakalstroi camp in Chelyabinsk, the Finnish members of the work army lived in dug-out-like barracks. Sketch from Aimo Salminen's book.

posthaste, and a thirty-kilometer barbed-wire fence to be lighted according to Gulag regulations. A strip ten meters wide was to be cleared outside the fence and sand sprinkled over it.

In May, inspectors reported that the "prisoners' living conditions were unsatisfactory." They were declared to have gotten so weak they could not sit up during interrogations. "New food norms, strict but not crippling" were initiated. According to Eskolin, inspectors from Moscow once executed seven camp managers who had sold for their own profit food intended for prisoners .

The first production line at the new metallurgical plant went into operation in February 1943—nine months from the time that the first trainload of prisoners arrived at the place. The factory produced only iron, but it was of the highest quality.

In the spring of 1943 with the delivery of United States aid to Moscow, conditions relaxed and improved slightly. The daily bread ration was now 500 grams, and a first check-up by doctors was made.

By the end of the year, there were nearly 44,000 people in the Chelyabinsk camp, some of them prisoners of war and criminals brought from labor reformatory camps elsewhere. There were 34,000 actual work army members. Beria singled out the camp for special commendation: it had met and surpassed the norms in quantity and quality.

The largest group at the camp were Germans, and more of them also died. "There were Germans there who could not speak a word of German. Only their family name was German," said Toivo Pietiläinen, the son of a Finnish border-hopper who later married Ebba Murto. He continued:

> It was worse than a prison camp. A prisoner at least got the food and clothing allowance due him; we had to buy them from our own wages. Many starved to death. I was just skin and bones too. I had to walk eight kilometers to work. Once I collapsed on the roadside, but luckily some men driving horses came along and picked me up. I was near death then. I came to on the following day.

Hundreds of Finns perished at Bakalstroi. We got the list of dead Finns and Ingrian Finns and counted a total of 659 names. Eila Lahti's father was brought to the camp on December 1942 and already died the following March. Veikko Katvala, the son of Kamensk Finns, died in June.

At one camp where there were Finns, a sixty-man group worked at digging graves. The bodies were buried in their underwear, unblessed, in shallow pits dug into the frozen ground. Sometimes there was not enough earth to cover them. Leo Pöllä, who worked at the burial ground, said that the bodies were thrown into common graves, up to 150 into a single pit. "They were brought in by the truckload, they had shriveled up for lack of food."

There were still Finns working at Bakalstroi in 1945 when the war ended. Actually they were freer to move now and they began to be paid a small amount. The German prisoners left and were replaced by Russians who had been prisoners of war in Finland, among others.

In January 1946 the newspapers announced that the ministry had ordered the repatriation of Finns and descendants of Finns in the Soviet Union to begin. Nothing happened. The guards did disappear from the watch towers that spring, the Finns were sent away from the factories, and some were able to get jobs elsewhere. Finally in early 1947 they were all sent home. They had to bind themselves not to say anything about what they had seen or heard.

When other Finnish women were beginning to be freed from the prison camps, for one of them the predicament was just beginning: Fanni Pyykkö was sentenced to twenty-five years.

Pyykkö had lost her daughter in Svirstroi in 1932 and her husband in Chelyabinsk in 1936; later the fact surfaced that Allan Pyykkö had been sentenced for spying and died in a prison camp in 1942. His sister, her second husband, and his brother were also imprisoned. Fanni Pyykkö herself was arrested for spying and was accused of anti-Soviet propaganda, right after May Day in 1942. She relates that she was beaten during the interrogations and tormented by sleep deprivation for a month and a half; altogether she was in a GPU investigation prison for a year.

Pyykkö served her eight-year sentence, first in a women's prison near Mariinski in Siberia where there were no other Finns. Then came a transfer to the Ural jails and by way of them to a camp northeast of Gorki. She got the information that sixteen-year-old Veijo had been forced to take a Russian passport and shortly before her sentence ended she heard that he had died. Freed in 1950, Pyykkö set out to find her son's grave. It was reportedly revealed that the hospital where he died had not performed a burial but had given the body to an anatomical institute for dissection, the usual fate of dead orphans.

One December night in 1953 six men came to arrest Pyykkö on the basis of a tip from an acquaintance. She was taken to the GPU investigations jail in Ural Solikamsk, suspected among other things of planning to murder either a party or Soviet national leader and, according to the story, even of planning to flee to Finland by submarine via Lake Ladoga. One of the informants, a woman who was to testify against her, attacked Pyykkö's sister Helli Marjomaa in a confused state of mind before the trial. The slender Marjomaa succeeded in killing her assailant with a block of wood during the struggle and was sentenced to ten years for it.

Pyykkö was close to death many times. She went on a hunger strike three times and also made a suicide attempt. The court pronounced sentence in the fall of 1953 on the basis of many articles in Section 58: "[Twenty-five] years in prison without right to appeal, property to be confiscated by the state." She wound up in a women's prison camp in Mordva.

Because of the chief prosecutor's objection, the supreme court of the Soviet Union took up the case. According to its decision, Pyykkö had suffered a stroke and no longer posed a "danger to society." In 1954 she was declared innocent in the prison camp hospital. In 1939 she had already written a letter of complaint to President Kalinin, and now she wrote to Voroshilov and traveled to Moscow for an audience with him. According to the latter's secretary, he was of the opinion that she should be allowed to go home.

Fanni Pyykkö stepped down from the train in the Helsinki station on the 10th of May in 1956. Her sister had been released along with prisoners-of-war a half year earlier. For years Fanni had traveled with poison tablets in her pocket in case the KGB should seize her. An old border-hopper Kalle Lehto relates that Finnish officials were about to deport her from Finland when her Soviet passport expired in 1956, and she had to contract a "paper marriage" with a Finn in order to be allowed to remain. (Perm state archives on the politically oppressed f. 1, op. 1, d. 10496)

Chapter Fifteen

The Wind Blows Over Them

In July 1939 Finland sent a second note to the Soviet Union regarding the return of the border-hoppers. The countries were heading toward the Winter War and, of course, the note had no effect. Immediately after the war, VALPO drew up the following summary regarding the border-hoppers:

> During 1930 to 1932, according to rough calculations, 12,000 to 15,000 "border-hoppers" have gone to Soviet Russia, of whom perhaps [fifty percent] have died. 2,014 individuals returned secretly to Finland from 1930 to [August 15, 1936]. From [August 15, 1936] to the latter part of 1939, we do not have accurate information at hand, but the number of those who have returned does not exceed [thirty]. By official means, from 1932 to [March 15, 1936] and during 1937 [to 19]39 a total of 265 individuals returned, [eighty-seven] of whom had applied to come back.
>
> Let it be further stated that in addition to those who have gone secretly to Russia, Finnish citizens have gone with passports via Sweden, either directly by boat to Leningrad or by way of Estonia, and also from America, over 4,000 individuals.

VALPO's calculations appear to show that 6,000 to 7,500 of the border-hoppers who left Finland had died in the Soviet Union during the 1930s.

One should also state that VALPO's figures on those returning after autumn 1936 seem too small. There was especially lively return activity during 1937. According to Kostiainen a total of at least 2,150 to 2,200 border-hoppers managed to get back secretly.

As was stated above, U.A. Käkönen claims that in 1939 the Finnish embassy had a card file of over 20,000 names of Finns who had turned to it for help. According to Käkönen it was "enlightening to interview" the border-hoppers. He said that in their naïveté they had calculated their Soviet wages in markkas at the official exchange rate, (one ruble = 9.30 markkas) so that they seemed almost princely. The exchange rate used in embassy circles was 1.50 to two markkas.

> As typical Finns, the border-hoppers could not refrain from complaining and worse still, comparing conditions in the Soviet Union to those in their homeland. When these facts were made known to their neighbors, the result was being reported for anti-state activities and transferred to compulsory labor camps or new job sites.

Tenaciously these people kept trying to get back home, either by writing or coming in person to the embassy to ask for help, Käkönen writes. Many reported being punished for having turned to the embassy.

From the Foreign Ministries letters to the police one can conclude that the border-hoppers were really not wanted back in Finland. Testimony was demanded regarding their relatives' willingness to receive them and ability to take care of "former Finnish citizens, now Soviet citizens." On the other hand, after the Winter War in 1940, the Foreign Ministry again tried to take up the case of the border-hoppers, justifying their return by the fact that Finland had many more prisoners of war than the Soviet Union, almost 5,500. Fruitless discussions on the issue were held with Moscow. The Foreign Ministry sent a list of 2,500 border-hoppers there when negotiations for putting the peace terms into effect were being carried on, but the negotiating committee headed by the new envoy, J.K. Paasikivi, decided that nothing would be gained by presenting it to the Russians. Even negotiations about Finns who had accidentally strayed across the border after the peace proved to be difficult.

According to Paasikivi there were some 5,000 depression-era "border-hoppers," and the great majority of them wanted to return to Finland. Many of them had been granted Soviet citizenship. Paasikivi brought up the subject in vain in his discussions with Molotov, who informed him that the question of a Soviet citizen's right to leave the country was legally a matter to be decided by the Supreme Soviet Praesidium, and that each case would be considered individually. "The borders of the Soviet Union are long, and we have to be strict about border crossing so that order can be maintained—so Molotov explained the matter," Paasikivi reported.

There was no progress on the matter of the border-hoppers, on which Yrjö-Koskinen had expended so much effort before the war, Paasikivi wrote. "The Soviet Union's view of the matter was different from that of the western countries." Some border-hoppers told of getting passports signed by Paasikivi from Moscow at this time, but they did not have the desired effect, even though Paasikivi's reputation in the Soviet Union was good.

For years now, Comintern agent Marija-Emma Martin-Schule, the chief figure in a "huge spy case," had been sitting in jail in Hämeenlinna. The Soviet Union would have accepted her, but Finland was considering an exchange for some of the border-hoppers who wanted to return. In the end, the Finns turned her over to the Germans in 1942. In Finland, as well as in the embassy, there arose a discussion of whether it was worthwhile to pursue the border-hoppers' case further. Was their return advantageous to Finland if she could not select those who were to return? The returnees could develop into a "restless and dissatisfied element," and could become a burden on social agencies. Officials began to view them as a lost cause; after the war they would no longer be of much benefit for anti-communist propaganda. In effect they were buried alive.

Later on, the SUPO looked with a good deal of suspicion on the border-hoppers who returned during the 1950s. They were watched with the help of neighbors. One thing that was checked on was whether they received leftist newspapers. In one instance, SUPO did not look favorably on the return of Maija Härmä in 1958 because she "had worked all her life in a foreign country" and would soon be of retirement age.

During the Continuation War (1940 to 1944), Engineer Captain Reino Castrén found in occupied eastern Karelia "Russian statistics" according to which 5,939 Finns had come to Soviet Karelia "on their own initiative" and 972 "not on their own initiative," for a total of 6,911. For all Finnish border-hoppers, Castrén heard the figure of 18,000 mentioned. Also found was a large storeroom full of border-hoppers' letters which had not been forwarded.

According to Karelian security ministry information, in 1947 there were 4,999 Finns in the republic. Since the recruiting of Ingrian Finns to come there had not yet begun, it can be assumed that they were chiefly immigrants from Finland and North America.

After the Continuation War, Finland was obligated to hand over the prisoners of war she was holding along with other Soviet citizens who had been brought to Finland. On her part, the Soviet Union promised to turn over "Finnish prisoners of war and other internees" in its territories. The agreement did not cover border-hoppers.

According to some border-hoppers and even some diplomats, it was useless to ask for help from Ambassador Cay Sundström, who took office in 1945. He took "a dim view" of the border-hoppers and their cases, probably because he wanted to please the Soviet Union in every way. On the other hand, his embassy stated the opinion in a memorandum of 1951 that "the group being repatriated should comprise all those who wanted to return to Finland, including the border-hoppers of the 1930s, 200 of whom were known." Sundström's successor, Eero A. Wuori was more understanding. One border-hopper said in reference to 1956:

> The envoy was now Vuori, whom I asked to rush my papers. He told me that they could not help the owners of Russian passports. I told Vuori that the embassy had not helped my sister or my son either, although they had Finnish passports. Vuori just showed me a map of Russia that had places marked with thumbtacks and said: "There are Finns with Russian passports living in those places. We do count them as Finns, although we can't help them."

Ambassador plenipotentiary Jorma Vanamo relates that taking care of the border-hoppers' cases consumed an appreciable amount of his time in Moscow both as an embassy assistant in Paasikivi's time between the wars and as the first embassy secretary during Sundström's term from 1945 to 1948. Vanamo also testifies that it was very difficult to get answers from the Soviets and that often the embassy's actions seemed only to make matters worse for the border-hoppers.

Vanamo's view was that the border-hoppers should be helped to return home in every possible way. "I can't escape the thought that the Soviet Union takes a negative view of the border-hoppers' return for the same reason that Finland desires it: the returning border-hoppers will have accurate and true information about 'Soviet actuality,' about the conditions of everyday life there."

Even during the 1950s, the Moscow embassy inquired of Vanamo, who had been transferred to Stockholm, on what statute or section of the law the Soviet Union based its claim that the border-hoppers were Soviet citizens. No such document ever appeared; perhaps it did not exist.

The border-hoppers were remembered often when Finland and the Soviet Union negotiated about prisoners of war. Their relatives wrote bitter letters to officials, for they suspected that civilians would be overlooked for the benefit of soldiers. Moscow was firmly of the opinion that the negotiations concerned only soldiers. The foreign ministry also decided in 1953 that "a blanket request for the return of all nationals" might result in the Soviet Union's demanding the return of thousands of their citizens still in Finland.

One day in 1951 the Finnish prisoners of war interned in a camp at Kiev and a few border-hoppers who had strayed into their midst read an official announcement in *Pravda* that there were no longer any prisoners of war in the Soviet Union, but only war criminals. They began a strike, which only resulted in those considered its instigators being taken away. As late as early 1954 there were still over sixty Finns in a camp at Krasnopolj who had crossed illegally or strayed by accident over the border. In the group were two prisoners-of-war. The Soviet Union sent all of them home together in February on a train by way of Vainikkala. There were Ural Finns in the group, at least one named Pentti Kosonen, who had left Kotka as an eleven-year old in 1931 and disappeared later from Kamensk. In 1953 to 1955, Finland still returned a few Soviet citizens who had served as volunteers in her armed forces, apparently to keep the door open for the return of Finns. In August 1955, Finland also pardoned and released a Russian spy, and Moscow turned over twenty-six Finns, most of whom were not prisoners of war. In the group returned in 1955 was a man named Mikael Hoikkala, whose liberation was at first celebrated gaily in Helsinki nightclubs. Only a month later Hoikkala stood facing charges of treason in court—the security police had revealed him to be a member of a spy cell.

Some Finns in camps and in Siberia told of their hopes being aroused when they heard a rumor in 1955 that German prisoners of war would be sent home. The amnesty law had indeed freed all those who had fought against the Soviet Union and those who had collaborated with the occupation forces, although only the Germans were mentioned specifically. But still the "paper war" and the waiting went on. Many seem to have appealed to President Voroshilov. In its letters, the Finnish embassy urged patience. Martta Piili wrote in a letter published a couple of years later that the embassy seemed to be making fun of her, and asked why even the "notable Finnish politician's son" (apparently embassy secretary Taneli Kekkonen) had not helped her.

Local militia functionaries explained that a Finnish passport was not enough, but that the Finnish embassy also had to provide a visa; the embassy corrected them—Soviet officials had to furnish a visa for leaving the country. These officials not only asked money for providing a visa (350 rubles) but also for the Finnish passport (100 rubles). At every phase, photographs were demanded, which had to be stamped with a seal that cost money. In addition, full and thorough vita sheets had to be written up in both Finnish and Russian.

Aimo Salminen relates that a full twenty-four photographs of him and his family members had to accompany his application. After that he was asked over and over again if he really wanted to return to the capitalist system. The return to Finland of his Russian-born children was impeded to the very end. For its part, VALPO opposed the arrival of his Russian-born wife. Felix Lankila, a logger imprisoned in Nizhni Tagil and later freed, lived with his wife in Siberia after the war. When the papers wrote about President Kekkonen's visit and the good relations with Finland, he mustered up the nerve to write to the Kalajoki workers' organization inquiring about relatives and friends. The contact resulted in Lankila's coming to visit Finland.

Lankila related that a large number of the Finnish border-hoppers were not on any records because they had not taken out Soviet citizenship. He said he had often been called to testify to a person's true name and identity when it was a case of a citizenship application or of being entered on the records.

During the summer of 1940, an investigation began in the Soviet Union of "distortions" which the NKVD's "arrest competition" had led to a couple of years earlier. In addition to foreigners, the victims had been "kulaks, eserries, and anti-revolutionaries." In the new purge, the sickle mowed down those who had actually carried out the persecution.

One fact that was discovered much later was that a secret NKVD group war tribunal in the Ural area had sentenced the Chelyabinsk area command's agents for "breaking socialist laws." We found in the files, for example, the decree which ordered the shooting of two of them, Fjodor Lapshin and Faddei Lugotsev. Three others were imprisoned. Two officials of the Nizhni Tagil NKVD had already been executed in 1939, and one was given a twenty-five-year sentence.

According to the decision of the war tribunal, the Chelyabinsk NKVD had devised charges against several thousand individuals, most of whom had been executed. Thus the Finnish victims had been only a part of the whole, but proportionally a large number of them had been shot.

According to the tribunal's decision, Lapshin had devised charges "artificially," based on the testimony of two NKVD secret agents, against an espionage and sabotage organization, most of whose members had been executed. The aforementioned secret agents had also been made "sacrificial lambs" along with members of that group.

The decision also revealed that the same NKVD unit had carried out other "group operations" in the Chelyabinsk area as well. At the leaders' orders a White Guard, cossack, and eserries anti-revolutionary organization had been invented, almost all of whose members had been sentenced to death. In addition Department 3 of the NKVD was ascertained to have carried out the "foreign operation" during which time nearly 500 Finns were arrested. Nikolai Fomkin, who had become so well known to the Finns was called on to answer the investigators' questions on many occasions. Nevertheless he is not known ever to have had to bear any responsibility for the Kamensk tragedy. M. Bykov, the head of the Kamensk NKVD, and his deputy Fomkin were dismissed from the NKVD in 1940 for the "falsification of investigative materials," and according to the Finns, Fomkin no longer had "any power" during the war.

Fomkin was supposed to tell what had happened to the Finns. According to him, over 200 Finnish men and women were arrested and sent by train to Chelyabinsk after the wired order for the mass arrest had arrived in mid-December of 1937. The Finns were tortured on the third floor of the Chelyabinsk NKVD, Room 509, as an investigator questioning the aforementioned Pjotr Suharev entered in the record.

After Stalin's death in 1953, the case was "opened" again. In 1955, for example, Voitsehovski, who had sent the "Polish wire" was interrogated. He then belonged to the leadership of the city of Chelyabinsk. He explained:

> In the summer of 1937, we carried out operational work to find out about possible anti-revolutionary activity among Polish and Baltic nationals in the Chelyabinsk area.
>
> At the end of the summer, Tshistov, the head of the Chelyabinsk NKVD area command, called an operative council, where he explained that a secret order had been received from the interior ministry and from Jezhov, secretary of the VKP(b)'s central committee, which revealed the existence of an anti-revolutionary organization, the so-called Polish military organization, in Moscow and many other cities. The tentacles of this huge anti-revolutionary organization extended from Moscow, Smolensk, and Minsk to other large centers, including Ural, for example.

> *During this council, Tshistov gave the order to begin arresting Poles,*
> *White Russians, and other individuals without delay.*

The interrogation of the interrogators made it clear that the statements extorted from the Finns had not been checked in any way. The records had been written "according to their own confessions." They named one another as recruiters. When the person interrogated had mentioned some individual by name, no effort had been made to check the truth of the statement with him, not even if he was in the same group of prisoners. The KGB declared that the NKVD had grossly broken the rules in the February-April 1938 interrogations in Chelyabinsk.

Suharev said in the 1940 hearings that people had been arrested for no reason and generally without any basis. "Several times I asked why a person had been arrested just because he had been a prisoner in Germany or was a foreigner. The chief answered that it was being done by order of the folk commissariat, plus the NKVD command and area chiefs' mandate."

According to Suharev the interrogations held in the spring of 1938 were so crude and their pace so ridiculous that it had to vitiate their quality. The investigators rushed into producing more and more records of interrogations. They were done in the same format and comprised only three to four sheets. Suharev's admissions were used in the rehabilitation of Finns in the 1950s. Investigators who had extorted confessions in Ural were still being executed at the end of the 1950s during Kruschev's "destalinization" phase.

Fomkin also wound up in another hearing in April 1958, when the Finns were being rehabilitated. Why had he been dismissed from his position of authority in the Kamensk NKVD? "I was retired, I think, because I had only an elementary school education. Besides, I had a stomach ulcer, and I already had [thirty-one] years of work in the NKVD." (In this establishment, one year of work was counted as two in figuring retirement.)

How had he carried out the investigations?

He had carried out operative work among the Finns and had had to take part in their interrogations. "I participated only a few times in the arrest and home searches of people belonging to other groups."

On what grounds had he signed, for example, the charge against Alfa Pekala-Kivinen of being an agent of Finland's espionage organization?

"I prepared and signed all the records of the border-hoppers' proceedings following the form and standards issued to me by my former chief."

Was there any evidence of Pekala-Kivinen's or other border-hoppers membership in a foreign intelligence organization? Fomkin was asked.

"After all this time, I don't remember, but I do remember that there was operative material on almost every one of them, but exactly what and in connection with whom it's hard to say."

Fomkin tried to shift the onus for the confessions onto the Finns themselves. "Since the border-hoppers wanted to return to Finland, they confessed without the use of any violence."

Fomkin was allowed to remain free in Kamensk-Uralski. He worked on job assignment in a war plant. According to Onni Kauppi, Fomkin's last position was as leader of the cadre group in the aluminum plant, and he died several years ago in Kamensk.

Salli Lappalainen was freed from the camp 2 January 1948, ten years to the day after her arrest. She was then ordered to work in Kontupohja, where she served first as a milkmaid and then as a welder. She was assigned to a barracks room which she shared with three other women.

In the spring of 1949, Salli Lappalainen's criminal case was re-opened for investigation. In his report on the case, the Petroskoi KGB investigator wrote that there was no basis in truth for the confession she had once made. The official closed the report with the following words, with which his superior concurred:

> It is declared:
> That the Lappalainen investigation case be returned to the archives.
> That no further measures be taken with regard to her.

In October 1950 the Kamensk-Uralski KGB informed Karelia that Salli Lappalainen had been interrogated only once in January 1938. The charge was based on her own confession, and there was no witness's information on her criminal activity. Veikko Nieminen, the person named as her recruiter had gone to Finland in 1937. "Thus the truthfulness of the confession she made of anti-soviet activity is open to suspicion."

The mills of justice ground slowly. Finally Lappalainen had a hearing with the Petroskoi KGB 28 November 1957. At that time new light was thrown on Veikko Nieminen, the "dangerous agent" on whose account she had been sentenced:

> I got to know Veikko Nieminen in the trade school. He was sickly, a little older than I was . . . in 1936 it was said that Allan Vuorio, Urho Karppinen, and Veikko Nieminen had gone somewhere else to work. It turned out, though, that they had gone to Finland, how I don't know.

I can't say anything bad about Nieminen. We didn't discuss politics, and so I can't say anything about his political viewpoints. He was very quiet and reserved by nature, and was ill with tuberculosis.

"Did Nieminen suggest that you join some organization?"

"He did not. We never discussed any organization . . . Veikko Nieminen never visited our lodgings or incited me to any kind of action, and I don't know if he was a Finnish agent . . ."

"Did you know border-hopper Metsämäki, Eino?"

"I don't know him or know of him."

Regarding her Bulgarian border-hopper husband, Vasili Genov, Lappalainen related that she had gotten to know him in Chelyabinsk in 1934. In Kamensk Vasili had been a filer in the factory. "He was a good person, and I can't say anything against him. He never spoke ill of the Soviet state. He earned well and in 1937 we were materially well off."

Lappalainen related that she had been interrogated for days on end, for many hours a day without sufficient rest. "In the end I was so tired that I was ready to sign whatever the interrogator demanded. At first I denied everything because it didn't correspond to the truth. I signed the answers I gave on [January 18] 1938 only under pressure." She had been told that there would be no consequences if she signed.

At the end of 1957, Salli sought rehabilitation, at which point information came from Kamensk that no one remembered her and her family. Regarding her asserted sabotage, the following was stated:

None of the old residents remember a crane's bucket load being dropped during the construction of the aluminum plant. Nor do these people know about S.I. Lappalainen's work in the garage. A worker at the UAZ garage recalls her outwardly as a person, but cannot characterize her politically or as a worker.

The Ural war tribunal restored Salli Juhontytär Lappalainen's reputation by an official declaration signed on 28 February 1958. Ten years had passed since she was freed from the camp. She retired in 1967.

The barrack in which Salli Lappalainen lived was built in 1949, and it was never renovated. There was no running water. Others kept writing everywhere to have her living conditions improved but always got a negative answer. She wrote of the matter to the Soviet-Karelia newspaper and even to the supreme council—in vain.

Salli Lappalainen died at the start of the 1990s. She was still living in the same place. Her entire life had been spent in barracks.

Aleksis and Gerda Saari were among those whose sentence was overthrown and whose reputation was restored at the end of the 1960s. In their files is the investigator's observation that there is no such relative as was claimed to have recruited Aleksis Saari to work as a spy and to blow up the Kamensk railroad.

One of the *troika* which had condemned Saari was still alive then, as well as the interpreter who had been present at the interrogation. The interpreter claimed that for the most part he had merely sat off to the side and that the Finns did not really understand what was happening. At first the member of the troika claimed that everything had gone properly and according to regulations—no one had been tortured. Then he admitted that the prisoners had been kept in cells where they could only stand until they confessed.

During the winter of 1990 the newspaper Kamenskij Rabotshij interviewed Aleksandr Kolesnikov, the assistant director of the Kamensk KGB. He said that the "*tshekists*," or the men who worked for the security apparatus, had been the first on whom the "blows of the reprisal apparatus had fallen." According to him, many honest *tshekists* had been sent to be shot or to concentration camps in the Sverdlovsk area. That was made possible by the fact that "in 1937 a criminal gang was formed" in the NKVD area command, the members of which were Bojarski, Kritshman, Mizrah, Plotkin, and Tshistov. "This gang drew up a false court case against the head of the command group, I. Reshetov and later against his assistant Samoilov." When these men were liquidated, the persecution of the NKVD rank and file began.

Kolesnikov related that immediately after Stalin's death, the "falsifiers were held responsible for their crimes." Among them was V. Katajev, the head of the Kamensk city NKVD, "who had dozens of human lives on his conscience."

A special task force of the command group had re-opened 8,766 cases, in which the NKVD triads had pronounced sentences during the 1930s. In the Sverdlovsk area, 10,391 persons had been rehabilitated. Their relatives were promised that any of their possessions which had been preserved, along with their case records, letters, and photographs would be given to them. A total of 670 people were not recognized as rehabilitated—"traitors, executioners, and security agency workers who had fabricated the criminal cases." The paper asserted that it had published the complete list of those who had had their reputation restored; however, there are few Finnish names on it. Only the following eighteen Kamensk Finns appear, and furthermore, some belong to the same family: Einari Hakola (properly Hakala) Niilo Hansen, Hanna Hilsa (Hölsä), Jenni Kemppainen, Antti Keronen, Adolf Kokkinen, Paavo Kokkonen, Aaro Kourunen, Aili Markkanen, Martti Meriläinen, Aleksandr (Aleksandra) Pekala, Valdemar Riuta (Riutta), Meeri Salonen, Selma Salonen, Aleksander Sinkkonen, Ida Sinkkonen, Martti Tekkeli (Tekkala), and Vilho Väänänen.

Ellen Närvänen, who had been left alone with one-year-old Raili when her husband disappeared, continued her efforts to get back to Finland. In 1935 she had gotten a Soviet passport from the Chelyabinsk militia, which was good for five years. In the spring of 1938 she had written everything she knew about her husband's fate to her Finnish relatives and asked for their help. She also wrote to the embassy in Moscow. Her relatives in Kemi went to work without delay and "most humbly" requested the foreign ministry to "get to work soon" on the family's case.

The Närvänens' campaign to return to Finland had begun under unfavorable auspices a year earlier. The Foreign Ministry had commented in August 1934 that "it saw no reason for the embassy to hasten their return." By that time three of the children in the family had already died. The ministry had been informed that Närvänen had taken part in communist activity in Finland. Other border-hoppers had also said that he had belonged to Osoaviahim and to the atheist society.

In May of 1939 Ellen Närvänen again sent an application to Finland's Moscow embassy, which referred it to the foreign ministry. In November, on the eve of the Winter War, Finland granted an entry permit and a six-month residence permit to the mother and daughter; VALPO did not oppose it. Relatives promised to guarantee the Närvänens' well-being, and the Kemi welfare board confirmed their ability to do so.

The next time the relatives inquired about the possibility of the mother and daughter's return was in 1946. During that year, a small group of Ural Finns who had kept their Finnish passports were able to come back.

Ellen Närvänen also asked for help and said that her husband had now been lost to the world for nine years. She was informed by the Foreign Ministry that she would have to re-apply for admission and that she should also turn to Soviet officials; they would have to give her permission to leave, since she had once taken out citizenship in that country.

Years went by. Raili grew up and finished school. She interpreted in the offices for her mother, who had not learned Russian adequately. The mother refused to give in. Papers went back and forth. Relatives made another commitment of support. Soviet officials testified that Närvänen was not a

Soviet citizen after all. Finland sent her a passport in 1948, with a three-month residency permit. "We urge their return, they are apparently Finnish citizens," read the ministry's message to the Moscow embassy.

Närvänen sent ten letters of confirming information to the Moscow embassy in 1947 to 1951. In the last letter from Baikalov in January 1951, she wrote:

> I the undersigned Finnish citizen. I send my Finnish passport to be renewed I beg the esteemed ambassador to return my passport by the end of this month. I must take my passport to the militia post here on the [first] day of February. I also ask the advice of the esteemed Finnish embassy who I should turn to for permission to travel to my Homeland. I have written many requests to this militia post. But they already told me not to write it's in vain. They don't give permission to travel to the Homeland. Respectfully requesting your reply.

This was the last message from Ellen Närvänen for a long time. Her relatives continued to write to her; Raili remembers getting Armi Kuusela's (Miss Universe, 1952) picture from Finland in 1952. Ellen Närvänen's pass grew old again.

Toward the end of 1953, after Stalin had died, the Moscow embassy informed the foreign ministry that it had received no answer to a letter it had sent to Närvänen a half year ago. Acting chargé d'affaires Ralph Enckell asserted that the lady could certainly write to the embassy on her own initiative if she wanted. Enckell was not "assured that insistence on this matter would be favorable to Mrs. Närvänen. It may be that her silence has to do with her daughter, who was born and grew up in the Soviet Union, and who is now seventeen years old, having been born October 1936."

> Nor does the embassy consider it favorable to Mrs. Närvänen that by continuing to send letters to her under these circumstances it keep active the perhaps unjustifiable effort to return to Finland.

In November 1954, Närvänen's boyfriend Robert Lyytikäinen got back to Finland; his wife had been arrested and had vanished in 1938. Lyytikäinen had served time in Finland as a member of the Red Guard, and now he was familiar with Russian prisons too. On arrival in Finland, Lyytikäinen reported that Ellen had been coerced into taking a Russian passport and threatened with jail and a "compulsory labor camp." Finally she had given in, fear-ing for the future of her daughter, who was studying to be a teacher, and for her own chances of getting work.

The Finnish girls had difficulties with the school offices as well as with the militia passport offices. At the Talitsa school, Raili Närvänen and Tamara Orell were called to meetings at which the rector and teacher tried to persuade them together and separately: "Finland is a capitalist land, where people live in misery. Do you know what it's like there?" "We know, we correspond with Finland." "You are thankless. You have been born and educated here. How dare you try to go to Finland?"

The foreign minister again advised Närvänen's sister that she was responsible for her relatives' welfare if they came to Finland. Out in backwoods Ural, the friends Raili and Tamara walked the fifty kilometers to the train to start out for Moscow to arrange for the papers, but chickened out at the last moment in the station. They had never been in a large city.

In May of 1956 Ellen and Raili Närvänen again received a three-month entry visa and finally they started off. The angry passport official in Baikalovo told them that they had to be at the Finnish border exactly on 17 June, or the whole matter would be nullified. They raised the money by selling their shanty. The trip to Leningrad took two weeks. Waiting for their tickets at the Hotel Astoria, others found out about their travel plans. One woman began to criticize Raili, demanding to know how she dared to leave the Soviet Union. They reached the border at the last minute.

The first thing they were told at the Soviet embassy was: "If you want to stay out of trouble, remember not to say anything about yourselves in Finland." They got a Finnish passport in 1958. Raili now lives in Helsinki and teaches Russian.

Their mother went to a clairvoyant and was given hints that her husband was alive somewhere where there were mountains and lakes. In the 1980s, the Närvänens received the false information from the Red Cross that Hiskias Närvänen had died in January 1939. Finally in 1995, after many inquiries, information arrived from Ural that Närvänen had been arrested "on the charge of belonging to a Finnish nationalist organization" and executed in Chelyabinsk in March 1938. The sentence was annulled and Närvänen posthumously rehabilitated in September 1957, nearly forty years before the information was given to his family.

Eeva and Hilkka Jordan never did get permission to move to Finland and remained in Baikalovo. Nor, in spite of many promises, did Sanni Orell (nee Lappalainen) and her daughter Tamara, born in Kamensk. The family had already obtained passports and permission to leave for the first time in

Kamensk a little before the arrests in November 1937; the Moscow embassy had also sent them money for travel.

VALPO reported in the winter of 1948 that the mother and daughter were "apparently Finnish citizens and free to enter Finland." The Foreign Ministry informed Moscow: "They may be returned home with the obligation to repay." However, in Ural the Orells were issued a sternly worded prohibition against leaving the country, and their Finnish passport grew old. In 1954 they were again granted Finnish passports valid for a year.

"At the passport desk" they were told that the visa cost 800 rubles for two people. In 1955 Sanni Orell asked for a men's suit from Finland so that she could sell it to get the money. Their relatives sent it. Mother and daughter were promised that the permission to travel was basically unencumbered, since they were still Finnish citizens. They were already beginning to buy homecoming gifts for their relatives. That year they were given Soviet passports and their 1956 application for exit visas were rejected with no reason given.

Reino Orell's sister, "Saima Pääkkönen of Hamina, a sausage-maker's wife," began to pressure Prime Minister Urho Kekkonen in 1956: her joy over the September Moscow agreement was beginning to dissipate. Why had they talked of only a few prisoners of war who would be pardoned and returned to Finland? Why had no information been given about the Finnish border-hoppers? There had already been announcements on the radio that Finns sentenced to prison camps could also return. "I myself will write to President K. Voroshilov in Moscow," Pääkkönen declared. She also wrote to the *Helsingin Sanomat*, which published her letter anonymously.

Pääkkönen did as she had threatened. On 24 February she sent a letter in Finnish to: "Mr. PRESIDENT comrade K.J. Voroshilov": it can be found in a Russian translation in the Orell's file in the Jekaterinburg archives. Reino Orell's brother also wrote to Voroshilov.

Pääkkönen begged pardon for daring to disturb the president with a letter, "but I hope that having read it, you will understand me." Then she explained her brother's and his family's vicissitudes in Russia down to the very last detail and explained the "paper war" that had been waged. Finally:

> I now turn to you, comrade President, in the belief that you can help us to get in touch with our relatives. When our president Paasikivi and prime minister Kekkonen met with you in Moscow last fall, the possibility that those who wished to could return to Finland was discussed. Your government took a favorable view of this matter, and all of us

who have relatives in the USSR were extraordinarily pleased. So help my brother. If he cannot return to Finland, please make it possible for him to write to us. Since so many years have passed, he presumably has already served his sentence, and we are ready to receive him, be he ill or well. Pity our old mother, and my brother's wife and daughter, who must still wait. Reading about your speech and your demeanor, I have been emboldened to turn to you with this great request.

The translation in the file is certified as correct and a certificate is appended: "We have requested a travel permit for Orell, Sanni Sonja and her daughter Tamara from the USSR's interior ministry's OVIR. [March 29, 1956] Razguljajev."

Raili Närvänen and Tamara Orell in the mood for departure from Ural in the 1950s. After a long struggle, Raili was able to move to Finland. Tamara never was.

By the winter of 1958, twenty years had passed since the execution of Reino Orell. His widow, along with his sister, was still seeking information about his fate. Now Salme Pääkkönen begged President Kekkonen's pardon in her letter "for turning to you in this same case, but since there is no help from anywhere, I have to keep trying to write."

Pääkkönen wrote that the Närvänens had long since come to Finland, and she asked for action on behalf of Reino, Sanni, and Tamara Orell. She said that nothing had been heard from the Foreign Ministry, to which the matter had been referred. Pääkkönen suggested that Kekkonen appeal to Nikita Kruschev.

Reino Orell had been arrested in Kamensk on 2 January 1938, and over the years there had been many kinds of reports about him. First his widow was informed that he had died of pneumonia in 1945, and the Soviet Red Cross answered an inquiry by saying that Orell had been sentenced to "a dis-

tant camp without correspondence privileges." According to Pääkkönen, "some kind of militia establishment" announced in 1956 that Reino had died of a middle-ear infection March 13, 1938. However, his sister-in-law Salli Lappalainen had told of seeing Reino in the Chelyabinsk jail in March 1938 healthy and in good condition before the girls were taken off to the camp.

"Now the same person can hardly die twice and go on living," wrote Pääkkönen. No help or response had been forthcoming "although I run to the post office every day to get the information I am waiting for," as she later wrote to Kekkonen. It devolved upon another Kekkonen to take care of the Orell case, Taneli Kekkonen at the Moscow embassy.

When Urho Kekkonen turned to the Foreign Minis-

Reino Orell. Relatives in Finland sent this photo to Tamara in Ural. News of Orell's fate was sought in vain for decades.

try, department head Enckell asserted that there was nothing they could do after they received word of Orell's death. "We have no influence on the wife and child's leaving the country."

Information we found in the KGB archives in Jekaterinburg states that Reino Orell had indeed died 13 March 1938—but that he had been shot. His daughter Tamara still lives in Russian Karelia. His widow died there in 1981. Once during the 1950s when visitors were first permitted to come from behind the eastern border, the doorbell of the Puonti family in Kotka rang, and a surprise visitor stood there: Fomin's wife, Olga.

Mrs. Fomin related that after her husband had died in Chelyabinsk, the family moved to Leningrad. They were caught there when the Germans encircled the city. Death by starvation was widespread, and once she herself had been in a heap of bodies, until someone noticed that she was still breathing. Her son Leo had become an officer.

Karin Puonti had become withdrawn after her bitter experiences and had destroyed her husband's letters from Kamensk. By a roundabout way they had heard how Niilo Puonti had been arrested and had vanished in the winter of 1937-1938. They had never sought a death certificate.

Letters from the Finns in Kamensk were constantly intercepted, and they were not permitted to be in contact with the Finnish embassy. Some of them, Uuno Saarenoja and Hilda Takalo, for example, succeeded, through the agency of acquaintances, in mailing their letters from Sverdlovsk. They got visas and got to Finland. As soon as they were able to move freely within the nation, some of the Finns went to Estonia, thinking that it would be easier to arrange for their return from there.

There were still some twenty Finns living in Kamensk-Uralski after 1958, when twenty years had gone by since that city's tragedy.* By now many of them have died there.

In Finland Chelyabinsk is best known from the fact that atomic waste from the Loviisa power plant was taken there until the end of 1995. In this area Stalin's atomic bomb was once developed secretly, sparing no sacrifice. The polluting effects of the 1950 and 1960 accidents in the Majak atomic plant extended to this area, where the city of Kamensk-Uralski is located.

---

*They were Allen, Elli, Elsa, and Onni Kauppi, Olavi Kemppainen (Kompanjon), Lempi Keränen, Elvi Koskinen, Hanna Mäntylä, Armas, Lyyli, and William Pitkänen, Andrei, Eeva, Rauno, and Vladimir Saarelainen (now Sarlanen), Selma, Rauno, and Torsti Salonen, Hilma Vaittinen.

On the windy steppes some fourteen kilometers from downtown Chelyabinsk lies the village of Shershnja. Here one finds Zolotaja Gora (Gold Mountain), the site of an old mining operation—some thirty pits. The place was mysterious and even frightful; many rumors about it circulated. From 1936 to 1943, the area was strictly isolated—a barbed-wire barrier and a guard barrack materialized there. Local people said that trucks were driven there at night and the sound of gunfire was heard.

The story is told that one of the men shot there was able to crawl away wounded and that one of the village women had nursed him back to health. The man's later fate is not known.

After the war, gold miners were given permission to explore the closed

Antti Fomin's son Leo became friends with young Finns in Ural. Like his father, he became an officer.

mines. They dug a pit in the slope to a depth of fifteen meters, and then began to tunnel horizontally. Immediately they struck an old mine shaft. The next day a man was lowered into the shaft with a light. He ran into fumes and an acrid stench: the bottom of the shaft was full of bodies and the admission of air had accelerated their decay. The mining operation ceased.

In the summer of 1989 the Chelyabinsk Memorial Society began to explore Zolotaja Gora with shovels and brooms as their tools. Opening the surface layer of one pit, the diggers were able to count the remains of 200 people buried near the surface of the earth.

Excavations were made at the site of four mine shafts, and bones were found in three of them. The victims lay face down with their arms spread wide. There were skulls everywhere, in the backs and temples of which one could see holes made by bullets fired at close range. Near the larger skulls there were smaller ones—those of women or children. Many of the bones and skulls were crushed. They had been compacted by a heavy weight—by tractors? Perhaps they had not fit easily into the mine shaft? Was room being made for more? Or had bullets been saved by crushing the victims' skulls?

There were charred individual items to be found—eyeglasses, crutches, canes, eau de cologne bottles, 1930s coins. . . . Right in the middle of every-thing there was a vodka bottle and glasses. Had the executioners partied on the grave? Burned coal had been dumped on the bodies. It looked as if holes had been opened later and lime dumped in to hasten their decomposition.

There were human remains on several levels; it was estimated that there could be as many as 30,000 victims. The executions had been carried out over a number of years, and those to be executed had been brought to Zolotaja Gora from at least Chelyabinsk, Ufa, Kurgan, Shadrinsk, Orenburg, Sverdlovsk, and Nizhni Tagil.

When the searchers opened the graves in 1989, a much-decorated vet-eran, eighty-one-year-old Aleksei Bespalov, former chairman of the Chelyabinsk action committee, appeared on the scene. According to his account he had been the "head of the secret political branch" from 1941 to 1943. He related that the battle against the anti-revolutionaries, the nation-alists, and the trotskyites had been hard and difficult. "Sometimes we didn't get to sleep for two or three nights. Our eyes were red and our heads ached. . . . It was hard to work."

But you were probably fighting against German spies and parachutists sent here during the war? he was asked.

No, it was a question of anti-revolutionaries. "Don't put down our role. They were hardened enemies: trotskyites, eserries, all kinds of nationalists, marketplace anti-soviets . . ."

In the 1950s, the city management ordered that a garbage dump be established at Zolotaja Gora. The re-burial of Stalin's victims occurred in September 1989; the remains of 360 executed were gathered up in fifteen coffins. The honorary chairman of the Memorial Society, Academician Andrei Sakharov addressed an audience of thousands of people: "People were taken, shot without any sort of trial or investigation. We swear by these open graves that this will never happen again . . ."

There is now a Memorial Society marker at the site. Near Chelyabinsk there is also a memorial financed by the Germans and dedicated to those who were in the work army. It stands in the middle of the villagers' potato fields. A memorial plaque to those who were its victims was affixed to the wall of the old NKVD building in October 1995.

Relatives (above) gathered before the security services building in Chelyabinsk exhibit pictures drawn by a victim of persecution of comrades who shared their fate. Center photo: Andrei Sakhavov. Memorial (at right) to the executed at the Zolotaja Goran mass grave near Chelyabinsk.

In 1996 a memorial to thousands who were executed was also erected near Jekaterinburg on the road to Moscow. It is said that on this spot 200 people were executed every night in January 1938. A group of Finnish names is inscribed on plaques there, beginning with Bruno Aalto, the Alhonen couple, and Väinö and Tuomas Ahonen. It is difficult to say if they were actually shot here (and not in Chelyabinsk) or if the inscribers merely found their names in the Jekaterinburg archives.

In Russia nowadays, every October 30th is observed as political prisoners' day. On that day in Chelyabinsk people are acquainted with a small, half-underground room, entered from an inner courtyard, in which the Finns too are supposed to have been shot in the late winter of 1938.

Very few of the Finnish border-hoppers and their children returned after the war and even after the death of Stalin, and for those few it was a slow process. But as early as 1946 or 1947, Tyyne Eskola and two mothers with their sons, Kerttu and Leo Moilanen, and Sointu Lindroos and Rauno Karjalainen, were able to get here. They were all detained at Vainikkala on the border and confined in a quarantine camp in Hanko.

Finns who had been invited could try to come on visits. Among the first, and they found it easiest to come, were the children of Ural Finns who had moved to Estonia, but it wasn't really easy for them either.

Aino and Sirkka Saarela barely managed to move completely from Estonia to Finland in December 1956, but after that the officials asserted that there had been anti-soviet propaganda in Finland, so return was again restricted. It was conjectured that Fanni Pyykkö's activities were the cause; Pyykkö wrote a bitter and detailed series of tales of her experiences in the *Kaleva* newspaper, which she later expanded into a book. The book is touching in its descriptions, but it clearly contains a host of errors—according to those who had also been there.

The return of the Saarelas had not been easy either. Relatives promised to guarantee their welfare in Finland and their passports cost 400 rubles each. Aino Saarela had written to President Voroshilov and at last a letter came from him saying that her papers were in order and could be picked up at the passport desk. She had to leave the country within three days.

The very first to return from Soviet Karelia, taking everyone completely by surprise, was Sylvi Ollikainen. When her brother invited her to come and visit relatives in 1956, he had heard of only one woman who had been allowed to move from Karelia to Finland with her children. After a "paper war" and seven months of waiting, Sylvi got to go to Finland for two months. She decided boldly that she would remain here.

It was not easy to get to the Soviet embassy in Helsinki, but the service there was courteous. Permission arrived from Moscow just when her visa and its extension for a month and a half had expired. When Sylvi Ollikainen signed her two-year visa, she was so nervous that she dropped the pen. "Calm down," said the official. "Good luck in your new life!"

Before the year ended, Sylvi was again a Finnish citizen. Ten years later Kerttu Järvinen returned from Ural. She had hopped the border in 1932 in the same boat as Sylvi.

Eeva Markkanen moved from Kamensk to Estonia with her only child in 1957; she had already lost three children in the Soviet Union. They moved in with Sirkka Laurila. The visit became a stay of over thirty years. Markkanen summoned up the courage to start looking for relatives in Finland through the Red Cross. "When my first relative, my cousin Irma from Summa, came to Tallinn in 1966, we went to the harbor with my daughter. A ship arrived, and it was so heart-warming to see the Finnish flag waving. I hadn't seen the Finnish flag since 1932."

Eeva got to go to Finland for the first time in 1967. Finland seemed like a fairyland. Mother, daughter, and granddaughter moved here for good at the start of the 1990s. Sixty years had passed since the little girl from Kotka had said: "I'm not going to Russia."

When President Mauno Koivisto made the surprising promise on television in the spring of 1990 that Finland would accept the Ingrians as returning emigrants, a stream of migration from Karelia, St. Petersburg, and Estonia began immediately. The descendants of people born in Finland and of the "reds" of 1918 were astonished: What was their position then? In Finland no one knew, or wanted to know anything about them; it was just as if the border-hoppers' tragedy and the Ural Finns, whose fates had once caused records to pile up by the meter on officials' shelves had been entirely forgotten.

Even in 1978 one of the "children of Kamensk" returned from her Finland visit to Siberia because her relatives conjectured that Finland might surrender her or that there might otherwise be trouble for her children. Finns also warned the otherwise fearful survivors that asking about their lost parents could only cause trouble for them.

Some still wrote to Soviet officials and in the early 1990s finally received a true account of the place and date of their parents' death and a certificate of rehabilitation. Some even received the court's decision with the sentence; this is to be shown only to relatives or upon authorization.

The Wahlstén sisters heard nothing about their parents for twenty years. In 1958 in answer to their inquiry they received the (false) information that

Going home! Eeva Markkanen leaving Estonia with her daughter to visit Finland in the summer of 1967.

Kirsti and Viljo Wahlstén had been given ten-year sentences and had died in a camp—the mother of a stomach illness in April 1944 and the father of pneumonia in March 1946. The burial place was unknown.*

In 1959 Eila was paid 1,048 rubles compensation for the illegal arrest of her father, of which she gave one half to Irma. Nothing was paid for her mother, for she had been only a housewife, although as an invalid she could no longer go to work in Kamensk.

From 1955 on the children of the "illegally repressed" had the right to collect their parents' two months' wages from the last place they had worked or its legitimate successor. A written application had to be sent in, together with a notarized copy of the rehabilitation certificate, school records, and a paper certifying the relationship. People started calling this compensation "hide money." Getting it sometimes required years of a "paper war."

The Wahlstén sisters continued writing to officials and finally during the glasnost period they received new information: their parents had been sentenced on 11 and 13 February 1938 "groundlessly, to be executed" for crimes against the revolution based on their own confessions. The father and mother, respectively, were shot on 10 and 13 of March 1938.

Irma, who had worked in a circus and wound up living in Krasnojarsk, was the first to return to Finland in 1990. She had previously been listed as Russian on her passport. "You should be happy," said the militia man when she asked to have the listing changed. "As a Finn you would have been banished to the ends of the earth."

Irma started working as a cleaning woman, concealing her heart condition so that she would not be fired. When her landlord heard that she had come from Russia, he locked her out. She slept on a hallway floor until the Helsinki welfare officials found her a place to stay in a home for women alcoholics. After a year's wait, she got a foreign resident's passport. Now she is a Finnish citizen.

The whole Wahlstén family was still listed as missing in the Kallio parish membership records. In August 1992 the announcement of the death of Kirsti and Viljo Wahlstén fifty-four years before was read in the church.

---

*From 1939 on, the official answer regarding all those who had been executed read: "Sentenced to ten years labor reformatory camp with no right to exchange letters or receive packages"; in 1945 officials were ordered to answer inquiries with the statement that the prisoners had died in the camps; from 1955 on, that information was accompanied by a death certificate containing a fake time, place, and cause of death invented by the KGB. From 1963 on those who inquired were given an otherwise truthful death certificate, but with the cause of death stricken out. False information continued to be given until 1989 when the orders described above were countermanded.

In 1968 Eila Wahlstén started out to visit Finland. She traveled for days from Kalmukia to get to Viipuri with her little boy but was turned back. But she did get to go to Finland for Christmas. Only during the perestroika period did she dare seek to have herself listed as Finnish on her passport. She moved to Finland in 1993 and applied for a residence permit. She had preserved her Finnish language unadulterated, although she had not met a Finn for twenty years.

Her knowledge of the language and an official statement from the congregation—according to the church records, Eila Wahlstén was born in Helsinki 20 February 1926—were not enough. Her application was rejected. The Foreign Residents Office declared that "anyone at all" could ask for a statement from a congregation, and demanded to see her birth certificate.

The center demanded that she leave the country or the police would come for her. "I can't go on living," she wrote in her diary. Someone advised her to lodge a complaint with the highest government court, which held that "apparently" she was Eila Wahlstén and let her stay temporarily. Her four children came to Finland. As we wrote the last lines of this book in the spring of 1997, Eila Wahlstén received word from the police department that she had been granted Finnish citizenship. Immediately afterward she was notified that she would not receive a citizen's pension.

The Tervonen children have finally found each other and three of them have moved to Kemi. Annikki and Helvi succeeded in getting residence permits in the early 1990s. Antti Tervonen, now a little over seventy years of age, who had run away, been lost for forty-five years, and had forgotten his Finnish, came on a visitor's visa. An attempt was made to send him back from Finland to the Ukraine, where he had sold his small house. His sisters' activism saved him.

The Tervonens, like all the children who dared to ask, were given false information about their parents' fate. They received the first death certificates in 1956, according to which Liisa Tervonen had died of stomach cancer at the age of forty-nine during the summer of 1944, and Isak Tervonen in the fall of 1952 of inflammation of the liver at the age of fifty-seven. The Tervonens were rehabilitated as innocent by decision of the Ural military district's war tribunal in 1958.

The true information arrived during the last days of the Soviet Union in the fall of 1991. It was fifty-three years late. Isak and Liisa Tervonen had died in Chelyabinsk 13 March 1938. Cause of death: *Rastrel* (shooting). The children were paid a small sum of money as compensation, to be divided among the four.

Onni Kauppi still lives in Kamensk as one of the last of the Finns. He worked as a lathe operator in the aluminum plant there for forty-five years. His wife, Elsa Tervonen, committed suicide, as did the couple's son. Kauppi says that his wife never recovered from the shock of 1938 and that both mother and son must be counted among the victims of the destruction wreaked upon the Finns.

The last of the Mohicans. Onni Kauppi has written of the Kamensk Finns and tried to enlighten the local residents about their fate. Picture from 1960.

Erkki Murto moved to Sortavala. For twenty years, he had been applying for a visitor's visa to Finland, which the authorities repeatedly rejected without giving a reason. Going to Moscow in 1966, Murto requested an audience with President Nikolai Podgorny. He had thought that the presentation of people's concerns to state leaders was pure propaganda, but he did get to ask the president why he could not visit relatives in the neighboring country. The visa came, and the man visited Finland many times.

Murto wrote to President Koivisto, was allowed to move to Finland, and as a Christmas gift in 1991, received the decree that Finnish citizenship was granted to Erkki Kallenpoika Murto "on condition that at the end of two years he relinquish his Russian citizenship." Murto was of the opinion that he had been given no alternative in the past when he took a Russian passport—the militia man had had a pistol lying on the desk.

Rauni Murto lives with her daughter's family in Karelia. She does not plan to move to Finland, since her ailing, Russian-speaking husband would probably not thrive here. "I know how a person feels when she loses her homeland," Rauni Murto says. "I'm a rootless person. When I was young, life went on somehow, but when I was older I got an ache in my heart like a stone. I'll carry that stone with me to the grave."

Rauni's older sister, who had remained in Finland, helped the family for as long as she lived. In the late 1950s the sisters traveled to Leningrad from different directions to meet each other for the first time in almost thirty years. A whole bus load of Finnish tourists wept during the meeting, Rauni says.

When the Soviet Union broke up in 1991, the children of Ural Finns wound up in an entirely new situation. In the last census, in Kazakhstan, for example, there were over a thousand Finns (and Ingrian Finns), many of whom had remained there after being freed from the camps. Now they became aware that they were living in independent Kazakhstan, where they were treated as Russians, that is, as outcasts. For these old, ill, and penniless people, lining up for reception at Finland's Moscow consulate is virtually impossible.

Among others, Dagmar "Tamara" Kurko, Elsi Alhonen, and the Saari sisters Etel and Rakel were left in Kazakhstan; to the latter officials had first given the misinformation that their mother had died of a heart attack. Etel and Rakel knew that they had relatives in Finland, but did not know their names and addresses. Rakel Saari became blind in her old age. The invalid Etel lived in a small room in an apartment building, from which she got out once a year on the average, and drew a pension of eighty markkas a month.

Dagmar Kurko is remembered as a frightened girl who always wept after she lost her parents, never spoke to anyone, and forgot her Finnish without ever adequately learning Russian. She and the ailing Elsi Alhonen-Juntunen live in Petropavlovsk in an eighty-year-old, tumble-down house that looks like a storage shed. They came to Finland on a visitor's visa in 1990. Lauri Vaittinen has died in Kazakhstan. Anja Hansen, who worked as a seamstress, got married and disappeared somewhere, and Eila Tamminen moved away.

In 1950 Niilo Hansen-Haug's relatives in Oulu heard only that "unfortunately his whereabouts are unknown." The last letter from Hansen-Haug came from Kamensk on Christmas Day 1936. Kristiina thanked people for

In 1989, after fifty-seven years, Rauni Murto came to Mussalo in Kotka to visit the house from which the Murto family left for the Soviet Union.

the packages and wrote about her lung disease, on account of which both the physician and the factory were trying to persuade her to go to a sanatorium for three months. She, however, wanted to go on working. A full year later, as we now know, she was executed along with her husband.

After leaving the children's home, Aune Koskinen studied to be a teacher in Kazakhstan. She reportedly denied her mother Elvi, who had returned from the camp and found her, for political reasons—after all, her mother had been condemned as an enemy of the people. Elvi Koskinen moved to Finland alone and died here. Saimi Heikkilä and Elli Eskolin were reportedly informed on by their own sons.

Suoma Lahti tells what her acquaintances from the camp days experienced: "During their years in the orphan home, the children were told: 'If your mothers come to get you, refuse to go, for they are enemies of the people who don't deserve your love.'"

Many of the border-hoppers had waited for years under wretched conditions in Karelia. Hilkka Sinkkonen, for example, who still lives in a twelve-square-meter room in a private house in Kontupohja tried in vain to come. Salli Lappalainen sent in her papers seven times before she got to come in response to an invitation.

With the death of her aunt in the 1960s Hilkka Sinkkonen has no longer applied to go to Finland. After decades of hard work, her pension is some one hundred rubles; she did not know that by showing her prison camp certificate she could get a slightly higher pension.

Sirkka Eloranta, born in a camp of Finnish parents, wound up in a prison camp children's home. There her mother, Aili Eloranta, found her on being released. Aili, who suffered from a heart condition, was still active in community life in the 1960s and died at the age of seventy-three in Kazakhstan. Sirkka, who had studied nursing, came from there to Soviet Karelia as a refugee when the Soviet Union collapsed. She waited about a year in Petroskoi for a visa to Finland; her earlier papers had lain idle in Moscow. She lived in a small room with her children.

After three years of trying, Sirkka Eloranta has made it to Finland, but only one of her three children has been able to come. Sirkka's Finnish half-brother has helped her to move and settle here.

Eloranta's children were asked at the consulate why they did not speak Finnish. They were put into the same waiting line with the Ingrians, whose waiting time is over half a year. For this reason, her daughter, who has a baby herself, had to travel thousands of kilometers to Moscow and back again to await the decision. After that another daughter came to Finland on a visit, but was returned to Russia when she tried to stay.

Elma Ronkainen stayed on to live in Karaganda when she was released from the prison camp. Now she lives with her daughter in Novosibirsk, but her sister Bertta is still in Karaganda. Elma Ronkainen writes that she just sits in her shanty; she has no friends, her health is poor, her wages are not paid, she has to carry wood and water a long way . . .

Before they skipped across the border in 1932, Alfa Pekala-Kivinen's mother smuggled liquor in order to support her family. In the Soviet Union, Alfa was sentenced to ten years in a labor camp and to perpetual banishment to Siberia. There she was completely isolated from other Finns, worked sixteen hours a day, while trying to raise a child that was born in the camp. Now eighty-five years old, having lost her father, mother, daughter, and husband during the 1930s, Alfa Pekala-Kivinen lives in Karelia, her sister Tyyne in far-off Krasnodar. One of the sisters died shortly after being released. Elsa Pekala is awaiting return to Finland in Kostamus. She lives alone in a two-room flat, where she washes the floor twice a day for exercise while she sings: "Finland is my home, the dear land where I was born . . ."

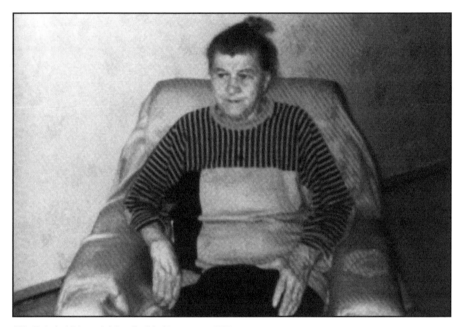

Alfa Pekala-Kivinen (eighty-five) in Kostamus, 1997.

Tyyne Rosendahl was sentenced to ten years in a camp and then to five years' banishment to Shadrinsk. She died there in 1976. Her two children, who were taken to children's homes, still live in Russia, Irma in Ural and Pentti in Siberia. Pentti Rosendahl, who happened to meet his poverty-stricken mother in Shadrinsk while he was in trade school, wrote:

> When I finished the school I got an unconditional work order for two years in Kurgan. From 1956 to1959 I discharged my obligations to the armed services. I married in 1960. I have two children, a girl Valentina

and a boy Andrei and one granddaughter Lena. Irma and I have many relatives in Finland. All of them promised to come and visit us, but apparently something prevented it. They have invited me to come and visit them, but I am forbidden to travel abroad since I work in a war plant, and now I don't have the funds to go anywhere. I haven't written to Finland for a long time.

It is a frosty day in January 1996. A cold east wind is blowing fine snow around the Helsinki railroad station. The last two passengers step down to the platform from the Moscow train. A small group is there to receive them. One of the women is disabled and moves cautiously and with great difficulty; she has to be helped. Her grown-up daughter Ljudmila is leading a brown spaniel made nervous by the odd smells.

Etel Saari has come home after sixty-three and one-half years. Her sister Lea died of cold and hunger in Kamensk in 1939. Her other sister Rakel lived to be seventy-one years old. Etel is the last member of the family that left Porvoo in 1932.

Notes

Page References

1   Markkanens' and Ollikainens' crossing: E Markkanen; S. Ollikainen; EK-
    Valpo XVI A 6c II, KA; Supo XXVII K-5799.
2   Lappalainens' crossing: S. Lappalainen.
4   Wahlsténs' crossing: E. Wahlstén; Ek-Valpo file 375, folder 3, report n. 74,
    7/32; Foreign Ministry (UM) written communication to the Moscow embassy
    1.24.33, UMA; Wahlsténs' personal files in both archives; Helsinki account
    books.
5   Saaris' crossing: Registration form: Saari, and letter 9.2.33, UMA 22 K.
5   Kakkinens' crossing: V. Kartineva.
6   Partanens' crossing: T. Kannas.
7   Estimate of 15,000 border crossers: Kostianen, p. 280.
7   Käkönens' claim: Käkönen, pp. 86-95.
7   With passports 1,400; [*Northern News*] 8.24.97.
7   Nykopp's account: Nykopp, p. 19.
7   Detentions by Finns: Kosonen-Pohjonen, pp.176, 190.
7   Detainees, distribution by years: Pogranitchnye. . . , p. 8; Koostiainen, p. 58.
8   Information from Kainuu: Kosonen-Pohjonen, p.178.
8   Unemployment in Kymi and Kotka: Viipuri district EK, situation report May
    1932, KA
8   Departures from the Kotka area, hiding aboard ship in Turku: Hakkapeliitta
    4.19.32; Isotalo, Chaps. 4 & 5; Uusi Suomi 11.22.32. Lost in Estonia: Tallinn

to the UM 12.21.31 and telephone report from Estonia 5.22.32, Ek-Valpo file 375; UMA file 40; Salminen I.1.

8   Detention at sea: Uusi Suomi 6.2.32; Kostiainen pp. 87-88.

9   Saarelas' departure: A. Peltola.

9   Kotka's Russian widows; US 2.29.32

9   Data from Petsamo, Terijoki, Joensuu: Ek Kemi Department 4.12.32, and Planting to the Interior Ministry 3.29.32, Ek-Valpo 375; EK Terijoki situation report March 1932, EK Joensuu 2.11.32

9   Ilomantsi and Kotka: Kansan Työ [People's Labor] 2.11.32; Helsingin Sanomat 2.6.32

10   Haukipudas, Syojärvi et. al.: Vapaus [Freedom] 7.18.32; US 7.2.32

10   Manninens' crossings: O. Manninen's notebook; Ek-Valpo XVI A6cI.

10   Kukko's sea voyage: Ruotu's account, EK-Valpo file 677; GAAOSO, folder 39603.

10   Laine family: S. Lahti; H. Rajala; Sevander, p. 54.

11   Jääskeläinens' story: E. Ranta.

11   Hartikainens' crossings: Harri's book; Immonen, p. 440.

11   J.W. Keto in the Soviet Union: Gustafsson, pp. 577-581

11   500 markkas for the trip: Advertisement 3.8.32, EK-Valpo file 375.

11   Behavior of the transporters: Nykopp, p 19; Flinkman, pp. 16-20; EK report no. 261m Hki 9.27.32, secret.

11   Riekki report: Riekki to the Foreign Ministry 8/32, EK file 375, folder 2.

12   Seppälä's story: Addendum to the transcript of interrogation 28/32, EK-Valpo Amp Finnish prisoners in Russia.

12   Account of the Murtos' crossing: EK-Valpo transcript of interrogation no. 178/32.

13   Murto family and Ilmari Murto: E. Murto; R. Murto; S. Ollikainen; GAAOSO f 1, op. 2, d 32793.

13   Soviet radio monitoring: Kostiainen, p. 44; Flinkman, pp. 10-11.

14   "The whole world knows . . .": YE statistical branch report Apr. 1933; UMA 22 K.

14   Ay-conference decision: HS 2.2.32

14   Leningrad radio Feb. 1933; YE statistical branch PM 3.11.33, UMA 22K.

15   "Potatoes and cabbage . . .": P. S. Report 10.17.32, EK-Valpo.

15   "With great skill . . .": Moscow embassy political report 2.25.32, UMA.

15   Pressure on the staff, welfare situation: Nykopp, pp. 10-11; Conquest II, p. 306

16   Famine and other reports: Moscow embassy political report 6.21 and 7.13.33.

16   Conquest's calculations: Conquest II, p. 306

16   Saarelas listen to the radio: A. Peltola.—Kuusinen was not in Karjala at the time and there is no confirmation of his radio talk.

16   Moscow Daily News: UM newspaper survey 1/34, UMA.

16   "News from fascist Finland": UM newspaper survey group 94, Russia, UMA.

16   Recruiter from Kemi: S. Karjalainen.

16   Recruiting Finnish-Americans: Hamlin, p;. 16; Koronen, p. 130; Takala in Karelia 3/93; Sevander P. 33, 38, 54; Kero, p. 36, 58.

17   Rovio's letter to Stalin: GAOPDF-archives, fond 3, op 5, delo 276.

17   Technical aid to Karelia: Kero pp. 30-31, 43, 76, 200; Carelia 3/93.

17   Finnish-Americans, their fate: Kero p. 18, 85; Carelia 3/93.

17   Cessation of activity: Sevander, pp. 41-42; Kero p. 58, 198.

17   Arrests, executions: Kero, p. 157; Carelia 3/93; M. Sevander.

18   Departure and contracts: Hamlin, pp. 19-20; Sevander, p. 71; Kero, p. 199; Hymy 3/96.

18   Disillusionment and "weeping": EK-Valpo newspaper survey 1/34.

18   Border-hoppers unwelcome: Riekki to the Interior Ministry 4.14.32, EK-Valpo file 375.

18   SKP leaflet: EK-Valpo file 375.

18   Free Labor warning: Free Labor 6.9.32.

19   EK does not believe there is recruitment: EK-Valpo file 375; Oulu sub-district, situation report, March 1942.

19   Russia refuses visas: Riekki to the Interior Ministry 4.14.32.

19   Maiski's words: Riekki's letter in an unnamed folder, UMA 22K.

19   Soviet embassy denies help to petitioners: EK Hki report 6.1.32, file 375.

19   Ek tests Kotka consulate: EK Viipuri situation report, Christmas 1932.

19   "Passports no longer denied": Jalanti PM, EK-Valpo XVI A 6c I.

19   Seppanen's story: EK-Valpo file 676.

20   Puontis' crossing: P. Kyyhkynen.

20   "'Butchers' try too . . .": Vapaus [Freedom] 5.16.32, 30.

20   Swindle in Helsinki: Pravda 10.12.32

21   Foreign Ministry memorandum: UM's PM 3.21.33, UMA.

21   "In some private letters . . .": Freedom 5.16.32. 30

21   Rovio and Stalin: Takala; "In Search of Eldorado," Carelia 3/93.

21   Announcement in Punainen Karjala [Red Karelia]: Punainen Karjala 5.24.32.

"IT WOULD BE NICE TO GET HOME"

23   Return to Finland: EK-Valpo XVI, file 375.

23   First interrogations: Salminen I, p. 30; EK Kemi transcript of interrogations 7.24.34; T. Laine.

23   Abuse of Saaristo: Kemppäinen's account, EK Valpo, file 676.

24   Ojala's account and Kingisepp: Lampila, p. 21: Salminen, p. 27.

24   Interrogation of Vilhelmina Murto: Interrogation 1932 in Murto folder GAAOSO fl. op 2, d 32792.

24   First words and meals: Apu [Aid] 38/94

24   Citizenship petition: Flinkman, p. 23: Huurre, p. 42; EK-Valpo file 378 and XVI A 6c I.

25   Investigation of men, wives' arrival:EK-Valpo file 375.

25   Number of border-hoppers in Kresty: Flinkman, p. 28; Ek file 378.
25   Women and children in Shpalernaya: Industrialnaja Karaganda 8.12.90; S. Lappalainen: O. Manninen's memory notebook .
25   Lehmus's account: Lehmus, pp. 114-115.
25   At the indoctrination building: Chief consulate of St. Petersburg's report 1/32, UMA; Lampila, p. 27.
25   Nykänen's death: A. Peltola
25   "We were locked up . . .": A. Vuorio's memory notebook and interview.
26   Ines Vuorio's letters: Vuorio folder, UMA 22K.
26   GPU's investigation, camps and job sites: Takala, p. 23.
26   Construction of the GPU Building: EK-Valpo situation report, 8/34 and XVI A 6b II; A. Rajala; Huurre, p. 161.
26   Boy's death: Karjala [Karelia] 11.23.33.
27   Hospitals and the disappearance of children: E. Markkanen; Aili Nikula's recollections; Salminen I, p. 88.
27   Jumping on the coffin: P. Kyyhkynen.
27   Complaints of 86 Finns: Rautkallio, p. 58.
27   Strike on the Mariinski Canal: V. Kartineva.
28   Strike at Kamajoki: Salminen I, pp. 68-69.
28   Strike in a Karelian logging site: EK's PM October 1934.
28   Strike of three Finns at Syväri: Flinkman, pp. 48-49.
28   Hunger strike at Kresty: Flinkman, pp. 56-57.
29   The Frisk incident: Valkama's account, EK-Valpo file 676.
29   Pyykkö's claim: Helenius, pp. 38-39.
29   The arrival of Finns at Svirstroi: EK Valpo XVI A 6b II; Kostiainen, p. 114; P. Kyyhkynen; Flinkman, pp. 34-36.
30   Flight of bachelors: HS 8.22.33; and 4.15.34; EK Valpo file 378; A. Peltola.
31   Arrest of 900: Carelia 5/97; S. Verigin, E. Laitinen.
31   Statement of 183 border-hoppers: Kostiainen, p. 170.
31   Siberian wolves: Apu [Aid] 28/94; T. Kannas; Flinkman, p. 53; Helenius, p. 31.
31   Vasenius's flight: Salminen I, p. 183.
32   Shipment to Siberia and Irkutsk: Kostiainen, p. 176; Karjala 11.23.33.
32   Red and black tablets: Flinkman, p. 37.
33   Osoaviahim and MOPR: EK-Valpo interrogation June 1936, Armas Jämsä's account; EK Valpo XVI A 6b II; EK Terijoki situation report no. 12/34.—Re. Osoaviahim in general, see Salomaa, pp. 285-292.
33   Puonti's lectures: Transcript of Vuorio's interrogation, EK Terijoki 8.1.36.
33   Puonti's crossing: P. Kyyhkynen.
33   Wage deductions: EK-Valpo XVI A 6b II.
34   Wahlstén's arrest: E. Wahlstén.
34   Informing on Puonti: P. Kyyhkynen.
34   Holopainen and the arrests: Flinkman, p. 39, 45; Helenius p 18, 74; EK file 677.

35   Aarne Kuusela: Rautkallio, p. 65.
35   Position of the Moscow SKP: Rautkallio, p. 65.
36   Death of children at Svirstroi: PS 11.19.32, EK-Valpo file 376; Flinkman, p. 40; A. Vuorio; Raitkallio, p. 71.
36   Laine's story: Hymy [Smile] no. 2/96.
36   "Strike forces": P. Kyyhkynen.
37   Abortion: A. Peltola's Memory notebook.
37   Conditions at Nevdubstroi: EK Sortavala situation report 2/33; Industrialnaya Karaganda 8.12.90; S. Lappalainen; A. Peltola.
37   Aid packages from Finland: EK-Oulu situation report 12/31; Kostiainen II; P. Kyyhkynen; R. Vorobieff.
37   Hansen-Haug's "large quantities": Letter from Rajajoki to Haukipudas 1933, exact date uncertain.
37   Westerlund's report: Westerlund to the UM 11.2.32, UMA.
37   Nuorteva goes to the barracks: Niemi, pp. 80-81.
38   Kaukonen and Ylen story: Westerlund to the UM 2.3.32 and 2.9.32, EK-Valpo file 375.
38   "We the undersigned": EK-Valpo file 375.
38   "It is not to the benefit . . .": Riekki to the UM 12.23.31, EK-Valpo file 375.
39   Paldans' petition: Paldan folder, UMA.
39   "I, the below-mentioned . . .": Karjalainen folder, UMA.
39   Withdrawal of petitions: Finland's Social Democrat 6.28.38.
39   Difficulties with passports and visas: Salminen I, p. 92, 123, 195, and II, p. 178.
39   Westerlund's message: Westerlund 2.9.32, file 375, KA.
38   Westerlund's recommendations at the year's end: Westerlund to Jalanti 1932, UMA 22 K; PM Salainen 12.3.32, Official measures, KA.
40   Yrjö Koskinen's viewpoint: From Moscow to the UM 1.21.33, UMA.
41   Westerlund ceases efforts: Westerlund to Hackzell 1.27.33, UMA.
41   Border-hoppers no longer ask for help: St. Petersburg 5.12.33, file 70. UMA 22 K.
41   Riekki denies spying: Riekki to UM 3.2.33, UMA.
41   Russian data about Finnish agents: Carelia 5/97.
41   EK Kemi district's opinion: EK Kemi 3.28.33, file 378.
43   Move to the Sarov camp: EK-Valpo XVI A 6c !; Addendum to EK Sortavala records 91/36; Apu [Aid] 38/94; Salminen I, p. 50; Rautkallio, p. 79; Helenius, p. 30; E. Wahlstén.
43   Svirstroi after others had left: EK-Valpo XVI A 6b II; Kostiainen, p. 114, Tuominen, p.181.
44   Train trip to Sarov: Aino Peltola's and Allan Vuorio's memory notebooks; P. Kyyhkynen; E. Wahlstén.
45   Women and children in Sarov: S. Hämäläinen; A. Peltola; A. Tervonen; H. Sinkkonen.
45   Yard, walls and church: EK-Valpo Finnish prisoners in Russia, interrogation

transcript signed by Rahikainen, KA; industrialnaya Karaganda 8.12.90; T. Kannas; V. Kartineva; Salminen I, p. 50.

45 Sarov dwellers and their number: EK Terijärvi 4.28.34, file 378; EK-Valpo XVI A 6c I and 6b II; Kostiainen, p. 187; Kivistös's series of reminiscences, Nykyposti [Current Post] 1987; A. Vuorio; A; Pekala-Kivinen.

45 The free and the confined: Kemppainen's account 1934, file 676, KA; Salminen I, p. 58; Isak Kaikkonen's letter 8.18.33.

46 Visiting children: P. Kyyhkynen; E. Wahlstén; H. Sinkkonen.

46 Irja Pekala's song: S. Ollikainen; Aino Peltola's memory notebook; A. Pekala-Kivinen.

46 Separation of boys from the others: Addendum to records 80/35, Finnish prisoners in Russia, KA; A. Vuorio.

46 Hunger and the death of Finns: ibid. 80/35; XVI A 6c I; EK Kemi record of interrogations 7.24.34, Kurvinen; Ajan Suunta [Trend of the Times] 11.3.33.

46 Närvänens: R. Vorobieff.

48 Skeleton Church: Tuura, pp. 134-35.

48 Fomkin, Hattunen, and interrogations: Ek-Valpo hlömappi 1770; Jämsä's account; Salminen I, p. 60.

48 Work assignments: Aili Nikula's recollections.

48 Feeding: Apu [Aid] 38/94; Letter from Sarov, Viljamaa folder, UMA.

48 Working conditions, the young in the woods: Addendum 80/35; A. Vuorio; V. Kartineva; T. Kannas.

49 Burial of the dead: V. Kartineva; Allan Vuorio's notebook.

49 About the commandant: T. Kannas; A. Vuorio.

49 Chaplin movie: Salminen I, p. 56.

49 State of mind among the Finns . . .": Mentioned in the transcript of Rahikainen's interrogation.

49 Escapes and petitions: border-hoppers' stories II, KA.

50 Osoaviahim and trade union meetings: Y. Kares, EK Sortavala situation survey.

50 Kanerva, Toijonen, and Gavroi: EK Valpo, Kataja's account, file 676, Pirttilä's account, file 677; T. Kannas.

50 Fomkin's background: GAAOSO Pekala folder, f 1, op 2, d26704-58.

50 Kosonen's background: EK-Valpo hlömappi 1770; O. Kosonen.

51 Women's letter to Mrs. Kosonen: EK-Valpo hlömappi 1770; O. Kosonen.

51 "Actually the clothing situation . . .": EK Sortavala, addendum to records 91/36 KA.

51 Fomkin satisfied with Finns: Salminen I, pp. 55, 60.

51 Fomkin and Varkkinen: Mattila's account, file 675, KA; Pirttilä's account, file 677; Lampela's account, file 677.

52 Kosonen as a socialist: EK Sortavala, Reisi's interrogation 9/36 KA.

52 Engineers gnaw at shoes: Vapaa Karjala [Free Karelia] and Inkeri. [Ingria].

52 Hyrsky's account: EK-Valpo hlömappi Hyrsky.

52   Fomkin on Kosola: border-hoppers' stories II, KA.
52   Saari informed on: L. Saari.
53   Laukkarinens informed on: GAAOSO Laukkarinen folder, f l, op 2, d42875.
54   Inspectors at Sarov: Helenius, pp. 39-40; Isotalo, pp. 107-108; XVI A 6c I,
     Jämsä's account, KA; P. Kyyhkynen; Kivistös' series of reminiscences in the
     Nykyposti [Current Post] 1987.
54   Saarenoja letter: Saarenoja folder, UMA.
57   Muuri boys: XVI A 6c I, KA.
54   Vartiainen: EK-Valpo hlömappi 1692.
54   Valkama: EK-Valpo hlömappi Valkamaa.
55   Saari's account of the sawmill: E. Saari.
55   Saari asks for stockings etc.: Letter from Svirstroi to Finland 9.2.32.
55   "We'll soon get a uniform . . .": Letter 11.22.32 in Saari folder, UMA
     (passport applications).
56   Saari on America: Letter to Finland 1.7.33.
57   Saari's petition: An undated hand-written petition in Saari folder, UMA.
57   Information about activity at the steam sawmill. EK-Valpo hlökortti Saari.
57   Riekki warns of agitators: Riekki to UM 3.2.33, UMA.
57   In general, however...": Yrjö-Koskinen to UM 1.21.33, UMA.
58   Ministry's memorandum: PM 3.21.33, UMA
58   Pakaslahti memo: PM 8.29.33, Pakaslahti.
59   Soviet Union does not acknowledge Finnish citizenship: File 70, Koistinen's
     memo 9.26.41, UMA.
59   Moscow's counterproposal: PM 3.21.33, UMA.
59   Shocking descriptions harmful: Um to Moscow embassy 5/33, file 70, UMA;
     secret wire from Moscow 11.5.33, same file.
59   Hackzell considers giving up: Hackzell 4.24.33, file 40, UMA.
60   Forms and accompanying letters: Embassy letter 6/33, file 70, UMA 22 K;
     Koistinen's memo 1941.
60   Ivalo's letter" Ivalo's letter 6.10.33 in Paldan folder UMA.
60   STT tells of agreement: EK-Valpo XVI A 6c I.
60   Lindqvist's letter: Lindqvist folder, UMA; EK Sortavala situation report.
60   Pakaslahti's statement: Pakaslahti's memo 11.30.33
61   Return of border-hoppers 1933-34: Koistinen's PM 1941.
61   "No citizenship": The phrase appears on the identification papers of border-
     hoppers who had been in Ural.
61   Nykopp's efforts: Nykopp, p. 9.

INTO THE URAL TRAP

63   1,300 Finns in Magnitogorsk: Rautkallio, p. 90.
63   First Finns: Isaak Kaikkonen's letter, 8.18.33.
63   A piece of sausage: P. Kyyhkynen.

64   Beginning journey, fire on the train: EK-Valpo file 264, Hyrsky; P. Kyyhkynen; Allan Vuorio's memory notebook.

64   Journey, arrival: T. Kannas; S. Lappalainen.

64   Magnitogorsk, Ural industry: Scott, p. 7, 70, 263; Kirillov I, p 113 and II, p. 55.

66   Foreign experts: Scott, pp. 74-76.

66   City and village: Addendum to records 80/35, EK Sortavala, KA; Scott, p. 64, 282.

66   Movement, sale of goods: Erkki Kuusinen folder, UMA 22 K (passport application); P. Kyyhkynen; S. Lappalainen.

66   Wages and food norms: Jämsä's account, EK-Valpo, KA; Scott, p. 57, 84.

67   Re. Osoaviahim: Finland's Social Democrat 6.28.38; Kostiainen, p. 155.

67   Re. Sanin-Sipinen: EK-Valpo hlömappi Sipinen; EK Terijoki, interrogation 66/37, Hyrsky; Logger's account, file 677, Murto's account, file 675, Viiala's account, file 675, KA.

67   Fomkin threatens Vuorio: A. Vuorio's notebook.

68   Trade school: Industrialnaya Karaganda 8.12.90; T. Kannas; Scott, p. 222; Solzhenitsyn III, pp. 347-348; O. Kauppi.

68   Getting food: T. Kannas; A. Vuorio.

68   Illness, death: Hymy 2/96; S. Karjalainen; P. Kyyhkynen.

68   EK's information about expulsions: EK Sortavala situation report Oct. 1934.

69   Banishments and Tara: EK memorandum PM Oct. 1934; Salminen I, p. 125, 134; Flinkman, p. 69.

69   "Banished people stay alive . . .": EK Sortavala situation report Oct. 1934.

69   "We have come to such a pass . . .": Kostiainen II.

69   Riekki's report: Riekki to the UM 10.8.34.

70   Emigrant sector: EK-Valpo file 677, Honkonen's account; S. Lappalainen.

70   Kuusela's and Sipinen's activities: Rautkallio, p. 90.

70   "Bone-rot in your brain": T. Kannas.

70   Palmén's question: EK-Valpo file 678, Samponen's account.

71   Kosonen's court case 1936; same file, Sinko's account.

71   Ahonen's jailing: EK-Valpo file 677, Kakkinen's account.

71   Magnitogorsk arrests: Scott, pp. 193, 32.

71   Border-hoppers' petitions; EK Sortavala situation reports.

71   Törölä's account: Adendum to report 80/35.

71   Liimatainen's reply: XVI A 6c II, KA.

72   Pukala's letter and fate: Letter from Magnitogorsk to Finland 2.13.34, Pukala folder, UMA; GAAOSO Pukala folder.

72   Pukala's background: P. Haapaniemi; Hymy 2/96; Orvo Virtanen folder, UMA.

73   "I most courteously beg . . .": Anna Orell's letter 2.9.34.

74   "I'll try it by myself . . .": Orell folder, UMA.

74   "I would like . . . with my family . . .": Pekala folder, UMA.

76   "Rauni and Erkki go . . .": Väinö Murto's letter 11.20.34.

76 Karvonen asks for help: Karvonen folder, UMA.

76 Katainen's letter: Katainen folder, UMA.

77 Hansen-Haug happening: Mother's letter to UM 2.20.36.

78 Pontus Artti's explanation: Artti's letter from Moscow to the treasurer's office 1.30.30.

78 The Laivo occurrence: Carelia 3/93; Sevander, p. 156.

79 The Puontis crossing and the start of their journey: Letter in the Puonti folder, UMA; UM's request to Moscow 7.17.33; P. Kyyhkynen.

79 EK's report on Puonti: EK's message in Puonti folder, UMA.

79 UM retracts its recommendation: UM's document to Moscow embassy 7.5.34.

79 Mrs. Puonti's return and the UM's replies: P. Kyyhkynen; Koistineni's letter 1.18.35; UM's letters 3.11.36 and 10.29.36.

79 EK changes its mind: EK to UM 1.12.37.

79 Re. Holsti: Karen Puonti's letter to Holsti 1.8.37.

80 Last stages of the Puonti case: UM's letter 4.28.37; Moscow embassy to UM 2.9.39; GAAOSO Puonti folder.

80 Statement on Viljamaa: EK to UM 10.27.33, Viljamaa folder, UMA.

80 Statement on Paldan: Paldan folder, UMA.

81 Hämäläinen's background: EK-Valpo hlömappi 5425, Hämäläinen; S. Hämäläinen.

81 Re. Holopainen: Holopainen folder, UMA; Moscow embassy to UM 9.27.39.

82 Yrjö Kares thwarts Lehtonen: To EK Sortavala headquarters 3.7.35.

82 Re. Malo: XVI A 6c II.

83 Re. Jelonen and Laukkanen: EK's letters to UM 5.18.34 and 5.4.34.

83 Re. Jokimies: EK letter 6.2.34, nameless folder, UMA.

85 Move to Chelyabinsk: Addendum to record 80/35; Rautkallio, p. 92; Sevander, p. 34.

85 Letter to O.V. Kuusinen: Rautkallio, pp. 48-49.

85 Strike over felt boots: Scott, pp. 117-118.

86 Finns in shopping lines: Scott, p. 117.

86 Fomin's arrival and background: Isotalo, p.124; Helenius, p. 43; O. Kauppi; Rautkallio, pp.91-93; Salomaa, p.311;—At least Rautkallio seems to confuse Fomin with Fomkin, thinking them one and the same man; it is hard to decide if Salomaa, using him as the chief source does the same—apparently so (see Salomaa, pp. 434-435). Neither has interviewed the border-hoppers, who remember Fomin and Fomkin well. Kostiainen also confuses Fomin and Fomkin (see Kostiainen, pp. 142-143, 250).

87 Hartikainen on Fomin: Harri, pp. 139-140; Hartikainen, pp. 29-30.

87 History of Chelyabinsk: Scott, p. 62,116; records 80/35.

87 A thousand Finns in the building: Kirsti Wahlstén's letter from Chelyabinsk, undated; S. Ollikainen.

88 Factories and Finnish work sites: Eemeli Nikula's letter 4.11.35; V. Kartineva; H. Sinkkonen; Jämsä's and Monto's accounts, file 675; Sevander, p. 82; Scott, p.267.

88   Wretched conditions and "panic": O. Kauppi; E. Wahlstén; Koskinen folder, UMA.
88   Re. Nikula: Letters 4.11.35 and 10.1.37; Aili Nikula's reminiscences.
89   "We were promised . . .": Viljo Wahlstén's letter 7.3., no year.
89   Sanin-Sipinen's opinion: Rautkallio, p. 92.
90   Riotous isolated: EK-Valpo hlömappi Hyrsky.
90   "Bosses" and clerical workers: Monto's account, File 675: Scott, p. 81, 282; Hamlin, p. 23; see also Kero, p. 210.
91   Consequences of "slacking": Hamlin, p. 58.
91   "Lately discipline . . .": EK Valpo report 80/35.
91   Fomkin recruits Hyrsky: EK-Valpo hlömappi Hyrsky.
91   Re. Eloranta: S. Eloranta.
92   Fomin's character and death: A. Vuorio; T. Kannas; Isotalo, p. 137; Helenius, p. 48.
92   Re. departures for trade school: T. Kannas; S. Ollikainen; Helenius, p. 48.
92   Return home of the Puonti women: P. Kyyhkynen; Helenius, p. 41.
93   Families left in Chelyabinsk: O. Kauppi; Helenius, p. 61; EK Terijoki interrogation 66/37, Hyrsky; R. Vorobieff.
83   Arrests: Helenius, p. 68; R. Vorobieff.

A PLACE NAMED KAMENSK

95   Name of the Finnish village: O. Kauppi.
96   The factory and its director: T. Laine.
97   Life in Kamensk: T. Laine; H. Sinkkonen; S. Lappalainen; A. Peltola.
97   Koskinen's letter to Finland: Koskinen folder, UMA.
97   Sewing workshops, Wahlsténs: the Kivinens' reminiscences in Nykyposti [Current Post] 1987; K. Wahlstén's letter from Kamensk 4.7.37.
97   Living conditions, rent: Kristiina Hansen-Haug's letter from Kamensk, undated.
97   Paldan's letter: Tyyne Paldan from Kamensk 5.5.37.
97   School: E Wahlstén; S. Eloranta; E. Markkanen.
98   Re. Eloranta: Neuvosto Karjala [Soviet Karelia] 8.18.67; S. Eloranta.
99   Kosonen's activities: EK-Valpo hlömappi 1770; Tyyne Paldan's letter 5.5.37; T. Laine.
99   Stakhanovism: Za Uralski Aliumini (ZUA) 1.15.36.—The paper's 1935 issues are missing.
99   Paper criticizes norms: ZUA 7.19.37.
100   Mason "Hapalainen": ZUA 9.11.37.
100   Number of Kamensk Finns: GAAOSO folder 26877, Orell; ZUA 3.23.89; Kamenski Rabotshi 4.28.93; Jämsä's account; addendum to EK record 443/37; EK Sortavala survey report 11/37; O. Kauppi; Interviews with those who had been in Kamensk.
102   Citizenship applications and test period: EK survey report 3/37; EK Valpo file

376.

102 Banishment abroad: Sbornik zakonodatelnih . . . p. 62.

103 Finnish citizenship and border-hoppers' passports: EK Valpo hlömappi 1770 and file 1394; XVI A 6c I and A 6b II.

103 "They all want . . .": EK Sortavala addendum to report 88/37.

103 Ivalo's letter: Ivalo to UM 10.27.36.

103 Move to Tashkent and Kazan: T. Laine.

104 From Amur AMP XIII C 1 b.

104 Arrest of 25 Finnish "agents": Letter from Head of Tatar NKVD to Jeshov, Tatar KGB archives, f. 109, op. 5, d. 32.

105 Kazan Executions: Tatar KGB archives, folder cited.

105 Laine in Uhta: T. Laine.

106 Varis brothers: GAAOSO Varis folder, Letter dated 1.4.38.

106 Flinkman in Uhta: Flinkman, p. 184.

106 Survey of border-hoppers: EK situation survey 1936, KA.

107 The Saaris' life in Kamensk: Letters from Kamensk 3.13.36; 10.8.36 and 9.9.36 (37?).

107 Puonti's last letters, Aalto's flight: P. Kyyhkynen.

108 Hyrsky pesuades Wahlstén: E. Wahlstén.

108 Re, Fomkin and his son: GAAOSO Pekala folder; S. Karjalainen.

108 Kosonen and other leaders: EK Valpo hlömapit Sipinen, Kosonen.

109 Sinko's account: EK Sortavala 1937, Sinko's interrogation, Finnish prisoners in Russia.

109 Re. Eloranta: S. Eloranta, A. Pekala.

109 Re. Tiainens: EK Terijoki interrogation record 66/37.

109 Fomkin as a jailer: Sinkko's interrogation, KA; T. Laine; Honkonen's and Roiha's accounts, file 677, KA.

109 Being taken to interrogation and prison: Helenius, p. 55; Sinkko's interrogation.

110 Sentences: EK Valpo hlömapit 1770.

110 Markkanen's fate: E. Markkanen.

110 Sanni Lappalainen offered money, questioned about returnees to Finland: A. Peltola; T. Romanova; Supo archives (XXVII K).

111 Recruiting of Aura: Supo archives XXVII K—Heikkilä, Saimi.

112 Re. Murtos: R. Murto and his letter to Finland.

112 "Honorable Sir Minister . . ." Kantonen folder, UMA.

113 Tervonens' quarrel: Annikki Tervonen.

114 Tervonens' letters: Tervonen folder, UMA.

114 Gerda Saari's letter: Letter from Kamensk to Porvoo 10.15.37.

115   Inquiry re. those wishing to return to Finland 1937; Pääkönen's letter to Kekkonen, Orell folder UMA.

116 Re. Juntunens: Letter 11.19.37, Juntunen folder UMA.

116 Re. Vilkman: GAAOSO Vilkman file.

298 / NO HOME FOR US HERE

117 "If you can wait . . .": EK Sortavala situation report 11/37.
117 Närvänen's information: Letter 3.17.38 Närvänen folder, UMA.
117 Liljerooses and Lahtinen: GAAOSO folder 43084 (Liljeroos) and folder 43082 (Lahtinen).
117 "Sometimes it seems very sad . . ." Kirsti Wahlstén's letter 4.7.37, hand copied by E. Wahlstén.
118 Home from the sewing workshop: Aili Nikula's reminiscences.
118 Waiting to leave and in school: E. Wahlstén; Irma Wahlstén's letter 6.2.36.
118 A woman visitor talks about Finland: Koskinen folder, UMA.
118 Paldan's arrest, wife's letter to Finland: E. Markkanen; E. Wahlstén; Tyyne Paldan's letter 5.5.37.
118 Christmas arrests: E. Wahlstén; P. Kyyhkynen; S. Hämäläinen; GAAOSO Puonti folder.
119 Tree celebration and picture of a girl's hand: Anni Kantonen's letter to Finland, Kantonen folder, UMA.
120 Last petitions in December: S. Ollikainen, Salonen folder, UMA.

THE RISE AND DESTRUCTION OF NIZHNI TAGIL

121 Working in Revda, Zlatoust etc.: Scott, p. 115, 267; Solzhenitsyn III, p. 56; Kostiainen, pp. 124-125; EK Valpo Sortavala, addendum to record 80/35, KA.
121 "Double-decker bunk in the barracks": K. Suvano.
121 Construction work at Tagil: Scott, p. 268; Supo Amp XIII X 1b, nro 12.12.57; Bolshaya Sovietskaya Ensiklopedia; Y. Siivonen.
123 Work tempo of Finns and Finnish-Americans: Sevander, p. 75; Aino Peltola's memory notebook.
123 "Our life is no . . .": Jordan folder, UMA.
123 "Alas, winter . . .": EK-Valpo Secret PS-report 1846/38, KA; Letter from Zlatoust; Tuura, pp.131-132.
123 Re. Ellen Närvänen: R. Vorobieff.
124 Re. Saarelas: Apu [Aid] 38/94; S. Saarela.
125 Tyyne Eskola's tale: A. Ppeltola; Supo XXVII K—1901.
125 Finnish village and number of residents: A. Peltola; S. Saarela; Apu [Aid] 38/94; for number in barracks see Supo XXVII K, Saarela, Aino; Y. Siivonen.
126 Re. Palmén: Apu [Aid] 38/94; Aino Peltola's memory notebook.
127 "banished . . . from Nizhni Tagil": File 683, KA.
127 Tagil's leaders sentenced and executed: Kirillov I, p. 201, 209, 213; Molotov, pp. 41-43; Conquest I, pp. 229, 260.
128 Sointu Lindroos's letter: Secret PS-report 1846/38.
129 NKVD celebration: Getty, p. 183.
129 Imprisonments 17 December: A. Peltola; Kostiainen, p 209; GAAOSO files on prisoners.
130 Tagil's prison camp concentration: Kirillov II, pp.3-4; Map of Gulag.

130   Other camps in the area: Dallin-Nicolaevsky, pp. 67-68.
130   Kirillov on punishments: Kirillov II, p. 71.
130   The Arvo Lampi happening: Letter, Russian security service governance for Sverdlovsk area 10.16.93; interviews with relatives.
131   Olkkonen's background: Vaasa HO's decision 2.29.32; Siltala p. 341, 409.
132   "When they took me to the border . . .": GAAOSO f 1 op 2 d 43619, Olkkonen, excerpt from interrogation transcript. Archives have noted on the transcript "Not for publication." We publish the excerpt with the relatives' permission.
133   Olkkonen's sentencing and death: GAAOSO, fl 1, op2, d 43080; Sverdlovsk area archives command's letter 1.24.97; Nizhni Tagil civil registry death certificate February 1997.
133   The Miettinen happening: GAAOSO Miettinen folder.
133   Finnish-Americans' fate: GAAOSO f 1 op 2 d 2283, Käkelä.

ESCAPEES AND EMBASSY PRISONERS

135   "Is that a way of sending in agents?": EK Terijoki 6/34, XVI A 6b I.
135   "They seem to be trying to recruit . . .": Valpo situation report 10/38. File 1394.
135   Twenty percent: Tuura, p. 138.
135   Report on Petsamo and Salla: XVI A 6c I.
135   Letter from a woman who had returned to Finland: Valpo's secret situation survey nro. 4, 4/41.
136   "We Finns were . . . domestic animals . . ."etc.: US 4.23.34; Karjala 4.25.34; XVI A 6b II.
136   "Hyena" journalism: Solanko to UM 10.1.37, UMA.
136   Flight of Vuorio etc. to Finland: Allan Vuoro's memory notebook and interview; EK Terijoki interrogation transcript nro. 94/36.
139   Kakkinens' flight: Kakkinen's account, file 677, KA; V. Kartineva.
140   Höglund's and Kunnas's cases: Höglund's and Kunnas's folders, Karjala security service archives.
141   Murtos' flight: Extract from Nykyposti 1992, no date.
141   Flinkman and border-hoppers, Flinkman and hunger strike: Flinkman p. 57, 201; see also Supo XXVII K—2113.
142   Hyryskys' flight and imprisonment: EK-Valpo hlömappi Hyrsky and file 264; Isotalo, p. 51.
142   Hyrsky in Finland: Rentola, pp. 296-301, 307.
143   "I've come to realize . . ." EK-Valpo hlömappi Hyrsky.
143   Re. Valkama: EK-Valpo hlömappi 2641.
143   RE. Huotari: Supo XXVII K—3816.
143   Lappalainen's flight: A. Peltola.
144   Alatalo's court case: Folder 29975 (Alatalo) Karjala security service archives.

144   Six who made it to Finland: file 683, KA.
144   Arrests at the gate: Isotalo, p. 192.126
145   "Every morning a few workers . . .": Raivaaja 11.22.89.
145   The NIkulas and Kivistö: Nykyposti series 1987; Aili Nikula's reminiscences; K. Suvano.
145   Yrjö Koskinen's "lies," "smuggling": E. Serjozhnikova.
145   "The only accessible road . . ." : Flinkman, p. 95.
145   Re. Perho: Käkönen pp. 86-95.
146   Disappearance of embassy workers: E. Serjozhnikova; J. Vanamo; S Lahti; H. Rajala.
146   Re. Karenius: Supo XIII c I b, Supo Hki 11.13.56.
146   "Finnish agents" revealed in Kazan: F 109, op 5, d 32, Tatar security service archives.
146   Re. Suoma Lahti and Anna Laine: S. Lahti; H. Rajala; Sevander, pp.78-79.
147   Re. Kilkkinen: Raivaaja 11.22.80; Flinkman, p. 230; J. Vanamo.
147   The fate of Suoma and her son: S. Lahti; H. Rajala; Raivaaja 11. 22.80; Sevander, p. 79.
147   1939 and 1941: Raivaaja 11.22.80; Nykopp, p. 138; Suomen Kuv alehti [Finland's Pictorial] September 1941.
148   Trio hides: T. Laine; J. Vanamo.
148   Huuskonen's experience: Huuskonen, p. 150.

OPERATION FINNS

149   Kirov's murder: Embassy's political reports 12.13.34 and 1.23.35 UMA.
149   Measures taken after the murder: Radzinski, pp. 358-359; Sbornik zakonodatelnyh. . . , p. 3.
149   Punishment of those without passports: Kirillov I, p. 165.
149   Re. Gylling, Karelia: Kero, pp. 161, 165, 170.
151   Resolution on Rovio: Takala, Carelia 9/91.
151   Order No. 55709: Gildi, pp. 246-247; Jokipii, p. 222.
151   Purge orders: Takala, Voprosy istorii..., p. 17.
151   Purge of Red officers: Voprosy istorii..., p. 118; Salomaa, pp. 305-307.
151   Support groups: Rautkallio, p. 140; I. Takala.
152   Attack in Vapaus [Freedom] paper: Kero, p. 189.
152   Finns and citizenship: Valpo situation report 8/38, KA.
152   Seventy-five percent of border-hoppers: Takala, Studia Slavica, p. 128.
152   Transport of border-hoppers: Jokipii, p. 322; Lampila, pp. 54-58, 65.
152   Holsti and Litvinov: Yrjö-Koskinen's missive to UM 7.12.38, KA.
152   Unfit for spying: Nykopp, p. 20.
153   Yrjö-Koskinen on terror: Political report 6.8.37, UMA.
153   "Further on . . ." Ibid.
153   Resolution of 7.2.37: Jokipii, pp. 222-223, Takala; Voprosy. . . , pp. 120-121.

154 Triads and dyads: Solzhenitsyn I, pp. 61, 212-213, Sbornik zakonodatelnyh. . . , p. 63.

154 Order no. 00447: Leningradski martirolog, pp. 41-42.

154 Approval of inreased number: Stepanov, pp. 16-18.

154 Order no. 00485: Rastrel po limitu, p.16; GAAOSO Katvala folder.

155 Rough draft of resolution re. Finns: Tshuhin, Severnyi Kurier 1.15.97.

155 Tenison's letter to Zakovsk: 5. albumi, Karelia security service archives.

155 Order to continue the operation: Moskovskye Novosti 6.21.92.

155 Permitting and prohibiting of torture: Radzinski, p. 378; Solzhenitsyn I, p. 83; Kirillov I.

155 Kruschev on Stalin's secret wire: Tuominen, p. 243.

156 Chargé d'affaires on the Stalin line: Political report 9.23.37, UMA.

156 Yrjö-Koskinen's report Political report 10.11.37.

156 Foreign communists' fate: Political report 11.15.37.

157 Prosecution quotas: Dallin-Nicolaevsky, p. 259: Solzhenitsyn I, pp. 62-63; Jokipii, pp. 223-224; Karjalan Sanomat [Karelia News] 2.19.97; Conquest I, p. 458.

157 "They told me . . .": Suoma Lahti's memory notebook.

157 "One of the judges . . .": Huurre, p. 222.

157 Combing through the card files: Dallin-Nicolaevsky, p. 259.

157 Paid informers: Radzinski, p. 389.

157 Number of prisoners in 1940: Argumenty i fakty, 11-16/1.1989.

158 "Many mass arrests": Valpo situation report, 4/38, file 1394, KA.

158 The wave swept by: Sevander, p.105; Huurre, pp. 153-154.

158 Karelia NKVD report: I. Takala, Studia Slavica, p. 139.

158 NKVD on the Finnish border-hoppers in Karelia: Carelia 3/93.

158 Numbers imprisoned and executed 1937-1938: Severnyi Kurier 1.15.97; Journal of History 1/91; Jokipii, p. 224, 323; Sevander, p. 101; Kostiainen, p. 118.

159 Kontupohja, Petroskoi: HS 2.25.90; Sevander, p. 71, 106; Kero, p. 190; Journal of History 1/91.

159 Fate of families of prisoners: Valpo situation report 3/39; Sevander, pp. 109, 110; Huurre, p. 165; Siimes in Punalippu [Red Flag] 8/88, I. Tshuhin, Severnyi Kurier 4.7.95.

159 Banishment to the east: Valpo Sortavala situation report 7/38 and 5/39, file 1416, KA.

159 Turn for the better from fall of 1938: Huurre, p. 222; Solzhenitsyn I, p. 66; Radzinski, p. 482; Getty, p. 189.

159 After the Winter War and 1941: Saarinen's statement, EK-Valpo XXXIV G 6, file 671; Lampila, p. 207; Solzhenitsyn III, pp. 106-108.

160 Rebellious areas: Kirillov I, p. 208.

160 NKVD Order 52623 comes to Ural: GAAOSO folders 26877, Orell (according to which Suharev signed his confession 4.3.40 and Fomkin 4.16.58) and 26808-58, Wahlstén; Gildi, p. 27.

160 Polish wire from Chelyabinsk: Kamenski Rabotshi 4.28.93.
161 Fomkin and "over 200" prisoners: GAAOSOO Pekala folder.
161 New group operation: GAAOSO Orell folder.
161 Leader complains of slow operation: Ibid.
163 Kniazev's account: GAAOSO f 1, op 2, d 22143, p. 61.
164 Victims of Operation Finns 1937-38: I. Takala.

THAT NEW YEAR'S NIGHT

165 Club celebration: S. Lappalainen.
165 Leaving for the dance: S. Ollikainen.
166 Soldiers in the barracks village: S. Hämäläinen; H. Sinkkonen.
166 Meeting in the dining hall: S. Lappalainen; S. Hämäläinen; R. Murto; H. Sinkkonen.
168 "A man in civilian clothes . . .": S. Hämäläinen.
168 Out of the dining room to the trains: Industrialnaya Karaganda 8.12.90; Helenius, p. 66; E. Murto; S. Hämäläinen.
168 Barracks rooms emptied: S. Hämäläinen, H. Sinkkonen, R. Murto; E. Wahlstén.
170 Re. Viuhko, Jelonen: S. Llappalainen; E. Markkanen.
170 Visitors from Finland: E. Wahlstén; E. Markkanen.
170 Return from the dance: S. Ollikainen; H. Sinkkonen.
171 Markkanen and the militiaman: E. Markkanen.

WHERE DOES THIS ROAD LEAD?

173 At the Sinarskaya station: Industrialnaya Karaganda 8.12.90; E. Wahlstén; S. Lappalainen; H. Sinkkonen; R. Murto; O Kauppi; S. Hämäläinen.
175 The young return to the barracks: T. Romanovna; S. Karjalainen; A. Tervonen.
175 Name of the barracks village: O. Kauppi.
176 "I saw a long line of cattle cars . . .": Helenius, p. 65.
176 Children taken from their mothers: Industrialnaya Karaganda 8.12.90; S. Lappalainen; S. Hämäläinen; E. Saari; H. Sinkkonen; S. Ollikainen; E. Wahlstén.
179 Chelyabinsk children's home: E. Murto; E. Wahlstén.
180 Encounter in the prison yard: S. Lappalainen.
180 Ollikainens meet in prison: S. Ollikainen.
180 Prisoners crowded: Conquest I, p. 267; Valpo's situation report 1939, KA; Mironova's turn to speak at Chelyabinsk 11.30.95, note by Eila Lahti-Argutina.
180 Women in cells: S. Ollikainen; H. Sinkkonen.
181 "Disclosed and liquidated. . . ,": GAAOSO Katvala folder.

181 Men's message to women's cell: S. Ollikainen; S. Lappalainen.
182 NKVD's interrogation procedures: EK-Valpo folder 671, KA; S. Hämäläinen; Helenius, p. 67.
182 Suharev's account: GAAOSO folder 26877 (Orell).
182 Kuikka incident: S. Ollikainen, S. Lappalainen.
182 Waterdrop torture: Solzhenitsyn I, pp. 83-95; Kuusinen, p. 209.
183 Interrogation procedures in Tara and Karelia: Salminen I, pp. 209-225; Huurre, p. 222.
184 Siiri Hämäläinen interrogations: Industrialnaya Karaganda 8.12.90; S. Hämäläinen.
185 Sylvi Ollikainen's interrogations and her father's confession: S. Ollikainen; GAAOSO Ollikainen folder.
186 Sinkkonens, Huotari: H. Sinkkonen; S. Karjalainen; O. Kauppi.
187 Course of the investigation: GAAOSO Orell folder.
187 Section 58: See, e.g., Leningradski martirolog I, p. 17; Kirillov I, p. 60.
188 Fictitious recruiters and false confessions: S. Ollikainen; Kuusinen, p. 214; HS 9.29.91.
189 Veikko Nieminen as a "recruiter" etc.: GAAOSO 25668-58 (Lappalainen).
191 Order for the arrest of Salli Lappalainen: Chelyabinsk area NKVD detention order no. 216, 1.2.38.
191 Record of iterrogation: Signed paper 1.19.38. GAAOSO Lappalainen folder.
192 Urho Murto's confession: GAAOSO folder 32793-P (Murto).
193 Sylvi Laukkarinen's confession: GAAOSO Laukkarinen folder.
193 Wahlstén's confession: GAAOSO folder 26808-58 (Wahlstén).
195 Tales about Katvala and other information: GAAOSO Katvala folder.
197 Al honens: GAAOSO Alhonen folder.
198 Saari's interrogations: L. Saari.
198 Sipinen's fate, and "special treatment": S. Eloranta; GAAOSO folder 26877.
198 Fomkin visits the cell: S. Ollikainen; Helenius, p. 67.
199 Markkanen's fate: GAAOSO folder 28514 (Markkanen); E. Markkanen.
199 Changes at the NKVD top: Andrew Gordievsky, p. 130.
199 Alatalo's confession and sentence: Alatalo folder, Karelian security service archives.
201 Veikko Ollikainen in Karelia: S. Ollikainen.
201 Interrogation and execution of six young people: Folders 14725 (Ollikainen), 11622 (Seppänen) etc., Karelian security service archives; death certificate no. 209 (Ollikainen), Prääsä 8.3.89.
202 "In the city of Nizhni Tagil . . .": Riekki to UM 1.24.38, KA.
202 "I did not dare . . . in the last letter . . .": Letter 3.17.38, Närvänen folder, UMA.
203 "Viljo Vahlstén and wife . . .": Wahlstén folder, UMA.

AMEN!

205 "25 years without correspondence privileges": Conquest I, p. 459; Rasstrelnye. . . , p. 191.
205 Execution of Saaris: L. Saari.
205 Hämäläinens' execution and Valpo's notification: GAAOSO file 177, Hämäläinen; EK-Valpo file 5425, KA.
206 Wahlsténs' execution: GAAOOSO folders 26808, 26809; death certificates; E. Wahlstén.
206 Hiskias and Fabian Närvänen: R. Vorobieff.
206 Sinkkonens' execution: Death certificates.
207 Conquest re. Lefortovo: Conquest I, pp. 457-458.
207 Hartikainen's assertion: Harri, p. 137.
208 Shootings in Karelia and Nizhni Tagil: Jokipii, p. 323; Karelian News 2.19.97; Kirillov II, p. 206.
208 Ural foreign national operation and Jekaterinburg: Kirillov II, pp. 208-209; Uralski Rabotshi 10.29.96.
210 Solzhenitsyn's horror: Solzhenitsyn I, p. 322.
210 Secret order circulated throughout NKVD: Solzhenitsyn III, p. 103; Kustaa Rovio: 3.13.38; Jokipii, p, 323; Salomaa, p. 308.
210 Executions in Uhta: Flinkman, pp. 168-169.
211 Mass grave at Zolotaja Goran: Mironova's statement at Chelyabinsk 10.30.95.
212 Decision to shoot Kirsti Wahlstén: GAAOSO f 1 op 2 d 29809.
212 Ebba Murto is saved: H. Sinkkonen; S. Lappalainen; HS 2.25.90.
213 Salli's mother's scream, execution: S. Lappalainen; GAAOSO Lappalainen folder.
213 Girls taken for sentencing and those pregnant: H. Sinkkonen.
214 Sentence: Statement of decision 4.11.49.
214 Dance in the corridor: H. Sinkkonen; S. Lappalainen.
214 "Where does this road lead?": S. Lappalainen.
215 Sylvi left alone in jail: S. Lappalainen.
215 Women do not know: Valpo situation report 1/41.
215 Takalo and Viman: Folders, UMA.
215 Hyrsky's letter to the Soviet Union: EK-Valpo hlömappi Hyrsky.
216 Kosonen replies to Turku, Kuusinen's fate: Kosonen's letter from Kamensk 7.16.38, KA; GAAOSO Kuusinen folder.
217 Valpo's knowledge of events: Valpo situation report 1/38 and 3/38. file 1394, KA.
217 "In early 1939 . . .": Valpo Terijoki situation report no 2, 3.6.39. file 1394, KA.
217 Voionmaa's letter: EK-Valpo, XVI A 6c II.
218 Yrjö-Koskinen's reply: Yrjö-Koskinen to UM 7.12.38, UMA
218 Change for the worse and Amen!: Yrjö-Koskinen to UM 11.3.38, KA.

THE CHILDREN OF KAMENSK

221 Elsa's and Lea's cards: Tervonen and Saari folders, UMA.
223 Lea Saari's fate: E. Saari; S. Karjalainen.
223 Women and children left in Kamensk: S. Karjalainen; O. Kauppi; E. Markkanen; R. Vorobieff; GAAOSO arrest information from January 1938.
223 Re. Markkanens: E. Markkanen.
224 Laurilas and Moilanens: S. Karjalainen.
224 A few men return: O. Kauppi; S. Karjalainen.
227 Automobile factory and commune: Hamlin, pp. 14-16; Kero, p. 30; Supo XIII C 1 b, Turku subdistr. 11.24.56.
227 The Kauppis' fate: O Kauppi; Red Flag 12/89; Sevander, pp. 75-77.
227 Women disappear 1 November: O. Kauppi; ZUA 3.23.89.
227 Meeri Salonen and Vorkuta: Työmies-Eteenpäin 4.19.91; GAAOSO Salonen folder; Salonen folder, UMA; in which the petition for a passport and photograph indicate that at least then the Salonens had a child; Dallin-Nicolaevsky, p. 73; A. Pekala.
227 Account by one who returned from Vorkuta: S. Hämäläinen.
227 Pekala and Fomkin's order: GAAOSO Pekala folder.
228 Aino Kuusinen's account: Kuusinen, pp. 213, 228-231; A. Pekala.
228 The remaining children to a children's home: E. Markkanen.
229 Deaths of children: E. Wahlstén.
230 Relatives separated, disruptive children removed: Sbornik zakonodatelnyh. . . , pp. 92, 100-101; Radzinski, p. 472.
230 Children at the militia post: R. Murto; E. Wahlstén.
231 Arrival in Arkhangelsk: H. Tervonen; R. Murto; E. Saari.
231 Talk to the Murto children: R. Murto.
231 Karhula sheriff's statement and the Murto's fate: Sheriff to UM 4.26.39, Murto folder, UMA; GAAOSO Murto folders: UM to Moscow embassy 8.15.39, Murto folder, UMA.
232 Reino Murto's fate: Annikki Tervonen; E. Murto; O. Kauppi.
233 Kamensk during the war: O. Kauppi' E. Saari; E. Markkanen.
233 Wrong information about Finns: O. Kauppi; Za Uralski Aliumini 2.17 and 3.23.89; Onni Kauppi's letter 2.11.90.
234 Tuominen on Chelyabinsk: Tuominen, p. 375.
234 In the children's home and at work during wartime: E. Saari; H. Tervonen; R. Murto; E. Wahlstén; H. Hämäläinen; S. Hämäläinen; Seura 2.17.95.
235 Antti Tervonen's disappearance: Antti Tervonen; H. Tervonen.
236 Etel Saari's fate: E Saari; L. Saari; E. Wahlstén.
237 Mothers and children in Nizhni Tagil: S. Saarela; A. Peltola.
238 Tyyne Eskola and her child's death: Suomenmaa 7.15.95.
238 Pellikka's story: Aino Peltola's memory notebook.
239 The Rosendahls' fate: GAAOSO f 1 op 2 d 29826 (Rosendahl); Pentti

Rosendahl's letter 1997.
239   Saarela's arrest: A Peltola; S. Saarela; Apu [Aid] 38/94.
240   In the children's homes, in school: T. Romanov; R. Vorobieff; S. Saarela.
241   "Send me a comb for lice": Apu [Aid] 38/94
242   Saarela in the prison camp: Apu [Aid] 38/94; Aino Peltola's notebook.

CAMP INMATES

243   Re; Karlag, Karabas: Sobesednik 25/89; S. Lappalainen; S. Lahti.
244   Siiri's prison number: HS 9.29.91.
244   Eloranta's daughter is born, winds up in morgue: S. Eloranta.
244   Women eat in the fields: H. Sinkkonen; S. Lahti.
245   Finnish prisoners of war: M. Lehtineva.
245   Plea for aid to Helsinki 1941: Valpo situation report 3.20.41.
245   Cows and wolves: S. Lappalainen; S. Lahti.
246   Railway construction, train derailment: HS 9.29.91.
246   Christmas songs, the Finnish language: S. Lahti; s. Lappalainen.
247   Camels and a dead Finn: S. Ollikainen; H. Sinkkonen.
247   Suoma Lahti arrives at the camp: S. Lahti's notebook; H. Rajala; O Kauppi;—
      Solzhenitsyn I, p. 392 relates that a half million people went through Karabas
      in a few years and mentions a man brought there in 1942 whose number was
      above 433,000; if that is true, the men probably had separate consecutive
      numbers from the women—or a tremendous number of prisoners flooded the
      camp in 1942.
249   Meeri Salonen's death: Kuusinen, pp. 229-231; A. Pekala.
249   "If I remember correctly . . .": Kuusinen, pp. 249-251; Germans into a work
      army: National defense committee's order 1.10.42, no. 1123; Solzhenitsyn I, p.
      68.
250   Finns taken into work army: Salminen II, pp. 93-101; Carelia 2/97
250   Sharp watch: O. Kauppi; L. Pöllä; HS 2.25.90; Sevander, p. 143, 159;
      Salminen II.
250   Eskolin story: Huuskonen, p. 165.
251   Deaths in camp: HS 2.25.90; Lampila, p. 255; Salminen II, pp. 103-112.
252   Seven executed: Huuskonen, p. 165.
252   Finnishing the factory: Simo Kajava's recollections.
252   "It was worse than . . .": HS 2.25.90.
252   659 Finnish names: Chelyabinsk GATSO-archive listing; Carelia 2/97;
      Otetsestvennyje arkhivy, 2/92.
252   Burial: Salminen II, p.114; HS 2.25.90.
253   Repatriation: Salminen 1, pp. 164-175.
253   Pyykkö: Helenius's book; Pyykkö's hlö card in Supo archives.

THE WIND BLOWS OVER THEM

255 Another note to the Soviet Union: Koistinen's report 1941, UMA.

255 Valpo's estimate of dead and returned: EK-Valpo XVI A 6c 1, KA;
     Kostiainen, p. 206.

256 "As typical Finns . . .": Käkönen pp. 86-95.

256 Paasikivi and Moscow: Koistinen's memorandum 1941; Paasikivi II, p. 35;
     Salminen II, p. 57.

257 Discussion—worthwhile to help the border-hoppers to return?: Suomen
     Kuvalehti [Finland's Pictorial] 3.31.94; Kostiainen p. 217.

257 Supo's attitude: Supo XXVII K and XIII G-10462.

257 Re. Castrén: Rinne's statement 9.18.41, EK Valpo file 376.

257 4,999 Finns: Carelia 3/93.

258 Turned over after the war: Law for expediting the armistice agreement
     9.23.44; T. Laasko; V. Laos.

258 Re. Sundström: T Laine; J. Vanamo; Salainen 1.13.1951, UMA 110 E6.

258 "The envoy was now Vuori . . .": Helenius, p. 234.

258 Documents not found during the 1950s: J. Vanamo.

259 Finns in the camps and in Siberia in the 50's: Flinkman, pp. 224, 230-232;
     Piili, pp. 134-136, 138, 142-144; Salminen II, pp. 197-200; Supo archives
     XXVII K—17725.

260 Re. Nizhni Tagil: Kirillov I, p. 213.

261 "Falsely under Tshistov's leadership . . ." Kamenski Rabotshi 4.28.93.

261 Fomkin's account and wired order December 1937: Ibid.; GAAOSO folder
     26887.

262 KGB declares NKVD had broken rules: GAAOSO folder 26887.

262 Fomkin's last days: S. Karjalainen; O. Kauppi's letter.

262 "Ural war tribunal . . .": Spravka 6.17.58, GAAOSO.

262 Fomkin's interrogation 1958: Interrogation 4.16.58 in Pekala folder,
     GAAOSO.

263 "It is declared that the Lappalainens . . .": GAAOSO folder 25668-58.

263 "Because of her anti-Soviet . . .": Kamensk KGB decision 10.26.50.

264 "None of the old residents . . .": Kamensk KGB, top secret, 12.27.57,
     GAAOSO folder Lappalainen.

264 Rehabilitation: Tribunal's decision 2.28.58; Karelian memorial's
     questionnaire: Lappalainen, Salli.

265 Saaris' rehabilitation: L. Saari.

265 Kolesnikov's newspaper interview: Kamenski Rabotshi 2.3.90.

266 Närvänen's struggle and return: Närvänen folder, UMA; Nameless file, UMA
     22 K; Supo archives XXVII K, XIII H-3420 and XIII B 26-2705.

267 "I, the undersigned . . .": Närvänen's letter to the embassy 1.15.51.

267 "Nor does the embassy consider . . .": Enckell's letter to UM 11.18.53.

268 Pressure on Raili and Tamara: R. Vorobieff.

268 Hiskias Närvänen's fate: Death certificate.
268 Re Jordans and Orells: T. Romanov; Moscow embassy to UM 11.15.37; Orell folder, UMA; Supo border-hoppers' archives (e.g. XXVIII K—1901).
269 "I now turn to you . . .": Orell folder, UMA.
270 Razguljajev's statement: GAAOSO folder 26877 (Orell).
272 Enckell's notification: Enckell's letter 2.22.58.
272 Reino Orell's death: GAAOSO Orell folder.
272 Fomina in Kotka: P. Kyyhkynen.
273 Zolotaja Goran discovery of bodies: Sotsialistitsheskaja Industrija 6.28.89; Pravda 9.21.89.
274 Estimate of 30,000 victims: Kamenski Rabotshi 7.9.90.
275 Jekaterinburg memorial: Uraalsk Rabotshi 10.29.96; A. Sarlanen.
275 Chelyabinsk memorial markers and days: Smena 7.12.89.
276 Hanko quarantine camp: Supo XXVII K.
276 Saarela's return: A. Peltola
277 Järvinens' return: Supo XXVII K—5799.
277 "In 1966 . . .": Eeva Markkanen's letter 3.20.97.
277 False information to inquirers: Rasstrelnyje. . . , p. 191.
279 Wahlsten's return: E. Wahlstén; I. Wahlstén.
280 Tervonens' return: Tervonen interview.
280 True and false information, rehabilitation: Punalippu [Red Flag] 12/89; Tervonens' death certificates 9.12.56 and 10.18.91.
281 Kauppi family's fate: O. Kauppi's letter; Punalippu [Red Flag] 12/89.
281 Erkki Murto's return: E. Murto; Nykyposti [Current Post] 1992.
282 Saaris and others in Kazakhstan: Seura 2.17.95.
282 Re. Hansen-Haugs: Kristiina Hansen-Haug's letter from Kamensk to Haukipudas 12/36; K. Haarala.
283 Rejecting their mothers: E. Saari; O. Kauppi; S. Ollikainen; S. Lahti; Supo's archives XVII K: Heikkilä, Saimi.
285 Alfa Pekala;s life: Letter to Finland 1.11.97; A Pekala.
285 "When I finished the school . . .": Pentti Rosendahl's letter from Kurgan, stamped 1.28.97.

Sources

Interviews and Informants:
Sirkka Eloranta, Anni Fomkina, Pekka Haapaniemi, Kalervo Haarala, Aleksei
Habarov, Ljudmila Habarova, Sirkka Hakala, Helli Hämäläinen, Siiri Hämäläinen,
Seppo Järvinen, Sirkka Kajalainen (Laurila), Tyyne Kannas (Leskinen), Viljo
Kartineva, Onni Kauppi, Olavi Kemppainen, Marjatta Klaus, Osmo Kosonen,
Pirkko Kyyhkynen (Puonti), Timo Laakso, Suoma Lahti, Toivo Laine,Vello Laos,
Salli Lappalainen, Matti Lehtineva, Jari Leino, Unto Lepokorpi, Eeva Markkanen,
Helena Miettinen, Erkki Murto, Rauni Murto, Sirkka Murto, Taisto Nikula, Sylvi
Ollikainen, Alfa Pekala, Aino Peltola (Saarela), Leevi Peltola, Tauno Pietiläinen,
Lauri Pukala, Irma Pynnönen, Leo Pöllä, Arvo Rajala, Helvi Rajala, Erkki Ranta,
Maria-Lisa Rodhin, Tamara Romanova (Orell), Irma Rosendahl, Pentti Rosendahl,
Albert Rusila, Meeri Räisänen (Murto), Sirkka Saarela, Kimmo Saares, Etel Saari,
Ljudmila Saari, Paula Sandell, Andrei Sarlanen, Edit Serjo?nikova (Ahonen), Yrjö
Siivonen, Seppo Sillanpää, Hilkka Sinkkonen, Irina Suomalainen, Kyllikki Suvano
(Nikula), Enni Tairola, Annikki Tervonen, Antti Tervonen, Helvi Tervonen, Eila
Wahlstén, Irma Wahlstén, Aune Vaittinen, Jorma Vanamo, Raili Vorobjeff
(Närvänen), Allan Vuorio, Tenho Ylätupa.

Archival Sources:
GAAOSO (Sverdlovskin area government institute state archives, Jekaterinburg).
GAOPDFK (State archives of Karelian civil and political movements and
      organizations).
GATSHO (Chelyjabinskin state archives).

Individual Files on Liquidated and Rehabilitated Finns:

National archives (KA), EK-Valpon [Finnish national police organizations]
—Subdistrict situation reports from the 1930s.
—Individual cards and files.
—Headquarters situation reports.
—Border conditions (XVI) [Emigration to Russia, border-hoppers' accounts,—
Finnish prisoners in Russia, official actions for the return of border-hppers, etc.]—
Russia (XXXIV) (Treatment of those arrested, methods of investigation, etc.
Perm. state archives on the politically repressed.
Security police (Supo) [Finnish] archives: Finnish abroad/immigrants to the Soviet
Union, Amp X ii C 1 b, files of border-hoppers who returned during the 1950s.
Foreign Ministry's archives (UMA), Helsinki:
—Card File of those gone secretly to Soviet Union.
—Moscow embassy's political reports 1931 to 1933 (5C18).
—Moscow embassy building (5G).
—Finnish citizens' reception in Soviet Union (E6 110).
—Passport applications with photographs, Moscow embassy.
—Finns gone secretly to the Soviet Union.
—Newspapers and periodicals, Russia 1930 to 1935.
—Aid to Finns abroad and arranging return of those without funds.
Karelian administrative archives of the Russian federation security service, Petroskoi.
Omsk administrative archives of the Russian federation security service, Omsk.
Tataria administrative archives of the Russian federation security service, Kazan.
Chelyabinsk administrative archives of the Russian federation security service.

Published Sources:
—Andrew Gordievsky: KGB. *The Inside Story*. London 1990.
—Bolshaja Sovetskaja Entsiklopedija. Moscow 1953.
—Conquest, Robert: *Den stora terrorn*. Stockholm 1971. (I)
—Conquest, Robert: *The Harvest of Sorrow*. London 1988. (II)
—Courtois, Stephane ym: *Le livre noir du communisme*. Pariisi 1997.
—Dallin-Nicolaevsky: *Forced Labor in Soviet Union*. New Haven 1947.
—Flinkman, Tauno: *Neljästi karkuteillä* [*Four Times a Fugitive*]. Helsinki 1957.
—Galitski, V.P.: Finskije vojeloplennye v lagerah NKVD. Moskova 1997.
—Getty, J. Arch: *Origins of the Great Purges*. Cambridge 1985.
—Gildi, L.A.: Rasstrely, ssylki, mutshenya [ ]. St. Petersburg 1996.
—Gustafsson, Paul: *Koulupoika, korpraali, konsuli* [*Schoolboy, Corporal, Consul*].
    Jyväskylä 1995.
—Hamlin, John: *Työmiehenä Venäjällä* [*A Worker in Russia*]. Porvoo 1934.
—Harri, Juho: *Kirottujen tarina* [*Tale of the Accused*]. Porvoo 1937.
—Hartikainen, Kaarlo J.: *Punaisten petojen luolissa* [*In the Den of the Red Beasts*]. Pori
    1933.

—Helenius, Fanni. Pitkä etappi. Kurikka, ei vuotta.

—Huurre, Kirsti: Sirpin ja moukarin alla [Under the Hammer and Sickle]. Porvoo 1942.

—Huuskonen, Taisto: Laps Suomen [Child of Finland]. Juva 1980.

—Immonen, Kari: Ryssästä saa puhua . . . [One Can Speak of Russia . . .]. Keuruu 1987.

—Isotalo, Kaarlo: Loikkarit [Border Hoppers]. Hämeenlinna 1969

—Jakovlev, Aleksandr: Po moshtsham i jelei [ ]. Moskova 1995.

—Jokipii, Mauno (ed.): Itämerensuomalaiset [Baltic Finns]. Jyväskylä 1995.

—Kangaspuro, Markku: Suomalainen vai venäläinen Karjala [Finnish or Russian Karelia]. Joensuu 1996.

—Kero, Reino: Neuvosto-Karjalaa rakentamassa [Building Soviet Karelia]. Helsinki 1983.

—Kirillov, V.M.: Istoria repressi v nizhnetagilskom regione Urala [ ] 1920-1950 gody I-II. N. T. 1996.

—Kirillov, V.M.: Kniga pamjati [ ]. Jekaterinburg 1994.

—Koronen, Matti: Finskije internatsionalisty v borbe za vlast sovetov [ ]. Leningrad 1969.

—Kosonen-Pohjonen: Isänmaan portinvartijat. Suomen rajojen vartiointi 1918-1994 [The Fatherland's Gatekeepers: Guarding Finland's Borders, 1918-1994]. Keuruu 1994.

—Kostiainen, Auvo: Loikkarit. Suuren lamakauden laiton siirtolaisuus Neuvostoliittoon [Border Hoppers: Illegal emigration to the Soviet Union during the Great Depression]. Keuruu 1988. (I).

—Kostiainen, Auvo: Neuvosto-Karjalasta ja "kaukaisen idän aromailta"—suoma laiskirjeitä Venäjältä ja Neuvostoliitosta. Turun historiallinen arkisto nro 40. (III) [From Soviet Karelia and the "far eastern steppes"—Finnish letters from Russia and the Soviet Union. Turku historical archives no. 40. (III)].

—Kuusinen, Aino: Jumala syöksee enkelinsä. Muistelmat vuosilta 1919-1965 [God Casts Out His Angel: Recollections from the Years 1919-1965]. Keuruu 1972.

—Käkönen, U.A.: Sotilasasiamiehenä Moskovassa 1939 [Military Attaché in Moscow 1939]. Keuruu 1966.

—Lahti-Argutina, Eila: Olimme joukko vieras vaan [We Were Only Outsiders]. Venäjänsuomalaiset vainonuhrit Neuvostoliitossa 1930-luvun alusta 1950-luvun alkuun. Vammala 2001.

—Lampila, Lea: Toivontähti. Loikkariperheen tarina [Star of Hope: Tale of a Boder-Hopper Family]. Juva 1991.

—Lehmus, August: Suomalaiset kommunistit Itä-Karjalassa [Finnish Communists in East-Karelia]. Tampere 1958.

—Leningradski martirolog 1937-1938. I-II [ ]. Pietari 1995, 1996.

—Map of GULAG. Riga Memorial Society 1993.

—Martin, Gilbert: Soviet History Atlas. London 1979.

—Molotov, V.M.: Uroki vreditelstva, diversii i shpionazha japonsko-nemetsko-trotskistskih agentov [ ]. Moskova 1937.

—Niemi, Irja: Neuvostokasvatti [Soviet-Reared]. Helsinki 1944.
—Nykopp, Johan: *Paasikiven mukana Moskovassa* [*With Paasikivi in Moscow*]. Helsinki 1975.
—Paasikivi, J.K.: *Toimintani Moskovassa ja Suomessa 1939-1941* [*My Activities in Moscow and Finland 1939-1941*]. Juva 1979.
—Piili, Martta: *Pakkotyövankina Siperiassa* [*Prisoner at Forced Labor in Siberia*]. Kuopio 1957.
—*Pogranitshnyje voiska SSSR 1929-1938* [ ]. Moskova 1972.
—Pyykkö, Fanni: *Pitkä etappi* [*A Long Time*]. Kurikka, undated.
—Radzinski, Edvard: Stalin. Juva 1996.
—*Rasstrelnyje spiski*, 1-2. Moskova 1993, 1994
—Rautkallio, Hannu: *Suuri viha. Stalinin suomalaiset uhrit 1930-luvulla* [*The Great Wrath: Stalin's Finnish victims in the 1930s*]. Juva 1995.
—Rentola, Kimmo: *Kenen joukoissa seisot? Suomalainen kommunismi ja sota 1937-1945* [*Whose Side Are You on? Finnish Communism and the War 1937-1945*]. Juva 1994.
—Salminen, Aimo: *Kuljin Stalinin Siperiaa* [*I traaveled Stalin's Siberia*]. Pieksämäki 1964. (I)
—Salminen, Aimo: *Paluu Stalinin Siperiasta* [*Return from Stalin's Siberia*]. Pieksämäki 1965. (II)
—Salomaa, Markku: *Punaupseerit* [*Red Officers*]. Juva 1992.
—*Sbornik dokumentov po istorii ugolovnogo zakonodatelstva SSSR i RSFSR 1917-1952 gg.* 1953.
—*Sbornik zakonodatelnyh i normativnyh aktov o repressijah i reabilitatsii zhertv polititsheskih repressij* [ ]. Moskova 1993.
—Scott, John: *Vad gör Ryssland bortom Ural?* [*What Is Russia Doing Beyond Ural?*] Stockholm 1943.
—Sevander, Mayme: *Red Exodus. Finnish-American Emigration to Russia*. Minnesota 1993.
—*Shema zheleznyh dorog SSSR*. Moskova 1968.
—Siltala, Juha: *Lapuan liike ja kyyditykset 1930* [*The Lapua Movement and Its Conveyances*]. Keuruu 1985.
—Solzhenitsyn, Aleksandr: *Vankileirien saaristo* [*Gulag Archipelago*] I-II. Tukholma 1974. III-IV. Tampere 1974. V-VII. Tampere 1978.
—*Stalin's Slave Camps*. Boston 1952.
—Stepanov, A.: *Rasstrel po limitu* [ ]. Kazan 1996.
—Takala, Irina: Repressivnaja politika v otnošenii finnov v Sovetskoi Karelii 30-godov. Studia slavica finlandensia. Tomus XI [ ]. 1994.
—Tuominen, Arvo Poika: *Kremlin kellot* [*Kremlin Bells*]. Helsinki 1957.
—Tuura, J.W.: *Työkansan viholliset* [*Working Folks' Enemies*]. Porvoo 1942.
—*Voprosy istorii jevropeiskogo severa*. [Kaksi Irina Takalan artikkelia.] (Two of Irina Takala's articles.) Petroskoi 1993.

Newspapers and Periodicals:
Apu [Help], *Argumenty i fakty* [ ], *Carelia* [ ], *Hakkapeliitta* [ ], *Helsingin Sanomat* [ ], *Historiallinen aikakauskirja* [Journal of History], *Hymy* [Smile], *Industrialnaja Karaganda* [ ], *Kaleva, Kamenski Rabotshi* [ ], *Karjala* [Karelia], *Karjalan Sanomat* [Karelia News], *Na smenu* [ ], *Neuvosto-Karjala* [Soviet Karelia], *Nykyposti* [Today's Post], *Oblastnaja gazeta, Punainen Karjala* [Red Karelia], *Raivaaja* [Pioneer], *Seura* [Society], *Severnyi Kurjer, Sotsialistitsheskaja Industrija, Suomen Kuvalehti* [Finland Pictorial], *Suomen sosialidemokraatti* [Finnish Social Democrat], *Uralski Rabotshi, Uusi Suomi* [New Finland], *Vapaa Karjala ja Inkeri* [Free Karelia and Ingraia], *Vapaus* [Freedom], *Za Uralski Aljumini.*

Index

Aalto, Bruno 193, 194, 275.
Aalto, Kalle 107,108, 139.
Aaltonen, Aleksanter 39.
Aaltonen, Väinö 105.
Åberg, Jaakko 121, 122.
Ahlgren, Wilhelm 78.
Aho, Eino 127.
Aho, Kalle 12.
Ahonen, Anni 71.
Ahonen, Edit 145,146.
Ahonen, Tuomas 275.
Ahonen, Väinö 275.
Äikäs, Lyyli 192, 194.
Akulov 96.
Alatalo, Eerik 104,105.
Alatalo, Väinö 144, 199, 200.
Alenius, Margit 213.
Alhonen, Elsi 234, 282.
Alhonen, Mari 275.
Alhonen, Viktor 197, 275.
Antikainen, Toivo 142.
Anttila, Eino 9.
Arpinen 54.
Artti, Pontus78.
Arvola, Hilda 223.
Aura, Emil 111.

Belyh 99.
Berija, Lavrenti 163, 199, 251.
Bespalov, Aleksei 274.
Biaudet, Eva 121.
Blücher, Vasili 231.
Bojarski 265.
Buharin, Nikolai 210.
Bykov, M. 261.

Chaplin, Charles 51.
Conquest, Robert 16, 207.

Dyster, Yrjö 229.

Eloranta, Aili 98, 99, 109, 213, 243, 245.
Eloranta, Kalle 91, 109.
Eloranta, Sirkka 244, 284.
Enckell, Ralph 267, 272.
Eskola, Irja 238.
Eskola, Matti 125.
Eskola, Tyyne 125, 238.
Eskolin, Elli 36, 223, 232, 283.
Eskolin, Onni 250, 252.
Eurén, Kerttu 157.

Flinkman, Tauno 13, 24, 31, 36, 106, 141, 147, 210.
Fomin, Antti 86, 92.

Fomin, Leo 273.
Fomina, Olga 272.
Fomkin, Nikolai 48, 50, 52, 67, 70, 86, 91, 92, 99, 108, 110. 116, 117, 142, 144, 160, 166, 189, 191, 198, 216, 227, 261, 262.
Fomkina, rouva 166, 171, 184.
Forström, Yrjö 85.
Friman, Arthur 91.
Frisk, Oskari 29.

Gavroi, Nikolai 50, 53, 70.
Genov, Vasili 165, 180, 181, 191.
Gylling, Edvard 14, 16, 149, 151.

Haapalainen, Erland 100.
Haapaniemi, Pentti 72, 104.
Hackzell, Antti 41.
Hackzell, Väinö 59.
Hakala, Einari 266.
Hakala, Iida 223.
Hakkarainen, Rafael 15.
Halvorsen, Erkki 27.
Halvorsen, Oskar 33.
Hanhela, Eino 125.
Hanhela, lapset 238.
Hansen-Haug, Anja 78, 98, 178, 282.
Hansen-Haug, Eero 78.
Hansen-Haug, Kristiina 78, 97, 282.
Hansen-Haug, Niilo 37, 78, 266, 282.
Harri, Juho 11.
Hartikainen, Anni 85.
Hartikainen, Kaarlo 11, 86, 207.
Hartikainen, Veli 85.
Hasala, Vilho 175, 201.
Hattunen 48.
Heikkilä, Inkeri 129.
Heikkilä, Isaak 129.
Heikkilä, Saimi 223, 283.
Heikkinen, Saimi 228.
Helistö, Selma 27, 223.
Hirvonen, Eino 129.
Hitler, Adolf 210.
Holopainen, Kaarlo 82.
Holopainen, Rudolf 34, 37.
Holsti, Rudolf 79, 152, 218.
Honkamäki, Mikko 193.
Huotari, Veikko 143, 186, 224, 233.
Huppunen, Sulo 189.
Huttunen, Hilja 223, 228.
Huurre, Kirsti 157.

Huuskonen, Taisto 148.
Hyrsky, Anna 142.
Hyrsky, Veli 52, 91, 92, 107, 141, 142, 196, 215.
Hämäläinen, Anna 81, 202, 205, doc.
Hämäläinen, Helli 177, 235, 233.
Hämäläinen, Juho 81, 118, 184, 202, 205.
Hämäläinen, Jukka 90.
Hämäläinen, Siiri 25, 100, 168, 171, 175, 177, 182, 184, 185, 213, 243,. 245, 247.
Hämäläinen, Tyyne 213, 245.
Härmä, Eero 126.
Härmä, Emil 85.
Härmä, Liisa 238.
Härmä, Maija 257.
Höglund, Albert 198.
Höglund, Alfons 140, 141.
Hölsä, Hanna 184, 266.

Irklis, P.A. 151.
Ivalo, Asko 60, 103.

Jagoda, Genrich 151, 153, 155.
Jalanti, Tauno 39.
Jalo, Erkki 148.
Jelonen, Aleksi 82.
Jelonen, Hilja 6, 37, 170, 223, 232.
Jelonen, Kerttu 228.
Jelonen, Laura 68.
Jezhov, Nikolai 105, 153, 154, 157, 162, 199, 261.
Jokimies, Kerttu 83.
Jokiniemi, Taneli 105.
Jordan, Arvo 27.
Jordan, Eeva 33, 123, 240, 242, 268.
Jordan, Hilkka 238, 268.
Juntunen, Anna 116.
Juntunen, Elsi 116.
Juntunen, Heimo 116.
Juntunen, Juuso 115.
Juntunen, Veikko 116.
Jämsä, Armas 101.
Järvelä, Eino 128.
Järvinen, Kerttu 223, 277.
Jääskeläinen, Edith 11.

Kabakov, I.D. 127.
Kaikkonen, Isak 63, 66.
Kakkinen, Anna 5, 71, 139.
Kakkinen, Tahvo 5, 139.

Kakkinen, Viljo 5, 39, 140.
Kalinin, Mihail 254.
Kallio, Erik 192, 193.
Kanerva 146, 147.
Kanerva, Henrik 128, 129.
Kangas, Eino 80.
Kantonen, Aino 80, 112.
Kantonen, Anni 119, 195.
Kantonen, Juho 80.
Karenius, Allan 146, 247.
Karenius, Oskari 146, 149.
Kares, K.R. 67.
Kares, Yrjö 82.
Kari, Aarne 193, 194, 233.
Karjalainen, Eino 39, 217.
Karjalainen, Rauno 238, 276.
Karppinen, Urho 263.
Kartineva, Viljo 27, 88.
Karttunen, Urho 136, 138.
Karvonen, Eino 76.
Katainen, Kirsti 76.
Katajev, V. 265.
Katajisto, Arvo 144, 147.
Katvala, Anna 174, 195, 196.
Katvala, Hugo 196.
Katvala, Reino 195, 196.
Katvala, Veikko 174, 223, 233, 252.
Kaukonen, Adam 37.
Kaukonen, Henrik 99, 165, 190.
Kauppi, Allen 272.
Kauppi, Elli 272.
Kauppi, Elsa 272.
Kauppi, Onni 101, 227, 232, 233, 263, 272, 282.
Kekkonen, Taneli 259, 271.
Kekkonen, Urho 259, 269, 270.
Kemppainen, Jenni 266.
Kemppainen, Olavi 177, 272.
Kero, Reino 13.
Keronen, Antti 266.
Keronen, Saimi 223.
Keränen, Lempi 272.
Keto, Jaakko W. 11.
Kilkkinen, Hilma 147.
Kilpelä, Matti 200.
Kirillov, Viktor ix, 130.
Kirov, Sergei 109, 149, 193, 233.
Kivistö, Toivo 53, 145, 147.
Knjazev 163.
Koivisto, Mauno 277, 281.
Koivuranta 12.

Kokkinen, Adolf 266.
Kokkonen, Paavo 266.
Kolesnikov, Aleksandr 265.
Kompanjon, Vladimir 177.
Komsula, Uuno 201.
Kortelainen, Aleksi 139.
Koskinen, Adolf 73, 88, 97.
Koskinen, Aune 283.
Koskinen, Elvi 223, 228, 272, 283.
Kosola, Vihtori 52, 67.
Kosonen, Jalmari 50, 52, 67, 70, 99, 108, 109, 198.
Kosonen, Lyyli 51.
Kosonen, Osmo 284.
Kosonen, Pentti 216, 233.
Kostiainen, Auvo viii, 7, 43, 256.
Kotkov, V. 128.
Kourunen, Aaro 266.
Kourunen, Hilda 223.
Kritshman 265.
Kruschev, Nikita 155, 262, 271.
Kuikka, Jussi 182.
Kujala, Emmi 232.
Kukko, Rudolf 10.
Kukkonen, Ida 228.
Kunnas, Teodor 140.
Kurko, Dagmar 177, 234, 282.
Kurko, Pentti 196.
Kuusela, Aarne 35, 36, 67, 70, 108.
Kuusela, Raili 267.
Kuusinen, Aino 183, 228, 248.
Kuusinen, Elsa 216.
Kuusinen, Erkki 118, 216.
Kuusinen, Mirjam 216.
Kuusinen, Otto Ville ix, 16, 33, 85, 206, 228.
Kuusisto, Matti 133.
Käkelä, Viljo 137.
Käkönen, U.A. 7, 256.
Kärkkäinen, 104.

Laakso, Edvard 133.
Lahti, Eila 252.
Lahti, Eino ix.
Lahti, Ida 247.
Lahti, Suoma 10, 146, 157, 247, 284.
Lahtinen, Yrjö 117.
Laine, Anna 147.
Laine, Helmi 99.
Laine, Toivo 8, 36, 100, 103, 105, 109, 137.
Laitinen, Nestori 109.
Laitinen, Tauno 191.

Laivo, Norma 78.
Lampi, Arvo 130, 131.
Lampi, Natalia 131.
Lankila, Feliks 133, 260.
Lappalainen, Anna 2, 66, 190, 191, 212.
Lappalainen, Hilda 143.
Lappalainen, Juho 2, 191.
Lappalainen, Salli 3, 46, 97, 165, 169, 171,
    173, 176, 180, 189, 191, 212, 213,
    214, 245, 248, 263, 265, 271, 284.
Lappalainen, Sanni 74, 110.
Lassila, Aukusti 109.
Laukkanen, Anna 83.
Laukkarinen, Fabian 53, 193.
Laukkarinen, Maila 235.
Laukkarinen, Sylvi 52, 53, 193.
Launonen, Väinö 109.
Laurila, Eino 123, 224.
Laurila, Lempi 224, 233.
Laurila, Sirkka 16, 68, 224, 277.
Lehikoinen, Heikki 127.
Lehikoinen, Toivo 23.
Lehmus, August 25.
Lehtinen, Ester 39.
Lehtonen, Arvo 82.
Lenin, V.I. 16, 68, 129, 241.
Lepokorpi, Esteri 223, 238.
Leskinen, Tyyne 46, 92.
Liimatainen, Reino 71.
Liljeroos, Juho 117.
Liljeroos, Olga 117.
Lindqvist, Liisa 186.
Lindroos, Sointu 123, 128, 217, 276.
Lindstedt 191.
Lindstén, Albin 109, 110.
Lintunen, Esteri 6, 92.
Litvinov, Maksim 59, 152, 218.
Lohilahti 63.
Lotov, Anatoli 236.
Lotta, Aino 247.
Lugovtsev, Faddei 260.
Luoto, Ensio 223, 233.
Luoto, Kauko 223.
Lyytikäinen, Robert 267.

Maiski, Ivan 19.
Malo, Iisakki 82.
Manninen, Oskar10.
Marjasin, L.M. 127.
Markkanen, Aili 2, 27, 110, 171, 266.
Markkanen, Eeva 2, 110, 171, 223, 228, 233,

277.
Markkanen, Eila 27.
Markkanen, Keijo 110, 223.
Markkanen, Robert 2, 110, 199.
Martin-Schule, Marija-Emma 257.
Marx, Karl 68.
Melanen, Maija 213, 244.
Meriläinen, Martti 266.
Metsämäki, Eino 139, 191, 193, 264.
Miettinen, Veikko 133.
Mironova, Svetlana 180, 181.
Mizrah 265.
Moilanen, Kerttu 223, 224, 238, 276.
Moilanen, Leo 238, 276.
Moilanen, Tauno 224.
Molotov, Vjatsheslav 127, 151, 256, 257.
Monto, Tuomas 90.
Murto, Ebba 12, 193, 212, 213, 232, 244,
    248, 252.
Murto, Elma 12, 232.
Murto, Erkki 12, 76, 97, 100, 102, 112, 169,
    178, 231, 232, 234, 281.
Murto, Ilmari 12, 112, 174, 206, 232.
Murto, Kalle 12, 80, 112, 141, 231.
Murto, Rauni 12, 76, 97, 112, 169, 178, 230,
    232, 234, 235, 282.
Murto, Reino 12, 167, 174, 196, 231, 232.
Murto, Urho 12, 112, 174, 192, 206, 232.
Murto, Veikko 12, 167, 174, 196, 223, 231,
    233.
Murto, Vilhelmiina 12, 24, 106, 174, 206,
    231, 232.
Murto, Vilho 231.
Murto, Väinö 12, 67, 74, 76, 112, 141, 231.
Mutta, Jooseppi 206.
Muuri 54.
Mäntylä, Hanna 223, 232, 272.

Nevalainen, Hilda 78.
Niemelä, Alma 223.
Nieminen, Veikko 136, 138, 189, 190, 191,
    201, 263.
Nieminen, Väinö 140.
Niilonen, Eeva 223.
Nikkari, Ester 223, 228.
Nicholas II 97.
Nikula, Aili 89, 145.
Nikula, Eemeli 88, 145.
Nikula, Kyllikki 121.
Nissilä, Yrjö 227.
Niva-aho, Heikki 103.

Nivel, Reijo 125.
Nuorteva, Kerttu 37.
Nuorteva, Santeri 37.
Nuutinen, Aatami 129.
Nykopp, Johan 7, 61, 152.
Nykänen, Matti 25.
Nyman, Arthur 142.
Närvänen, Alpo 46.
Närvänen, Alvari 46.
Närvänen, Ellen 46, 93, 117, 123, 203, 223, 238, 266, 268, 271.
Närvänen, Fabian 206.
Närvänen, Hiskias 46, 93, 202. 206, 268.
Närvänen, Kerttu 46.
Närvänen, Raili 93, 123, 240, 241, 266, 268.

Ojala, Hilja 24.
Okudzhava, S. 128.
Olkkonen, Jaakko 131, 132, 133.
Ollikainen, Albin 1, 180, 185, 186, 201.
Ollikainen, Oiva 171, 223.
Ollikainen, Sylvi 1, 100, 166, 171, 180, 181, 185, 186, 201, 213, 214, 245, 248, 276.
Ollikainen, Veikko 92, 201.
Ordzhonikidze, Sergo 127.
Orell, Anna 73.
Orell, Reino 73, 110, 167, 269, 272.
Orell, Sanni 173, 175, 223, 239, 240, 268, 270.
Orell, Tamara 110, 173, 175, 238, 240, 268, 272.

Paasikivi, J.K. 256, 258, 269.
Paasonen, Aladár 145.
Pakaslahti, Aaro 58, 59, 60, 70.
Paldan, Olga 118.
Paldan, Otto 39, 80, 118, 206.
Paldan, Tyyne 39, 97, 118.
Paldan, Väinö 105, 206.
Palmén, Thure 70, 127.
Panova 99.
Partanen, Aleksander 195, 198.
Partanen, Tyyne 6.
Pasanen, Kalle 186.
Patrikainen, Lauri 45, 70, 74.
Pekala, Aleksandra 74, 266.
Pekala, Alfa 46, 125, 223, 227, 228, 262, 285.
Pekala, Irja 49, 112, 182, 189, 248.
Pekala, Maunu 74.

Pekala, Tyyne 223, 232, 238, 285.
Pellikka, Kusti 238.
Peltoniemi, Juho 109.
Perho, Akseli 145.
Peter the Great 95.
Pietiläinen, Tauno 252.
Pihlajamäki, Ester 228.
Pihlajaniemi, Ester 223.
Piili, Martta 259.
Piispanen, Eino 201.
Pitkänen, Armas 272.
Pitkänen, Lyyli 272.
Pitkänen, William 272.
Plotkin 265.
Podgornyi, Nikolai 281.
Puhakka, Jaakko 195, 196.
Pukala, Armas 72.
Pukala, Kalle 72, 104.
Puonti, Karin 33, 34, 66, 71, 78, 79, 92, 272.
Puonti, Niilo 20, 33, 37, 78, 92, 107, 118, 272.
Puonti, Pirkko 27, 33, 46, 68, 78, 92, 107.
Puupää, Pekka 188.
Pynnönen, Tyyne 93, 175, 223, 224, 232.
Pyykkö, Allan 93, 253.
Pyykkö, Fanni 29, 31, 34, 92, 93, 109, 176, 182, 253, 254, 276.
Pyykkö, Veijo 253.
Pääkkönen, Salme 269, 270.
Pöllä, Leo 253.

Qvintus, Impi 70, 108, 189.

Rajala, Arvo 181.
Rautkallio, Hannu ix, 86.
Razguljajev 270.
Reinikainen, Kauko 201.
Reshetov, I. 265.
Riekki, Esko 11, 19, 38, 42, 43, 57, 69, 70, 71, 153, 201.
Riikola 71.
Riipinen, Juho 239.
Riutta, Valdemar 266.
Roiha, Antti 197.
Roiha, Jalmari 83.
Rongaljoff, Juri 177.
Ronkainen, Bertta 284.
Ronkainen, Elma 213, 284.
Ronkainen, Oiva 177.
Rosendahl, Andrei 285.
Rosendahl, Irma 239, 285.

Rosendahl, Pentti 239, 285.
Rosendahl, Tyyne 233, 238, 239, 285.
Rosendahl, Valentina 285.
Rosenström, Kalle 125.
Rovio, Kustaa 16, 21, 86, 151, 152, 210.
Runeberg, J.L. 188.
Räkä, Toivo 192.
Räty, Eevi 17, 223.

Saarela, Aino 9, 16, 24, 43, 124, 125, 129, 237, 239, 242, 276.
Saarela, Artturi 124, 125.
Saarela, Sirkka 124, 238, 239, 241, 277.
Saarelainen, Andrei 272.
Saarelainen, Eeva 223, 232, 272.
Saarelainen, Rauno 272.
Saarelainen, Vladimir 272.
Saarenoja, Uuno 54, 224, 233, 272.
Saarenoja, Viola 53, 54.
Saari, Aleksis 5, 52, 55, 57, 107, 198, 205, 265.
Saari, Etel 5, 55, 57, 107, 114, 176, 177, 222, 236, 282, 286.
Saari, Gerda 5, 56, 57, 107, 114, 176, 198, 205, 265.
Saari, Lea 5, 52, 55, 57, 107, 114, 222, 223, 286.
Saari, Ljudmila 286.
Saari, Rakel 5, 57, 107, 222, 235, 237, 282, 286.
Saariniemi, Betty 223.
Saariniemi, Hannes 105.
Saaristo, Viljo 23.
Saaristo, Ville 200.
Saharov, Andrei 274.
Salminen, Aimo 27, 28, 183, 260.
Salo, Irja 176.
Salo, Sinikka 176.
Salomaa, Markku 86.
Salonen, Maire 228.
Salonen, Meeri 120, 227, 249, 266.
Salonen, Rauno 272.
Salonen, Selma 223, 227, 266, 272.
Salonen, Torsti 272.
Samoilov 265.
Samsonov 191.
Scott, John 86, 90.
Seppälä, Lauri 12.
Seppänen, Jaakko 19.
Seppänen, Viktor 201.
Sevander, Mayme 17.

Sinkko, David 109.
Sinkkonen, Aleksander 170, 186, 206, 266.
Sinkkonen, Hilkka 167, 169, 171, 174, 180, 186, 213, 215, 248, 284.
Sinkkonen, Ida 167, 169, 206, 266.
Sipinen, Onni 67, 70, 88, 89, 108, 198.
Sirola, Yrjö 16.
Solzhenitsyn, Aleksandr 1156, 182, 210.
Stahanov, Aleksei 99.
Stalin, Josif 17, 21, 99, 145, 146, 151, 153, 155, 189, 199, 210, 241, 261, 265, 267, 274.
Stenman, Laina 170, 223.
Stenman, Oskari 170.
Suharev, Pjotr 160, 162, 182, 262.
Sundström, Cay 140, 258.
Suokas, Matti 224, 243.
Svedberg, Edvin 121.

Takala, Irina 17.
Takalo, Hilda 93, 215, 232, 272.
Tamminen, Eila 229, 282.
Tekkala, Martti 266.
Tennilä, Matti 105.
Terho, Toivo 201.
Tervonen, Annikki 46, 100, 113, 175, 177, 221, 223, 232, 280.
Tervonen, Antti 113, 176, 221, 235, 280.
Tervonen, Elsa 113, 168, 175, 177, 221, 223, 232, 238, 281.
Tervonen, Helvi 113, 177, 221, 280.
Tervonen, Isak 83, 113, 280.
Tervonen, Liisa 280.
Tervonen, Tauno 113.
Tiainen, Väinö 109.
Toijonen, Kustaa Adolf 50.
Tomunov 185.
Tshistov 261, 262, 265.
Tshuhin, Ivan 158.
Tuhatshevski, Mihail 231.
Tuominen, Arvo Poika ix, 44, 234.
Tuominen, Onni 109.
Tykkyläinen, Väinö 126.
Tyyskä, Aleksander 78.
Törölä, Tauno 71.

Vahlroos, Eero 92.
Vaittinen, Akuliina 173.
Vaittinen, Hilma 101, 101, 108, 173, 232, 272.
Vaittinen, Lauri 173, 282.

Vaittinen, Pentti 233.
Valaskivi, Armida 4.
Valkama, Pauli 54, 55, 143.
Vanamo, Jorma 258.
Varis, Eero 106.
Varis, Toivo 106.
Varkkinen, Paavo 51.
Vartiainen, Kalle 54, 206.
Vasenius, Uljas 31.
Venho, Tuomas 109.
Viitala, Maria 228.
Viljamaa, Elli 228, 233.
Viljamaa, Juho 80, 195, 196.
Vilkin 100.
Vilkman, Ida 1116, 197.
Vilkman, Margit 246.
Vilppula, Tauno 211.
Viman, Vilhelm 215.
Virkki, Matti 66.
Virtanen, Orvo 72.
Viuhko, Hellä 98, 223.
Viuhko, Pauli 70, 108, 185, 198.
Voionmaa, Väinö 217.
Voitsehovsk 261.
Voroshilov, Kliment 254, 259, 269, 276.
Voutilainen, H. 53.
Vuorio, Allan 25, 26, 33, 36, 48, 49, 67, 100,
    136, 138, 191, 196, 263.
Vuorio, Ines 26.
Vuorio, Juho 25, 124, 128.
Vuorio, Margit 26, 229.
Vyshinski, Andrei 105.
Väänänen, Vilho 266.

Wahlstén, Eila ix, 4, 46, 89, 102, 108, 167,
    169, 176, 177, 203, 230, 235, 236,
    280.
Wahlstén, Irma 4, 176, 178, 203, 229, 230,
    236, 279.
Wahlstén, Kirsti 4, 87, 89, 97, 117, 145, 176,
    194, 206, 212, 279.
Wahlstén, Lydia 203.
Wahlstén, Viljo 4, 34, 89, 108, 118, 167, 193,
    194, 203, 206, 279.
Westerlund, Eino 37, 38, 39, 40, 41, 43.
Wuori, Eero A. 258.

Ylén, Väinö 43.
Ylätupa, Tenho 20.
Yrjö-Koskinen, Aarno 25, 46, 61, 63, 126,
    128, 133, 136, 187, 220.